Lecture Notes in Computer Science 14625

Founding Editors

Gerhard Goos
Juris Hartmanis

Editorial Board Members

The series Lecture Notes in Computer Science (LNCS), including its subseries Lecture Notes in Artificial Intelligence (LNAI) and Lecture Notes in Bioinformatics (LNBI), has established itself as a medium for the publication of new developments in computer science and information technology research, teaching, and education.

LNCS enjoys close cooperation with the computer science R & D community, the series counts many renowned academics among its volume editors and paper authors, and collaborates with prestigious societies. Its mission is to serve this international community by providing an invaluable service, mainly focused on the publication of conference and workshop proceedings and postproceedings. LNCS commenced publication in 1973.

Samia Bouzefrane · Damien Sauveron
Editors

Information Security Theory and Practice

14th IFIP WG 11.2 International Conference, WISTP 2024
Paris, France, February 29 – March 1, 2024
Proceedings

 Springer

Editors
Samia Bouzefrane ⓘ
Cedric Lab, Cnam
Paris, France

Damien Sauveron ⓘ
University of Limoges
Limoges Cédex, France

ISSN 0302-9743   ISSN 1611-3349 (electronic)
Lecture Notes in Computer Science
ISBN 978-3-031-60390-7   ISBN 978-3-031-60391-4 (eBook)
https://doi.org/10.1007/978-3-031-60391-4

This Springer imprint is published by the registered company Springer Nature Switzerland AG
The registered company address is: Gewerbestrasse 11, 6330 Cham, Switzerland

If disposing of this product, please recycle the paper.

Preface

Future ICT technologies, such as the concepts of Ambient Intelligence, Cyber-physical Systems, and Internet of Things, provide a vision of the Information Society in which: a) people and physical systems are surrounded by intelligent interactive interfaces and objects, and b) environments are capable of recognizing and reacting to the presence of different individuals or events in a seamless, unobtrusive, and invisible manner. The success of future ICT technologies will depend on how secure these systems are and to what extent they protect the privacy of individuals and individuals trust them.

The Workshop in Information Security Theory and Practice (WISTP) was established in 2007 as a platform to unite researchers and practitioners in various fields and foster collaboration and exchange between the research and industrial/consumer communities. The WISTP 2024 conference aimed to provide an elicited forum for researchers and industrial practitioners to present and discuss emerging trends in security and privacy, including experimental studies of fielded systems, while exploring the application of security technology, and highlighting successful system implementations.

WISTP 2024 was hosted by Cnam (Conservatoire National des Arts et Métiers) a French public institute created in 1794 and dedicated to life-long education. Cnam is based in the heart of Paris and is associated to the museum of arts and crafts. WISTP 2024 was organized by the CEDRIC Lab of Cnam, the University of Limoges, and the association ASELKIM with the cooperation of IFIP WG 11.2 Pervasive Systems Security.

We had 30 submissions and the program committee accepted 12 papers. Every submission was assigned to two members of the program committee for review. The accepted papers originated from: Algeria, Australia, Canada, China, Germany, India, France, Morocco, the Netherlands, and the USA. Three brilliant invited speakers completed the technical program. The first speaker was Youakim Badr, a tenured Full Professor of data analytics and artificial intelligence at the Pennsylvania State University – Great Valley. His talk was entitled "Securing the Future: Addressing Cybersecurity Risks in Large Language Models". The second speaker was José Lopes Esteves, the deputy head of the Wireless Security Laboratory at ANSSI, the French Cybersecurity Agency. The talk dealt with "Electromagnetic Security: when Maxwell meets Bell-Lapadula". The third speaker was Jean-Jacques Quisquater, a Belgian cryptographer and a professor at the University of Louvain (UCLouvain). He received, with Claus P. Schnorr, the RSA Award for Excellence in Mathematics and the ESORICS Outstanding Research Award in 2013. He holds 17 patents in the field of smart cards. His talk was titled "Post-quantum cryptography everywhere very soon for everybody".

We would like to thank the authors for their high-quality paper contributions, the chairs and the members of the technical program committee for reviewing the submitted papers and selecting a high-quality program, and the general chairs for their support. Our special thanks go also to the organizing committee members for their great help, and to the sponsor institutions.

We hope that all the participants enjoyed this hybrid conference, especially to those who came to enjoy visiting Cnam and Paris.

March 2024

Samia Bouzefrane
Damien Sauveron
Soumya Banerjee

Organization

General Chairs

Samia Bouzefrane   Cnam, France
Damien Sauveron   University of Limoges, France

Program Chair

Soumya Banerjee   Transa Solutions, Ireland

Technical Program Committee

Alessio Merlo   University of Genoa, Italy
Céline Chevalier   Université Panthéon-Assas Paris II, France
Claudio Ardagna   Università degli Studi di Milano, Italy
Dave Singelee   Katholieke Universiteit Leuven, Belgium
Denis Trcek   University of Ljubljana, Slovakia
Emmanuel Conchon   University of Limoges, XLIM, UMR CNRS
                                  7252, France
Gabriele Costa   IMT Lucca, Italy
Javier Lopez   UMA, Spain
Joachim Posegga   Univ. of Passau, Germany
Kadri Benamar   University of Tlemcen, Algeria
Kouichi Sakurai   Kyushu University, Japan
Maryline Laurent   Télécom SudParis, France
Mehmet Sabir Kiraz   Montfort University, France
Nouredine Tamani   ISEP, France
Olivier Levillain   Télécom SudParis, Institut Polytechnique de
                                  Paris, France
Serge Chaumette   University of Bordeaux, France
Siraj A. Shaikh   Coventry University, UK
Sjouke Mauw   University of Luxembourg, Luxembourg
Stefano Zanero   Politecnico di Milano, Italy
Tassos Dimitriou   Computer Technology Institute, Greece and
                                  Kuwait University, Kuwait
Thibaut Heckmann   Centre de Recherche de la Gendarmerie Nationale
                                  (CREOGN), France

Umut Uludag	TUBITAK-BILGEM-UEKAE, Turkey
Yong Guan	Iowa State University, USA
Yulliwas Ameur	Cnam, France

Organizing Committee

Rezak Aziz	Conservatoire National des Arts et Métiers, France
Lydia Ouaili	Conservatoire National des Arts et Métiers, France
Mustapha Kamal Benramdane	Conservatoire National des Arts et Métiers, France
Kaoutar Sadouki	Conservatoire National des Arts et Métiers, France
Bastien Buil	Orange Innovation Caen, France

Webmaster

| Rezak Aziz | Conservatoire National des Arts et Métiers, France |

Steering Committee

Angelos Bilas	FORTH-ICS & University of Crete, Greece
Olivier Blazy	XLIM, University of Limoges, France
Konstantinos Markantonakis	ISG-SCC, Royal Holloway University of London, UK
Joachim Posegga	Institute of IT-Security and Security Law at the University of Passau, Germany
Jean-Jacques Quisquater	Catholic University of Louvain, Belgium
Damien Sauveron	XLIM, University of Limoges, France
Chan Yeob Yeun	Khalifa University, UAE

Sponsoring Institutions

Conservatoire National des Arts et Métiers, France
University of Limoges, France

Contents

SPAWN: Seamless Proximity-Based Authentication by Utilizing
the Existent WiFi Environment 1
Philipp Jakubeit, Andreas Peter, and Maarten van Steen

MQfilTTr: Strengthening Smart Home Privacy Through MQTT Traffic
Manipulation 17
Henrich C. Pöhls, Sven Gebauer, Fabian Scharnböck,
Korbinian Spielvogel, and Joachim Posegga

Combining Cryptography and Discrete-Event Systems to Study Sensor
and Actuator Cyberattacks 33
Ahmed Khoumsi, Mohammed Erradi, and Fahd Adni

Towards Interconnected Quantum Networks: A Requirements Analysis 49
Swantje Kastrup and Nils gentschen Felde

A Similarity Approach for the Classification of Mitigations in Public
Cybersecurity Repositories into NIST-SP 800-53 Catalog 64
Ahmed Elmarkez, Soraya Mesli-Kesraoui, Flavio Oquendo,
Pascal Berruet, and Djamal Kesraoui

Top Cyber Threats: The Rise of Ransomware 80
Amir Djenna, Mohamed Belaoued, and Nourdine Lifa

Enhancing Security in Blockchain Enabled IoT Networks Empowered
with zk-SNARKs and Physically Unclonable Functions 96
Pranav Unni, Saumya Banerjee, and Samia Bouzefrane

Security Challenges and Countermeasures in Blockchain's Peer-to-Peer
Architecture 111
Hussein Kazem, Nour El Madhoun, Samia Bouzefrane,
and Pierrick Conord

A Bitcoin-Based Digital Identity Model for the Internet of Things 128
Youakim Badr, Xiaoyang Zhu, Samia Saad-Bouzefrane,
and Soumya Banerjee

Towards a Time-Dependent Approach for User Privacy Expression
and Enforcement 146
Nouredine Tamani

Privacy Preserving Federated Learning: A Novel Approach for Combining
Differential Privacy and Homomorphic Encryption 162
    Rezak Aziz, Soumya Banerjee, and Samia Bouzefrane

Distributed Backdoor Attacks in Federated Learning Generated
by DynamicTriggers 178
    Jian Wang, Hong Shen, Xuehua Liu, Hua Zhou, and Yuli Li

Author Index 195

SPAWN: Seamless Proximity-Based Authentication by Utilizing the Existent WiFi Environment

Philipp Jakubeit[1]([✉])[ID], Andreas Peter[1,2][ID], and Maarten van Steen[1][ID]

[1] University of Twente, Drienerlolaan 5, 7522 NB Enschede, Netherlands
p.jakubeit@utwente.nl
[2] Carl von Ossietzky Universität Oldenburg, Ammerländer Heerstraße 114-118,
26129 Oldenburg, Germany

Abstract. Our objective is to create a transparent authentication factor using existing hardware and information already present. Transparent authentication refers to not burdening the user with interaction, and therefore a transparent authentication factor is applicable not only at the beginning of a session but continuously during an authenticated session. We choose to utilize the WiFi environment of a user, as it is ubiquitous in terms of the presence of WiFi signals and user hardware. As we intend our contribution as an addition to stand-alone passwords or existing multifactor-authentication schemes, we decided to build on the concept of separated authentication channels used in state-of-the-art multifactor authentication. To do so, we require two devices. Measuring the WiFi environment from two points enables us to use the proximity of devices as the additional authentication claim. In this work, we demonstrate that it is feasible to use WiFi to identify the proximity of devices. We analyze two scenarios, a semi-densely populated apartment environment and a densely populated office environment in terms of WiFi access points. In the apartment scenario, we show that SPAWN provides at least as much entropy as a traditional password, while not requiring the user to retype a low-entropy token. In the office scenario, this amount of entropy can still be derived in 74% of the measures. By applying private set metrics, we investigate and demonstrate that a device's proximity can be employed as an authentication factor without compromising privacy.

1 Introduction

We are faced with the increasing prevalence of multifactor-authentication (MFA) systems on a daily basis. According to the Global Password Security Report [14], 57% of online businesses had adopted MFA schemes in 2019. The most common form of MFA in use is two-factor authentication (2FA), which combines a knowledge factor (the user's password) and a possession factor (a code sent via SMS or an app). NIST describes the use of MFA as a 'security enhancement' [22]. However, most 2FA schemes lack usability by requiring user input. This is confirmed by a 2023 MFA report, which shows that 33% of the users turn off

© IFIP International Federation for Information Processing 2024
Published by Springer Nature Switzerland AG 2024
S. Bouzefrane and D. Sauveron (Eds.): WISTP 2024, LNCS 14625, pp. 1–16, 2024.
https://doi.org/10.1007/978-3-031-60391-4_1

MFA due to its annoyance [18]. Furthermore, authentication is still only used at the beginning of an authenticated session. While some more secure systems such as banking applications use strict session timeouts, systems that continuously evaluate the user's authenticity are virtually nonexistent.

We propose SPAWN, a seamless, proximity-based authentication mechanism that utilizes the user's WiFi environment as an additional, transparent authentication factor. The concept is that when a user is required to multifactor authenticate, a second device is in close proximity. This is true for traditional two-factor authentication, as the second device must be accessible for the user to receive and retype the token. The main aspect of the multifactor scheme to date is to have two separate communication channels with the service to provide reassurance of the user's authenticity. However, the user is kept in the loop to retype a one-time token. We bypass the user involvement in utilizing environmental measurements. Having a device nearby provides sufficient information to confirm that the entity is likely to be the user the entity claims to be. Therefore, SPAWN can be used as a transparent factor in MFA systems. A *transparent authentication* factor allows a user to be authenticated without the user's participation in the authentication process. Furthermore, due to its transparency, SPAWN can be used as a continuous authentication factor. A *continuous authentication* factor allows the system to authenticate a user continuously, not only at the beginning of an authenticated session, but on demand. We can even use SPAWN for multiple devices in the user's vicinity. For example, when an infant wants to access an online streaming service, it may not be sufficient for the smartphone to be close to the smart TV, but also for the smartphone of a legal guardian to be in proximity to allow for a valid authentication.

SPAWN works by measuring the WiFi environment of the user on at least two devices. We measure the user's WiFi environment in terms of existing WiFi access points (AP) in the surroundings of the two devices and take advantage of the uniqueness demonstrated of a WiFi fingerprint [8]. These measurements are encrypted with a fresh key and sent to the service for comparison. The fresh key is derived from a session key and a session-specific identifier. The latter is communicated by the service, while the former is created and communicated via a software-spawned hotspot by one of the user devices. This mechanism allows SPAWN to provide the WiFi-based proximity authentication factor while protecting the confidentiality of the measurements. Our main contributions are:

- We investigate the feasibility of using the WiFi environment of a user to determine if devices are in close proximity.
- We demonstrate that it is feasible to use WiFi to identify the proximity of devices and investigate the guarantees that can be obtained.
- We show that the proximity of the device can be used as an authentication factor.
- We show that it is possible to assert proximity of devices without compromising privacy (each device only learns its own measurement, and the service only learns the number of APs per measurement and their intersection size).

2 Related Work

Different systems have been proposed for secure, transparent, and continuous authentication. One area of research is behavioral profiling, which utilizes user dynamics such as call and application usage, to detect irregularities [2]. Another field of study is the use of input devices, with keystroke dynamics being used to authenticate a user [1]. Modern input devices, such as touchscreens, have been used to develop biometric profiles with a classification success rate of 100% in less than four seconds [3]. Even the position that a user holds the device can be used for user recognition [19]. However, all of these methods involve some form of classification, which is time consuming and computationally expensive. In contrast, SPAWN requires only a comparison without prior training.

Since 2020, tracking infectious diseases has become a popular area of research. This involves measuring the proximity of devices of different users, usually using Bluetooth or WiFi. For example, WiFi network logs from enterprise networks are used to reconstruct device trajectories for contact tracing [23]. However, this is limited to enterprise environments and requires access to enterprise WiFi logs. Another approach is to require changes to existing routers [27]. Again, training and classification add to the costs of such systems.

Regarding the proximity of devices, several paths are researched. An agreed frequency can be used to measure proximity [4]. Synthesized signal-strength data on different channels is used to increase the entropy of proximity-based key generation [13]. WiFi signals and WiFi technical specifications can be used to determine the proximity of devices [16]. The channel state information (CSI) of the ambient WiFi signals is used to determine the proximity of devices [21]. Additional hardware in terms of backscatter tags is used [15] and auditory proximity detection [6]. However, SPAWN is a unique approach as it measures the environment of the two devices in terms of observable APs, regardless of the state of the WiFi connection. Note that we do not compare to distance-bounding protocols, as they aim to establish an upper bound on the physical distance, while we evaluate the similarity of the WiFi environment to infer proximity.

To compare observed APs and ensure the desired privacy guarantees, we employ a technique known as private set intersection cardinality (PSI-CA). There are several ways to implement PSI-CA. One way is to use multiparty computation combined with oblivious transfer [17]. Another approach is a generic transformation to construct PSI from key agreement protocols [20]. Lastly, functional encryption can be used to realize PSI and PSI-CA [24].

3 System Description

SPAWN has two interacting parties: a user who intends to conduct authentication and a service validating the user's authentication attempt. Analogously to traditional 2FA schemes, we require at least three devices, two user devices, and the service. The service acts as a third party *validator*, verifying the authentication claims. The first device of the user is the *claimant*, which produces the claim to be validated. All other user devices are *attesters*, supporting the claimant's claim against the validator. Having only communication channels between the devices and the service could further improve the security of our authentication scheme, as it mitigates man-in-the-middle and eavesdropping attacks. However, this requires more data than is accessible via operating system (OS) abstractions (see Sect. 6). Therefore, we assume not only a separate communication channel with the validator but also an additional one-way connection between the user devices. In Fig. 1 we show the three devices and their connectivity.

SPAWN ensures that the user devices and the validator are familiar with each other and can communicate securely. Both user devices perform a WiFi measurement, and the validator evaluates the similarity of these measurements. For this evaluation, we utilize the degree of overlap in the measurements and the ratio of overlap to all observed APs. Considering both the number of shared APs and the proportion of overlap to observed APs, allows us to determine how much information is shared by the devices' measurements and how similar the two measurements are. The establishment of asymmetrically secured communication between the devices and the validator creates an initial level of trust. Both the device and the validator know that their

Validator

Claimant   Attester

Fig. 1. This figure illustrates the communication channels between a laptop a smartphone, and the validator.

communication is confidential and authenticated. Further, the asymmetrically secured communication allows for non-repudiation, thus ensuring the integrity and accountability of the communication. Furthermore, symmetrically secured communication between the two user devices creates a secondary level of trust by providing confidentiality, integrity, and authentication based on the possession of the symmetric key. Additionally, the utilization of current environmental measurements is necessary to achieve a third level of trust due to showing an overlap in the measured WiFi environment, which upholds a previously specified amount of shared information and required similarity. This third level of trust guarantees the desired proximity claim for transparent authentication. Furthermore, including the measurements is crucial in preventing relay attacks, providing recency due to a service nonce, and proximity due to the overlap of APs in the measurements.

3.1   Identity Assertions and Security Foundations

The major components of SPAWN are the WiFi-capable user devices. We require at least $n = 2$ user devices $\{D_1, \ldots, D_n\}$ to determine proximity. Additionally, we require the validator for verification. We assume that D_1 is the claimant. *The claimant* collects WiFi measurements and communicates with the validator under encryption, for example, using a TLS-secured channel. In addition, it can communicate with the second user device, the attester. Each device D_j for $j \in \{2, \ldots, n\}$ functions as an attester. *The attester* should confirm the authentication claim of the claimant. It collects WiFi measurements and communicates with the validator under encryption. In addition, it has a means of communication with the claimant. This *device-to-device* (D2D) communication in SPAWN is required to ensure up-to-dateness. We assume that the devices are capable of communicating wirelessly. We realize wireless communication using a *SoftSpot*, a software-spawned WiFi hotspot. Additionally, we assume means of direct communication for the initialization of a pre-shared key (e.g., NFC, cable connection). The *pre-shared key* (PSK) serves multiple purposes: A private PSK facilitates a trust relationship between user devices and guarantees the confidentiality and integrity of data exchanged between devices. Explicitly, the PSK protects against replay and man-in-the-middle attacks.

3.2 Conducting and Comparing Measurement

To make measurements, recall the devices D_i for $i \in \{1, \ldots, n\}$. Each device is tasked with performing a WiFi measurement of the surrounding APs. We assume that the measurement $\mathbf{M}_i$ for a device D_i includes the media access control (MAC) address and the service set identifier (SSID) of each observed AP, represented by $MAC(AP)$ and $SSID(AP)$, respectively. These two pieces of information are available on all operating systems (OSs) without requiring privileged access rights. Therefore, the measurement is a set of tuples of the MAC address and SSID for each observed AP. We assume $\mathbf{env}(D_i)$ to be the WiFi environment, measurable in the current position of the device D_i. The measurement is defined as the set: $\mathbf{M}_i = \{(MAC(AP), SSID(AP)) | AP \in \mathbf{env}(D_i)\}$.

To compare the measurements, the validator must validate the proximity of the claimant device and the attester device. To do so, the validator compares the set of APs measured by the devices. If only one device is required to be in proximity, the validator compares only two measurements. If more devices are required, the validator evaluates each attester's measurement against the claimant's measurement, for example, D_1 and D_2 as well as D_1 and D_3.

Requirements. For each participating party, the validator, the claimant device D_1, and each attester device D_j, we require that each device D_i learns no more than its own measured set of APs $\mathbf{M}_i$. The validator learns none of the sets $\mathbf{M}_i$.

Outsourced private set intersection cardinality (PSI-CA) protocols fulfill these requirements by letting the participating user devices learn nothing more than their sets and the validator the intersection cardinality of the sets. PSI-CA is a cryptographic primitive in which only the cardinality of the intersection of two private input sets is learned. Contrary to most of the solutions in the literature, we require an outsourced evaluation in which neither of the parties learns cardinality [10,24]. Only the third-party validator should acquire this knowledge. The second requirement in our use case is that the applied solution is either noninteractive or employs mechanisms to prevent cheating from the participating parties. We require this, as we apply PSI-CA to derive an authentication claim.

3.3 Authentication Process

The authentication process is divided into three stages: initialization, authentication request, and validation of the authentication claim. We provide a visual representation of these stages in Fig. 2. In addition, we discuss user participation and session management.

Initialization. Initialization is carried out once to bind the devices to each other. Each claimant and attester device are registered at the validator to participate in the SPAWN-based authentication. We assume that this is handled by dedicated software "apps," from the validator, running on the user devices. Furthermore, we assume that these apps provided by the validator communicate and establish an encrypted channel between the device and the validator. For the binding of the claimant and the attester, we assume previously mentioned close-proximity communication in the form of NFC or a cabled connection. The two apps will offer ways of generating and exchanging a shared secret between them. We call this randomly generated key the PSK. The key can be generated locally or by a key exchange forwarded by the validator. Local PSK generation involves either one device that takes the role of key generation or a multiparty approach. In the case of a lead device, the key is simply exchanged locally. Alternatively, a key exchange could be conducted through the validator. We discuss the security implications of these two scenarios in Sect. 5. Furthermore, the devices will store each other's MAC address as an identifier.

Authentication Request. An authentication request can be triggered by the claimant device or the validator. The claimant and the validator have a one-round exchange about a request being scheduled. Additionally, the validator sends a fresh nonce to the claimant device. The claimant starts listening to the WiFi environment for the attester's MAC address. In parallel, the validator requests confirmation from the attester device. In the following, the attester device does several things. The attester device generates a random 32-byte session key (SEK) and encrypts it with the PSK, $enc_{PSK}(SEK)$, before spawning a SoftSpot, with $enc_{PSK}(SEK)$ as the SSID.

As soon as the claimant device measures the SoftSpot of the attester device (identified by the MAC address), it does three things. First, the claimant device decrypts the SEK by applying the PSK, $dec_{PSK}(enc_{PSK}(SEK))$. Second, the claimant, D_1 conducts measurements $\mathbf{M}_1$ (dropping the SoftSpot) and encrypts the observed AP representation set with a key derived from the SEK and the nonce, $key = SEK\|nonce$. Third, it sends the ciphertext set to the validator. Given an encryption function $enc_{key}(message)$ and the set of measurements $\mathbf{M}_i$, the set of ciphertext $\mathbf{C}_i$ is defined as $\mathbf{C}_i = \{enc_{key}(m)|m \in \mathbf{M}_i\}$.

The validator communicates the nonce to the attester device and that it has received a claim. The attester device (D_2) stops the SoftSpot, measures the WiFi environment, creates $key = SEK\|nonce$ and encrypts its measurements $\mathbf{M}_2$ with key to receive $\mathbf{C}_2$.

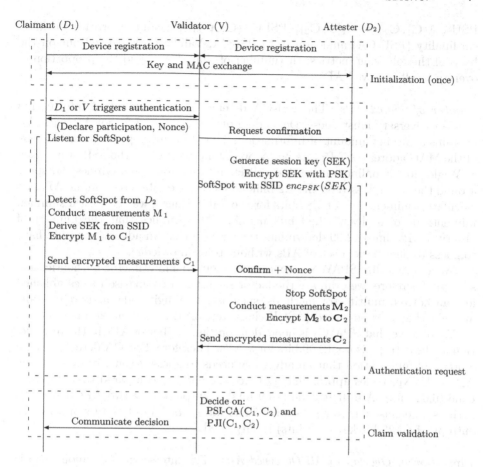

Fig. 2. This figure shows the steps of the SPAWN authentication process with two user devices, one acting as the claimant and the other as the attester, and a service as the validator V. Furthermore, the three phases of the authentication process (initialization, authentication request, and claim validation) are depicted. Session management is not included in the figure, as it deals with when the authentication request and claim validation are used together. The two solid bars on the left and right in the authentication-request phase represent the time that the user device listens to the SoftSpot and must keep the SoftSpot active.

Claim Validation. The claimant has provided a set of ciphertext $\mathbf{C}_1$, which the validator validates against the set of ciphertext received $\mathbf{C}_2$ from the attester device. As the sets are encrypted, the validator cannot access the content but can determine only the cardinality of each set, $|\mathbf{C}_1|$ and $|\mathbf{C}_2|$. When comparing the encrypted elements of the sets, the validator can calculate the cardinality of the intersection of the two sets by computing PSI-CA$(\mathbf{C}_1, \mathbf{C}_2) = |\mathbf{C}_1 \cap \mathbf{C}_2|$. Knowing the cardinality of both sets and the cardinality of their intersection, the validator can then compute the cardinality of the union of the two sets applying

PSU-CA($\mathbf{C}_1, \mathbf{C}_2$) = $|\mathbf{C}_1| + |\mathbf{C}_2| -$ PSI-CA($\mathbf{C}_1, \mathbf{C}_2$). We call this private set union cardinality (PSU-CA) analogously to PSI-CA. Validation is carried out on the basis of the following metrics: the number of shared APs and the proportion of overlap to all observed APs.

Number of Shared APs. The PSI-CA determines the amount of information that an adversary must guess. Depending on the data used for an AP, each AP contains a varying amount of information. The literature reports a min-entropy of the MAC address of 7.15-bits [9]. As we intend to also use the SSID we looked at Wigle [26], an online service that collects information about wireless hotspots around the world. Based on the 1.2 billion (short-scale) observed unique APs, we calculate a min-entropy of 5.84 bits for the SSID. Hence, we get a total summed min-entropy of at least 12.99 bits per AP. This implies that the number of observed APs times 12.99 determines the entropy that an adversary would have to guess to determine a set of APs without prior knowledge.

We aim to utilize SPAWN as an enhancement to a multifactor-authentication system. Therefore, we evaluate the factor strength in comparison to established and authorized multifactor methods, such as a two-digit code, a six-digit code, an eight-character password (ASCII characters 32-127), and a 128-bit key.

We observe that SPAWN is dependent on the number of APs in the intersection as the entropy is $k \times 12.99$ bits for k APs. Therefore, PSI-CA determines the amount of information that an adversary needs to guess. Even with a matching AP, SPAWNprovides approximately twice the entropy compared to a two-digit code (6.64 bits). A 6-digit code (19.9 bits) is surpassed by two APs. Five APs surpass an eight-character password (52.44 bits), and from ten APs onward the entropy of a 128-bit key (128 bits) is surpassed.

Proportion of Overlap to All Observed APs. The intersection-to-union ratio is known as the Jaccard index (JI) [7]. It is defined by the cardinality of the intersection divided by the cardinality of the union and is shown to be capable of fingerprinting a location based on WiFi [8]. In our setting, we compute the private JI (PJI) by PJI($\mathbf{C}_1, \mathbf{C}_2$) = $\frac{\text{PSI-CA}(\mathbf{C}_1, \mathbf{C}_2)}{\text{PSU-CA}(\mathbf{C}_1, \mathbf{C}_2)}$. We utilize the PJI as a distance metric that is specific to the location and can be calibrated. Although PSI-CA establishes the minimum information required at the intersection, PJI determines the similarity between the measurements. To consider the location and the device used, we propose a dynamic approach. During calibration, the system calculates the standard PJI for the given location and operates transparently unless the PJI deviates significantly. In such cases, the user must decide on the legitimacy of the authentication attempt.

User Involvement. In general, SPAWN can be used as a transparent authentication factor. However, we require a user in the loop during three scenarios.

Calibration of a Location. WiFi is characterized by high variability in coverage and density, as shown in the literature [8]. Therefore, there cannot be a standard solution, but there needs to be a calibration per location. We assume that a user is prompted with a confirmation request to determine the location's PSI-CA and PJI. This happens the first couple of times defined by the specific application.

An Uncertain SPAWN Claim. Even with a location-specific calibration phase that involves a user, an attester measurement can differ too much from a claimant measurement. In this case, the attester device is prompted with an authentication request, and the claimant device is notified of the denied attempt. If the PCI-CA still contains sufficient APs for the desired security level, the expected PJI could be adapted according to the new and confirmed measurements.

Device Compromise. In case of noticing theft or loss of a device, the user is the fastest hope of detection. Therefore, the user is compelled by the user's own security to notify the validator about a missing device. This is especially relevant, as proximity to the absent device would be enough to confirm a login.

Session Management. The session covers the entire period from beginning to end. The start of the session is the moment when authentication takes place. In certain contexts, such as banking or other more secure systems, a session is timed out. Although continuous authentication is not a novel concept [5], it is hardly ever deployed. SPAWN allows transparent and therefore continuous authentication. In practice, a validator can initiate proximity validation at any time during the session. The validator requests the two devices to measure their environment and thereby can dynamically detect proximity. As a result, the session can also be terminated due to a failed proximity claim validation.

3.4   Instantiation

The PSI-CA protocol proposed in [24] fits both requirements of SPAWN precisely, the requirement of an external validator and the noninteractiveness. In [24] the validator is called the evaluator with the requirement that only the evaluator learns PSI-CA and that the participating parties learn nothing more than their own set. The proposed noninteractive protocol is an efficient two-client functional encryption (2C-FE) based PSI and PSI-CA scheme.

For small set sizes, the system proposed by [24] is quite efficient. We presume to deal with small set sizes, with an estimated maximum of about 100 APs in a user's WiFi environment [8]. We guarantee by the PSK and local SoftSpot that users indeed have the same matching key and utilize the nonce shared by the validator as a session-specific identifier. Therefore, the only remaining question is how to instantiate the PRF.

Instantiating PRF. The PRF can be constructed based on a block cipher, a keyed hash function, or a hash-based message authentication code [24]. We chose the latter and instantiated the PRF required by applying KMAC, the Keccak-based message authentication code [11]. By choosing KMAC, we can independently adapt the key and output size. Furthermore, it is based on Keccak, the latest secure hash algorithm to be standardized by NIST [11].

2C-FE based PSI-CA [24]

Assumptions: A pseudo-random function PRF

1. **Setup** Choose a PRF from an ensemble of PRFs and assume matching client keys.
2. **Encrypt** Each client encrypts each set element together with a session-specific identifier by applying the chosen PRF for each set element and outputs the set of encrypted and identifier-tagged elements.
3. **Evaluate** The evaluator computes the set intersection's cardinality of the encrypted sets and derives the cardinality of the original set intersections.

4   Results

We decided to present two scenarios since considering all possible WiFi environments is infeasible: a semi-densely populated apartment environment with a maximum of 34 APs observed and a densely populated office environment with a maximum of 87 APs observed. We conducted measurements at both locations with three devices: an off-the-shelf laptop, with an Intel Alder Lake-P PCH CNVi WiFi chip, an Android device from Asus, the ZenFone 8, and an embedded WiFi chip on a Raspberry Pi 4, the Broadcom BCM4345[1]. Interestingly, at both locations, the maximum number of APs was measured by the embedded chipset. Figure 3 illustrates that, in the exemplary apartment environment, the measurements between a laptop and an Android device yield over 99% of instances where the entropy surpasses that of a password-based authentication factor. Similarly, when considering embedded hardware and the laptop, 100% of the measurements exhibit a number of shared APs such that the harvested entropy exceeds that of the minimum assumption for passwords. We conducted about 1800 measurements on the laptop, more than double on the embedded device, and 32 measurements on the Android device. Figure 4 illustrates that, in the office environment, the measurements between a laptop and an Android device yield nearly 74% of instances where the entropy surpasses that of a password-based authentication factor. Similarly, when considering embedded hardware and the laptop, almost 88% of the measurements exhibit a number of APs such that the harvested entropy surpasses that of the minimum assumption for passwords. We conducted about 3600 measurements on the laptop, about 340 measurements on the embedded device, and 14 measurements on the Android device.

---

[1] https://gitlab.com/wifi-spawn/data.

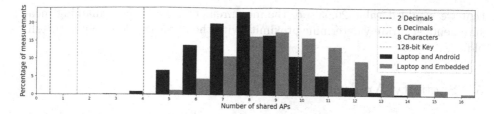

Fig. 3. This bar plot at an apartment illustrates the AP overlap between the laptop and the embedded device, as well as between the laptop and the Android device. Additionally, we use vertical dashed lines to represent the number of APs needed to achieve the entropy of other specified authentication methods, 2 and 6 digit numbers, 8-character passwords, and 128-bit keys. Everything to the right of a dashed line performs better.

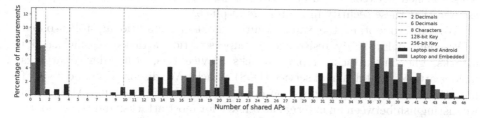

Fig. 4. This bar plot at an office illustrates the AP overlap between the laptop and the embedded device, as well as between the laptop and the Android device. We use vertical dashed lines again to represent the number of APs needed to achieve the entropy of other specified authentication methods.

In addition to the overlap (i.e., intersection) of the APs measured by different devices, we determine the proximity to a measured location by applying the PJI. This can be done in two ways: dynamically or statically.

Dynamically determining proximity can be performed by letting the user confirm that the measured PJI is indeed sufficient and that the user wants to be authenticated in this setting. This allows us to tune the threshold at the validator based on the user's feedback. Note that in the office scenario (Fig. 4) we observe an intersection of zero. This measurement cannot be used for transparent authentication, and in the situation of zero overlap, the system is required to prompt the user.

Statically determining proximity can be performed analogously to the threshold determined for location fingerprinting [8]. To achieve this, a close-by, *off-site* location is required during configuration. The threshold could then be the mean of the maximum similarity observed in the measurement at the off-site location and the minimum similarity observed in an on-site measurement [8]. We conducted 18 off-site measurements in front of the door to the apartment and the office. For the apartment, this implies that we would devalue 4.29% of the measurements. For the office, we conducted nine off-site measurements and observed that we would devalue 26.53% of the measurements, while the remaining measurements accurately determine proximity with the statically determined threshold.

5   Security Analysis

Under normal operation, we consider the participation of two entities: the user and the validator. The user possesses a minimum of two devices and asserts the proximity of these devices, which is verified by the validator. During the initialization phase, device binding occurs, resulting in the user having an application (app) on each device. These applications are equipped with secure communication capabilities with the validator (e.g., TLS). Additionally, a pre-shared key is established between the user devices as part of the initialization phase. We assume that these security measures are in place.

We aim to obtain the same security goals as traditional, token-based, 2FA schemes. Explicitly resistance to impersonation attacks, parallel session attacks, guessing attacks, replay attacks, device loss, stolen-device attacks, insider attacks, and denial of service (DoS) attacks. We discuss DoS and a spoofing attack in the next paragraph on jamming and WiFi poisoning. After which we distinguish between an external adversary for most attacks, and the validator and the user as adversaries for insider attacks.

Jamming and Poisoning the WiFi Environment. As WiFi APs communicate wirelessly and can be created easily, jamming and poisoning are possible. If jamming attempts are conducted, the validator would notice a scarce presence of APs for authentication and would revert to a token-based 2FA. Poisoning the WiFi environment is also possible. However, it would only enrich the environment in terms of APs. To build an attack upon a poisoned environment without having access to the devices, an adversary would be required to capture the device to validator communication and hence be capable of decrypting the secure communication of the validator and the device. As we expect state-of-the-art security, such attacks will be infeasible if the scheme is implemented correctly.

External Adversary Goals and Options. The primary aim of an external adversary is to obtain unauthorized authentication. To acquire location-specific WiFi details, the adversary has two options. One option is to take control of a WiFi-enabled device near the user, while the other is to physically access the user's location. However, gaining physical access to a protected location, such as an apartment or an office to conduct a valid adversary measurement M_A, is feasible only for a limited number of entities that are sufficiently close and authorized. Similarly, accessing WiFi-enabled hardware is also restricted to a limited number of entities who have the ability to gain access to a device near the user. However, both measurements are encrypted by the *key*, which includes a fresh nonce. Therefore, even an adversary that has a sufficiently similar WiFi measurement M_A does not gain any additional advantage in relation to the objective as both PCI-CA and PJI are computed on the encrypted set of measurements. The adversary has no means of computing C_A from M_A without the *key* or breaking the underlying encryption. The only benefit for an adversary who obtained a valid measurement M_A is the opportunity to extract location-specific data. However, this data extraction can also occur without the use of SPAWN.

To ensure that the validator deals with a genuine user, both user devices are preregistered. Preregistration entails a device-validator bound, implying that logging in can only be conducted by the claimant device. If both devices are compromised, the user's account is protected by the built-in security mechanisms of the claimant device and the user's password (assuming an MFA use case). If the attester device is compromised, the adversary's capabilities are even more limited compared to the traditional second-factor token setting. This is because the claimant device is preregistered, and the adversary can only deny user access but cannot gain access using only the attester device. However, if the claimant device is compromised, the adversary can gain illicit authentication by bypassing the first authentication factor (e.g., password) and the security mechanisms of the claimant device. The only additional requirement is that the adversary must physically be close to the user with the attester device or poison the user's environment and the environment of the attester device with the same fake AP. In summary, an adversary can circumvent SPAWN only if they have access to the claimant device *and* can successfully bypass the first authentication factor *and* be sufficiently close. This shows why device loss should be immediately communicated to the validator (see Sect. 3.3). Note that having access to the user device and bypassing the first authentication factor would also compromise traditional authentication schemes. 2FA might withstand such attempts if only the claimant device is controlled by the adversary, however, we consider requiring physical proximity sufficient as SPAWN is intended as an extension to traditional 2FA schemes.

Corrupted Validator Goals and Options. The objective is to learn sensitive private inputs from its users. This objective is independent of the security model chosen, either honest but curious, or malicious. In the case of an honest but curious model, the validator fulfills its duties and attempts to gather as much information as possible. In this scenario, the validator can be utilized to transmit key-exchange information, as it also carries out the transmission without the risk of a man-in-the-middle attack. In the case of a malicious model, the validator is not considered trustworthy and will take the necessary actions to obtain location-specific data. Therefore, a key exchange via the service should not be conducted to ensure that the user information is still secured by the PSK.

Malicious User Goals and Options. A malicious user may have the intention of misleading the system to prove proximity when there is no proximity by not providing the correct location information. Such behavior can also occur in traditional multifactor-authentication systems. For example, a user might ask their family or colleagues to forward a token for confirmation. Similarly, in the case of SPAWN, the user could share the set of ciphertexts or manipulate the WiFi environment to deceive the system. However, executing such an attack to falsely claim proximity requires more advanced techniques than simply sharing a few digits, as in traditional 2FA schemes. It would involve reverse-engineering and modifying the validator's app or creating an entirely artificial WiFi environment to accurately replay a request. Both are more complex endeavors than simply retyping a number in traditional multifactor-authentication schemes.

6   Discussion

Multi-Device Proximity. It is possible to use multiple devices as attesters instead of just one. When there are multiple attesters, each claimant and attester pair should follow the procedures outlined above for a single pair of devices. This approach is particularly advantageous when there is a second authority involved.

Device-to-Validator only Communication Model. We also considered developing a communication model for the devices that relies only on validator channels and eliminates the need for D2D communication. However, the abstractions of received packets in OSes do not provide sufficient detail. The only reason for D2D communication is to ensure the actuality of the data on both devices. By enabling the WiFi hardware to operate in 'monitor mode' with detailed, timestamped beacon frames, we can obtain actuality from the received packets only. However, constantly monitoring the WiFi environment would require dedicated hardware, as it continuously blocks the WiFi antenna for packet reception. Alternatively, we could introduce a new element to the beacon frames that the OSes would be required to pass on to the user. This new element could include something as simple as timestamps or even new features as provided by WiFi direct [25].

7   Conclusion

We showed that the user's WiFi environment can be used to determine proximity between devices. The measurement capabilities of different devices vary, however, the information present is sufficiently distinctive to conclude proximity, and therefore provides an additional authentication factor. We showed that guessing the correct set of WiFi APs is between 74% and 100% of the cases harder than guessing a random eight-character password. We further showed that with off-site measurements SPAWN can be calibrated to recognize sufficiently close devices statically. The only additional aspect that we require is the validator's software on the claimant device. We assume an app for this paper; however, a simple browser extension would suffice. With minor changes such as WiFi timestamps or other unique information, we could remove the D2D part and further optimize the usability and security of SPAWN. However, without additional requirements except for an installed app, SPAWN provides transparent and thus continuous authentication capabilities. This elevates usability while increasing security by being continuously applicable throughout the session.

References

1. Crawford, H., Ahmadzadeh, E.: Authentication on the go: assessing the effect of movement on mobile device keystroke dynamics. In: Thirteenth Symposium on Usable Privacy and Security, pp. 163–173 (2017)
2. Crawford, H., Renaud, K.: Understanding user perceptions of transparent authentication on a mobile device. J. Trust Manage. **1**, 1–28 (2014)
3. Dee, T., Richardson, I., Tyagi, A.: Continuous transparent mobile device touchscreen soft keyboard biometric authentication. In: 32nd International Conference on VLSI Design, pp. 539–540. IEEE (2019)
4. Ghose, N., Gupta, K., Lazos, L., Li, M., Xu, Z., Li, J.: ZITA: zero-interaction two-factor authentication using contact traces and in-band proximity verification. IEEE Trans. Mob. Comput. **23**, 6318–6333 (2023)
5. Richard, P.: Security: active authentication. IT Professional **15**(4), 4–7 (2013)
6. Han, D., Chen, Y., Li, T., Zhang, R., Zhang, Y., Hedgpeth, T.: Proximity-proof: secure and usable mobile two-factor authentication. In: Proceedings of the 24th Annual International Conference on Mobile Computing and Networking, pp. 401–415 (2018)
7. Jaccard, P.: Étude comparative de la distribution florale dans une portion des alpes et des jura. Bull. Soc. Vaudoise Sci. Nat. **37**, 547–579 (1901)
8. Jakubeit, P., Peter, A., van Steen, M.: The measurable environment as nonintrusive authentication factor on the example of WiFi beacon frames. In: Saracino, A., Mori, P. (eds.)International Workshop on Emerging Technologies for Authorization and Authentication, pp. 48–69. Springer, Cham (2022). https://doi.org/10.1007/978-3-031-25467-3_4
9. Jakubeit, P., Peter, A., van Steen, M.: LocKey: location-based key extraction from the WiFi environment in the user's vicinity. In: Proceedings of the Eighteenth International Conference on Information Security Practice and Experience (2023)
10. Jolfaei, A.A., Mala, H., Zarezadeh, M.: EO-PSI-CA: efficient outsourced private set intersection cardinality. J. Inf. Secur. Appl. **65**, 102996 (2022)
11. Kelsey, J., Chang, S., Perlner, R.: Nist special publication 800–185: sha-3 derived functions: cshake, kmac, tuplehash and parallelhash. Tech. Rep., National Institute of Standards and Technology, Gaithersburg, MD (2016)
12. Konig, R., Renner, R., Schaffner, C.: The operational meaning of min-and max-entropy. IEEE Trans. Inf. Theory **55**, 4337–4347 (2009)
13. Li, Z., Wang, H., Fang, H.: Group-based cooperation on symmetric key generation for wireless body area networks. IEEE Internet Things J. **4**(6), 1955–1963 (2017)
14. LastPass by LogMeIn. The 3rd annual global password security report. Tillgänglig (2019). https://lp-cdn.lastpass.com/lporcamedia/document-library/lastpass/pdf/en/LMI0828a-IAM-LastPass-State-of-the-Password-Report.pdf
15. Luo, Z., Wang, W., Qu, J., Jiang, T., Zhang, Q.: ShieldScatter: improving IoT security with backscatter assistance. In: Proceedings of the 16th ACM conference on Embedded Networked Sensor Systems, pp. 185–198 (2018)
16. Pierson, T.J., Peters, T., Peterson, R., Kotz, D.: Proximity detection with single-antenna IoT devices. In: The 25th Annual International Conference on Mobile Computing and Networking, pp. 1–15 (2019)
17. Pinkas, B., Schneider, T., Weinert, C., Wieder, U.: Efficient circuit-based PSI via cuckoo hashing. In: Nielsen, J.B., Rijmen, V. (eds.) EUROCRYPT 2018. LNCS, vol. 10822, pp. 125–157. Springer, Cham (2018). https://doi.org/10.1007/978-3-319-78372-7_5

18. Prove. State of MFA Report (2023). https://www.prove.com/blog/prove-identity-2023-state-of-mfa-report-consumer-attitudes-multi-factor-authentication
19. Primo, A., Phoha, V.V., Kumar, R., Serwadda, A.: Context-aware active authentication using smartphone accelerometer measurements. In: Proceedings of the IEEE Conference on Computer Vision and Pattern Recognition Workshops, pp. 98–105 (2014)
20. Rosulek, M., Trieu, N.: Compact and malicious private set intersection for small sets. In: Proceedings of the 2021 ACM SIGSAC Conference on Computer and Communications Security, pp. 1166–1181 (2021)
21. Shah, S.W., Kanhere, S.S.: Wi-Auth: Wifi based second factor user authentication. In: Proceedings of the 14th EAI International Conference on Mobile and Ubiquitous Systems: Computing, Networking and Services, pp. 393–402 (2017)
22. NIST special Publication 800-79-2. Guidelines for the authorization of personal identity (2022). https://www.nist.gov/itl/applied-cybersecurity/back-basics-multi-factor-authentication-mfa
23. Trivedi, A., Zakaria, C., Balan, R., Becker, A., Corey, G., Shenoy, P.: WiFiTrace: network-based contact tracing for infectious diseases using passive WiFi sensing. Proc. ACM Interact. Mob. Wearable Ubiquitous Technol. 5(1), 1–26 (2021)
24. van de Kamp, T., Stritzl, D., Jonker, W., Peter, A.: Two-client and multi-client functional encryption for set intersection. In: Jang-Jaccard, J., Guo, F. (eds.) ACISP 2019. LNCS, vol. 11547, pp. 97–115. Springer, Cham (2019). https://doi.org/10.1007/978-3-030-21548-4_6
25. WiFi Alliance: WiFi Direct (2023). https://www.wi-fi.org/discover-wi-fi/wi-fi-direct
26. Wigle: WiFi Network Database (2022). https://wigle.net/
27. Yuen, B., et al.: Wi-fi and bluetooth contact tracing without user intervention. IEEE Access 10, 91027–91044 (2022)

MQfilTTr: Strengthening Smart Home Privacy Through MQTT Traffic Manipulation

Henrich C. Pöhls[✉], Sven Gebauer, Fabian Scharnböck, Korbinian Spielvogel, and Joachim Posegga

Chair of IT-Security, University of Passau, Passau, Germany
hp@sec.uni-passau.de

Abstract. We present the software design for an easily extendable architecture that prevents leakage of privacy-relevant data in messages sent from smart home environments to external servers outside of a smart home. Such problems arise since users are mostly unable to control which data leaves the local network unfiltered. We address this situation by a privacy-enforcing hub architecture located at the smart home gateway; our approach enables manipulation of e.g. MQTT messages in order to block or rewrite data before it leaves the smart home. We exemplify our architecture for information dissemination control using MQTT, since it is a well-established and frequently used communication protocol in Internet of Things applications. Our performance analysis demonstrates a comparably low overhead that can easily be tolerated. We also discuss how brown field (e.g. existing) devices can be integrated into such an approach which also highlights our extension of modeling the network protocol's sender and receiver functions separately facilitating Node-RED; moreover we investigate the danger of circumventing such a hub architecture by exploiting metadata side channels; both these issues have not been sufficiently addressed in previous works, which we extend in this work.

Keywords: information dissemination · MQTT · privacy · Internet of Things

1 Introduction

Smart home devices tend to be closely linked to cloud services. A *cloud* is defined as "[...] a pool of configurable computing resources" [19] which can serve necessary resources for executing services or as storage for large amounts of data [19]. Manufacturers of *Internet of Things* (IoT) devices usually provide their users with a device-external application to configure the device. These applications mostly connect to "[...] the manufacturers cloud" [13], but these clouds often introduce additional threats: Kazim and Zhu [16] argue that one of the major threats in cloud computing includes data breaches. Other problems are data

© IFIP International Federation for Information Processing 2024
Published by Springer Nature Switzerland AG 2024
S. Bouzefrane and D. Sauveron (Eds.): WISTP 2024, LNCS 14625, pp. 17–32, 2024.
https://doi.org/10.1007/978-3-031-60391-4_2

loss, identity/account hijacking or denial of service attacks [16]. These threats are still very relevant, as the recent case of Eufy has shown [2,6,20–22,28].

While the integration of cloud resources often adds significant value to IoT- and in particular smart home-applications [19], it remains important to mitigate the additional risks associated with it. Providing this control with fine-grained control over messages and their contents is the motivation behind the work described in our paper. Given that smart home devices' revenue has tripled over the last five years and is expected to grow 50% further by 2025 [18] the users themselves are still poorly prepared to deal with issues like protecting confidentiality of their data or maintaining privacy-preserving properties of applications.

The reason for these privacy issues is that user data usually leaves their network and is saved and processed by external cloud services [15]. The lack of restrictions a user can enforce on data transmitted by smart home devices to cloud services is a serious security concern because it allows smart home platform providers to access "[...] virtually all smart home data in the clear" [34]. This empowers providers to infer sensitive information about the smart home owner, like presence or absence from home, its energy consumption, visitors (in case of using security cameras or microphones), and much more, but leaves the user powerless. In this paper we address this by locally enforcing rules on the contents of the messages that contain the data before it is sent to cloud services via a smart hub (MQFILTTR). The hub is located between the smart home devices and the cloud/platform providers and acts as a kind of information dissemination control boundary. The hub decides which data is allowed to leave the local network and whether it should be partially obfuscated, or reduced in its resolution (e.g. sending averages less frequently), to protect sensitive information [15,34]. This allows users to avoid completely trusting smart home cloud providers and allows them to regain some control over their personal data [17].

Within the European Union, the Data protection law (GDPR [9]) even requires service providers to —among other things— "minimise the amount of collected data" [8] and that the data subject, which is the individual person whose personal data is handled, needs to be able to intervene. Further, there is the recommendation that "device manufacturers should limit as much as possible the amount of data leaving devices" [8]. Notably, keeping cloud communication and data collection to a minimum is not necessarily in the interest of the cloud provider. Even the opposite is true, as a recent case from November 2022 illustrates: EUFY is a manufacturer and distributor of various *Internet of Things* (IoT) devices including security cameras [2]. Contrary to all marketing promises not to upload anything into the cloud, its products *intentionally* uploaded and even processed non-anonymised, privacy-relevant data like security camera footage and applied face recognition technology to label faces with *cross-account* unique identifiers. This case also showed that users lost control over personal data once it had left the home network: Despite having been deleted in the app, these photos remained publicly accessible, even after users deleted their Eufy account [6,20–22,28].

Our paper presents a way to enforce data protection via a so-called smart hub. We reproduce parts of the Peekaboo architecture by Jin et al. [15] and identify weaknesses as well as potential improvements. Our main focus is on the core architecture and on scalar and tabular data rather than audio and video processing using machine learning that was targeted in Peekaboo. This avoids the complexity associated with audio/video formats and special hardware needed for machine learning acceleration that was needed in Peekaboo. We have extended that concept with dedicated modules for the communication protocol, so we can translate from insecure to secure versions of the same protocol or even completely switch the protocol between the data's source and the sink on the cloud. Without the need to for machine learning, we demonstrate the great applicability of the general principle of data minimisation on the side of the data generator (e.g. at the discretion of the data subject). We tackle the problem by locally processing data such that the quality and amount of information is sufficient for the smart home providers to still provide their services. At the same time, we obfuscate, reduce or compute aggregated data to respect the user's privacy and prevent malicious entities from inferring precise personal information.

2   Related Work

Since the inception of the Internet of Things (IoT), privacy violations concerning end-users have emerged as a significant concern. Several works have delved into the underlying challenges and potential remedies [14,30,35]. Fernandes et al. [10] proposed an early approach to encourage app developers and vendors to support user privacy policies on the app or server side. Other works, e.g. by Hong et al. [13], introduced policy languages such as "Bark", which can be used to establish rules and boundaries in natural language, regulating device access and device behaviour based on user's specifications. However, the difficulty of verifying vendor adherence to these rules necessitates alternative solutions that run on the user's end. In recent years, hub-based architectures have gained prominence as state-of-the-art solutions; here a so called hub as a central gateway is used to address security, privacy, and additionally compatibility issues arising from IoT device heterogeneity, as demonstrated by Anthi et al. [3].

As part of the hub-based architecture research, Zavalyshyn et al. [33] presented "HomePad," an advanced privacy-aware home hub that enables users to supervise data processing and utilisation in smart home applications. Employing a modularised application framework with explicit data flow, HomePad utilises automated Prolog-based data flow verification to ensure compliance with user-defined privacy policies. Its expressive privacy policy specification further empowers users with comprehensive runtime data control within their smart home environment.

Additionally, "Peekaboo" from Jin et al. [15] employs a central gateway (hub) offering operators for preprocessing data into the desired format, acting as an intermediary between smart home devices and external networks. This allows users to retain control over their sensitive data. Similarly, Chi et al. [4] introduces "PFirewall", a mediator between IoT devices and their associated cloud.

While Peekaboo utilises predefined operators specified by developers to obfuscate outgoing data, PFirewall adopts a "policy-based data filter" [4] for automated data-minimisation policies. For example, the outgoing temperature data can be manipulated to prevent meaningful information inference by the cloud provider, and outgoing data may be blocked if it does not trigger an event.

In light of privacy concerns hindering IoT adoption, Davies et al. [5] propose "Privacy Mediators", locally-controlled software components that interpose on raw sensor streams. These mediators, situated in the same administrative domain as the sensors, dynamically enforce privacy policies of the respective owners or users. To facilitate Privacy Mediators' implementation, logical points of presence are established through "cloudlets" [5]. Cloudlets are locally-administered data centers at the Internet's edge, supporting code mobility and aligning with natural boundaries of trust and responsibility for individuals and organisations.

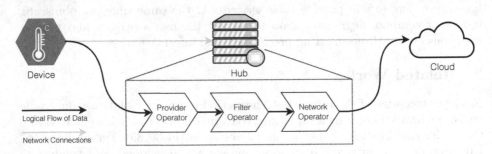

Fig. 1. High level architecture of using a hub or gateway [15]

3   Design Improvements of MQFILTTR

In this section, we present the design aspects of our proposal MQFILTTR, which extends ideas from the Peekaboo [15] architecture (seen in Fig. 1). In the following we focus on challenges and improvements we made to the existing work.

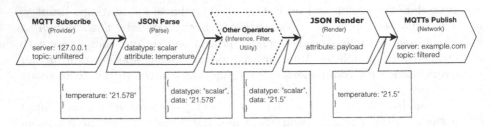

Fig. 2. Example of a MQFILTTR pipeline using separate provider/network operator (which upgrade the connection's security from MQTT to MQTT-over-TLS) and parse/render operator (which reduce the data's resolution)

Central is the *hub*, an in-home trusted device that mediates communication between IoT devices and the cloud. The hub enforces rules, such as limiting data transfer or pre-processing data locally before it is sent to the cloud. Rules for each device are specified in a *manifest* provided by the device's manufacturer, trusted third parties or the user. Rules are implemented as data processing pipelines by combining pre-defined *operators*. These operators can analyse, manipulate and spoof data; additionally they can communicate with the network in order to receive and send data.

Many smart home protocols like Z-Wave and Zigbee already use central *hubs* (also called *bridges*, *controllers*, or *coordinators*) to enable communication between their devices and the Internet [7,32]. It is therefore conceivable to integrate the hub with such bridges in the future, resulting in a single box that handles protocol translation as well as privacy and security. An existing open-source, protocol-independent smart home controller like Home Assistant can already act as (or integrate with) a Zigbee coordinator [11] and Z-Wave controller [12] through the use of external USB dongles.

3.1   MQFILTTR Separates Data Translation and Data Communication

In the related work Peekaboo [15], *provider* and *network* operators (see Fig. 1) do two things, first they handle communication protocols like HTTP or MQTT, second they translate data from and to Peekaboo's internal JSON format. We extended this and MQFILTTR separates these two functionalities into two extra operators for each pipeline. Examples of such protocols include MQTT and HTTP as well as plain TCP or UDP. Translation between data formats includes, for example, conversion between big-endian, little-endian or ASCII-encoded numbers, extracting payload data from JSON objects, or converting between different audio/video/image formats. We call these new categories of operators *parse* and *render* operators. Parse operators take data from provider operators and convert it to Peekaboo's format. Render operators perform this conversion in the other direction and pass the "rendered" packets on to a network operator.

Figure 2 shows an example pipeline using these operators. Its network operator receives JSON data via MQTT by subscribing to a topic on a locally running broker. Then the parse operator extracts the scalar payload from the "payload" attribute. At the end of the pipeline, a render operator builds a JSON object containing the filtered data as the "payload" attribute. This new JSON object is then sent by the network operator via an MQTT publish request to a broker in the cloud using *MQTT-over-TLS* (MQTTs).

Finally, this separation enables reuse of existing generic networking code as one only needs to implement custom *parse* and *render* operators.

3.2   MQFILTTR Isolates at the Network Level

In order to make sure that devices do not bypass the hub and communicate directly with the cloud, network traffic from these devices needs to be restricted.

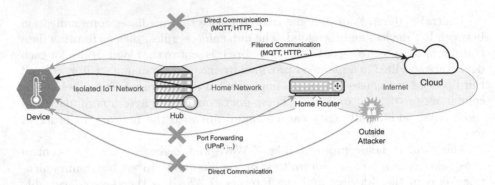

Fig. 3. Network topology isolates IoT network: all communication is via the hub in order to block unwanted communication from and to the device

For this purpose, the network architecture of MQFILTTR builds upon the fact that all the protected IoT devices connect to a separate Wi-Fi network created by the MQFILTTR hub, as shown in Fig. 3. The MQFILTTR hub effectively acts as a firewall and only allows connections to the hub itself, but not to the internet. By this, MQFILTTR can also prevent insecure or malicious devices from interfering with devices on the user's regular home network, or becoming accessible over the public internet through *Universal Plug and Play* (UPnP) port forwarding if the home router is insecurely configured or has vulnerabilities.

This kind of network isolation comes with additional challenges:

Devices might rely on basic network services like *Network Time Protocol* (NTP), which need to be provided by the hub in the restricted network. Therefore, the MQFILTTR hub runs an NTP proxy, a DHCP server, and in future also other services like local DNS.

Devices need to able to receive notifications or direct firmware updates from the cloud. Jin et al. [15] list such cloud-to-device communication as an aspect for future work and suggest to address it by extending device manifests to also cover communication patterns beyond device-to-cloud connections. MQFILTTR also did not look into this aspect; our focus is on device-to-cloud communication as the most crucial direction for privacy violations.

3.3   MQFILTTR Offloads Encryption to the Hub

As a proxy for all communication between devices and the cloud, MQFILTTR can also translate between different protocols. Of note is a translation between plaintext protocols and their counterparts that use *Transport Layer Security* (TLS) in order to secure communication with the desired cloud server during its traversal over the public Internet. For example, a MQFILTTR pipeline can use a plaintext MQTT provider operator for communication in the local network, while using an MQTT-over-TLS network operator for encrypted connections to the cloud (as depicted in Fig. 2). The hub can thereby provide secure communication to local devices which might not have enough computing power for TLS on their own. This approach can mitigate some of MQTT's current security problems described by Spielvogel et al. [29], allowing device manufacturers to declare security aspects like the need for TLS proxying in the device's manifest.

4 Implementation

This section presents our prototype implementation.

4.1 Challenges of Reusing Pekaboo's Code

Jin et al. [15] provide an open source implementation of a Peekaboo hub on GitHub[1]. However, setting up a working instance of this hub proved to be challenging because of some issues in the codebase. This includes incomplete documentation, some invalid code[2], as well as incomplete implementations of operators, causing them to silently fail for certain input data types. The *noisify* operator, for example, does not handle scalar values[3] despite its documentation stating otherwise[4]. Additionally, its error handling fails in case of unsupported input data[5]. Therefore, we implemented MQFILTTR from scratch[6] to focus on the extension and generalisation of the hub and pipeline architecture rather than fighting with details in the existing implementation of Peekaboo.

4.2 Operators and Runtime Environment

The original Peekaboo implementation [15] is based on *Node-RED*[7], a "programming tool for wiring together hardware devices, APIs and online services" [23]. We also decided to choose the Node-RED framework for MQFILTTR as it is more established than their alternatives[8] and in general we chose flow-based programming because it provides useful advantages compared to implementations in usual programming languages in this pipeline context, e.g. the reusable

---

[1] https://github.com/CMUChimpsLab/Peekaboo.

[2] https://github.com/CMUChimpsLab/Peekaboo/blob/
66865aabb81bd322e939343e14588fcea8eb58a4/peekaboo-applications/hello-visitor-camera/detector.py#L22.

[3] https://github.com/CMUChimpsLab/Peekaboo/blob/
2ef5203cb123f320ef8ca4b3866ba4191f618322/peekaboo-operators/node-red-contrib-peekaboo/noisify.js#L97.

[4] https://github.com/CMUChimpsLab/Peekaboo/blob/
2ef5203cb123f320ef8ca4b3866ba4191f618322/peekaboo-operators/node-red-contrib-peekaboo/noisify.html#L178.

[5] https://github.com/CMUChimpsLab/Peekaboo/blob/
2ef5203cb123f320ef8ca4b3866ba4191f618322/peekaboo-operators/node-red-contrib-peekaboo/noisify.js#L100.

[6] Our source is available on request and will be made available after publication.

[7] https://github.com/node-red/node-red.

[8] Node-RED has over 3k forks and 16k stars on GitHub, while TotalJS [31] only has over 400 forks and 4k stars.

component-oriented structure of "flows" and their asynchronous nature. In Node-RED a so called flow is constructed by connecting several nodes (see Fig. 5).

Node-RED already provides built-in nodes for network communication using MQTT and HTTP as well as plain TCP and UDP. [23–26]. This enables code re-use and MQFILTTR directly facilitates them as provider and network operators to achieve our separation between communication and translation (described Sect. 3.1). Moreover, implementing provider and network operator as nodes makes them independent from each other allowing translation between different input and output protocols at ease. This enables simple TLS proxying as described in Sect. 3.3, without the need for any additional specialised code. Further, we implemented two pairs of nodes for simple parse/render operators in Node-RED. One operator pair works with plain input/output data. The other supports simple JSON-based formats.

4.3 Additional Hub Services for Basic Network Services

To provide even isolated IoT devices basic network services, the hub offers additional network services: First, communication via MQTT requires an MQTT broker; so MQFILTTR runs an instance of *Mosquitto*[9]. MQTT provider operators connect to this local broker, while MQTT network operators directly connect to the cloud. For communication via HTTP, no extra service is necessary because Node-RED's existing HTTP socket can be used to accept connections to HTTP provider nodes. Second, a usable environment in the isolated IoT network (see Sect. 3.2) is provided by running a DHCP server using *systemd-networkd*, a DNS server using *bind9* and an NTP proxy using *ntpd*. Importantly, the DNS server provides only local name resolution, and does not forward requests to the Internet. This prevents malicious but isolated devices from using DNS tunneling via tools like *iodine*[10] to bypass the hub.

4.4 Prototype Environment

To illustrate the capabilities and simplicity of the underlying concept, a prototype environment was built around the hub implementation. Figure 4a depicts the IoT device ('SENSOR') which exposes the temperature sensing capabilities. It sends temperature data along with metadata (current timestamp) via MQTT to the server ('CLOUD') at intervals of one second. The latter stores all temperature values and simulates a mobile app by outputting the current value via a web interface (depicted on the right-hand side in Fig. 6). We use *Raspberry Pi 4* (4 GB RAM) single-board computers as the client, the server, and the MQFILTTR hub; an *Adafruit TMP117* measures the temperature.

Without a Hub. The IoT device is connected via a third party hosted Wi-Fi network to the cloud. Without a hub, the IoT device can send data directly and unfiltered and sends temperature and metadata to the cloud at an interval of 1s.

---

[9] https://mosquitto.org.
[10] https://github.com/yarrick/iodine.

With MQfilTTr as a Hub. This time, the IoT device needs to be connected to the hub's Wi-Fi network. It must not be connected to any other Wi-Fi network in order to allow the hub to intercept network traffic. Only in this configuration can we ensure an isolation on network level. Then, all requests go through the hub's filtering service; direct connections to the cloud, including behavior analytic services, can be blocked (DNS-level and direct connections). To regain some control over the leakage of temperature and metadata, with a high frequency, the MQFILTTR hub lowers the data push interval by aggregating temperature values for five seconds and sends just one message containing the average. The metadata is also altered and set to the current time. Furthermore, the conversions ensure that transmitted data indeed contains only numerical values as well as a timestamp.

(a) Test setup: Hub (middle) between a mockup IoT sensor (left) and the device's cloud server (right).

(b) Brown field setup: Hub (left) between a weather station (right) and its cloud server (on the Internet).

Fig. 4. MQFILTTR setup as hub

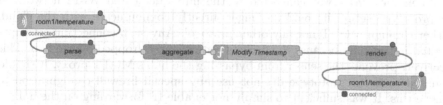

Fig. 5. MQFILTTR's pipeline in Node-RED: (1) listen to incoming MQTT messages on a topic; (2) parse raw data into an internal state; (3) aggregate data over time; (4) render simulated metadata; (5) publish the new data as outgoing MQTT message

Fig. 6. MQFILTTR at work: Instead of a steady flow of information leaking MQTT messages from the sensor (top left) MQFILTTR only lets the cloud's web interface (right) see one aggregated (bottom left) MQTT message.

5   Evaluation and Discussion

First of all, the aggregation pipeline of our prototype successfully reduces the amount of data packets transmitted to the cloud: As shown in Fig. 6, the cloud server receives only one MQTT message for every five original messages sent by the IoT device. This reduces the temporal resolution of the data, but the result is still useful for e.g. controlling a home heating system, as long as the reaction time is not expected to be near-instantaneous e.g. for controlling a home distillery.

5.1   Security Functions

It should also be possible to encrypt communication between the hub and cloud without any changes affecting the sensor.

When the sensor was connected to the hub's dedicated Wi-Fi network in our prototype setup, it could no longer directly communicate with the cloud, neither through MQTT nor any other protocol. Any such connection attempts resulted in timeouts because the packets were silently dropped by the hub. This effectively prevents the sensor from bypassing the hub's MQTT proxy. It should be noted that our prototype did not use any special firewall configuration to achieve this. It was sufficient to simply not enable IP forwarding on the hub.

In the other direction, the hub also blocked direct communication to the sensor, from both the home network and the internet. This further increases the overall security of the setup by reducing its total attack surface.

As described in Sect. 3.3, when the sensor was properly configured to send its data to the hub, we could also successfully encrypt the traffic between the hub and cloud using TLS. The only two components that need to be reconfigured in this case are the MQTT server in the cloud and the network operator in the hub's pipeline. For all other components, especially the sensor itself, this change it completely transparent.

5.2 Performance

Since our setup introduces an additional device (the hub) into the communication channel between sensor and cloud, it is possible that this new device has an impact on performance.

We did a simple performance evaluation by sending a large amount of temperature data packets through our prototype's aggregation pipeline, and measuring the time until the last aggregated packet arrived in the cloud. We generated one million packets with random temperature values, for a total size of 57 MiB, and sent them to the hub using the mosquitto_pub command line tool. In our prototype setup with TLS enabled between the hub and cloud, processing these packets took 53 seconds. This results in a throughput of 8.6 Mbit/s or 18.868 Packets/s, which should be enough even for large personal IoT setups. The apparent bottlenecks in this test are Mosquitto and Node-RED on the hub, as we could continuously see both processes at 100% CPU usage on the Raspberry PI running the hub.

When image or video data is pre-processed on the hub using local machine learning models, the performance of the overall application can also be impacted through reduced accuracy. Since our implementation only focuses on numeric data, evaluating this type of accuracy-related performance is out of scope of this work.

5.3 Potential Metadata Side Channels

Usually, data sent by the IoT device to the cloud contains further metadata *within* the payload. Examples are the device's serial number, the soft- or hardware's version or the device's current time. While the hub processes the camera footage or temperature data itself in a predefined way, attention must also be paid to its metadata. Theoretically, such a timestamp field could not just contain the current time, but also other privacy-relevant data. If there is a malicious background, it is also possible for the device to do this inconsistently and switch between expected metadata output and information leaks based on e.g. the time of day. Furthermore, with seriously malicious intentions, it is also possible to encode hidden messages in simple raw data, e.g. integers. Even using the digits from a temperature measurement, one could encode letters into numbers or even broadcast the bits (0, 1) as temperature data. This risk can never be completely eliminated and becomes more and more difficult to prevent with more complex data, e.g. with images.

For this reason, the entire payload must be examined, possibly restricted or – depending on how the server handles incomplete content structures – simulated.

5.4   Integration of Existing Devices (Brown Field)

When applying such a hub-system to the real world, one major problem is that there are already a lot of smart devices out there that expect to have free network access in order to communicate directly with the cloud. Fully restricting their network access could likely limit or break their functionality, so taking a filtering approach is required to balance usability and privacy. However, filtering the data sent by these devices is also non-trivial due to a lack of vendor-provided manifests and documentation, and could even be infeasible if their communication is properly encrypted and the connection to the cloud server is properly authenticated. We assume that some devices would enable re-configuring the device's API endpoint such that the traffic is readable to the hub, either by downgrading the security or switching to a different service and then using our new layer of protocol abstraction (see Sect. 3.1) to translate between the local protocol and the remote protocol.

We conducted an experimental evaluation using the Ecowitt weather station GW1101 (as shown in Fig. 4b). The Ecowitt ecosystem offers various additional functionalities to users, contingent on their consent to publish recorded data to the Ecowitt Cloud. From a privacy perspective, constantly sending precise data at high frequency may raise concerns regarding the potential violation of user privacy. We configured the GW1101 weather station to transmit all data, originally destined for the Ecowitt cloud, to our PEEQABOO hub instead. This gave us the opportunity to exercise control over the frequency and granularity of sensor data, enabling us to selectively determine when, what, and how to relay data to the Ecowitt Cloud. Notably, this approach is not limited to the specific Ecowitt Cloud; rather, it is extendable to any cloud server designed to handle sensor data[11]. In our specific experiment, the hub transmitted aggregated data to the cloud at an hourly interval, diverging from the original 16-second update frequency employed for specific sensor outputs, such as temperature and wind speed. Thus, our modular design allows an easy integration of brown-field devices by implementing protocol receivers and senders. In any case, on one side MQFILTTR's abstract provider and network operators can retrieve raw sensor data from brownfield devices by encapsulating the logic necessary to understand the device's messages at the hub. On the other side they are able to direct the output of the data mangling pipeline to any location, including new ones(See footnote 11), or with heightened security (e.g. upgrading to TLS secured MQTT).

6   Conclusion

This paper discusses the design, prototype implementation and evaluation of our proxy/hub MQFILTTR aimed at increasing users privacy by withholding or manipulating MQTT-based messages at a trusted central gateway at the user's network. We thereby evaluated the following claims:

---

[11] https://www.linkedin.com/pulse/collecting-presenting-weather-sensor-data-using-ecowitts-jonas-frantz/.

- The suitability of the privacy proxy or hub concept as a general design pattern for information dissemination control or data minimisation.
- Its lightweight realisation in terms of performance for MQTT-based alphanumerical content.
- Extending the Peekaboo approach [15] with more fine grained modules to separate translation and communication of data.

In the following we briefly discuss above points and future work.

6.1 Proxy/Hub Approach as a Design Pattern

Regarding EUFY's recent privacy incident (see Sect. 1), a hub based IoT concept could not only have monitored and warned that a data exchange was taking place, but it could also have prevented the communication in the first place. As mentioned in the related work, the use of a proxy is a fundamental software/network design pattern[12]. Those patterns shall "codify basic security knowledge in a structured and understandable way" [27]. They have been extended to privacy design patterns: the proxy concept can be found on curated lists of design patterns[13]. We showed in this work that hubs like our MQFILTTR are concrete tools to implement the building blocks necessary to achieve information dissemination control and provide means of data minimisation for this proxy pattern.

6.2 MQTT Manipulation Is Lightweight, but Still Effective

By concentrating solely on text rather than including image or video content, as in existing works [15], we avoided the need of heavy AI functionality, and therefore showed that the proxy/hub pattern is easily implementable based on existing open-source components like Node-RED. It is also lightweight as we showed in Sect. 5.2 and could be run on most newer home routers at least for a small number of devices or small number of parallel flows.

6.3 Extension to Separate Translation and Communication of Data

We decoupled the data translation nodes from those handling the communication, which was originally a combined step in related work like Pekaboo [15] (cmp. Fig. 1). This results in greater flexibility for pipelines in the MQFILTTR design; for example a pipeline could accept non encrypted MQTT plaintext messages on the local encrypted Wi-Fi side of the hub and emit properly secured TLS encrypted MQTT messages that leave the home network and traverse the internet to the cloud back-end server. This increased security could be offered by a generic pipeline/flow that the administrators could add independently of the additional flows to actually change the MQTT messages' content or frequency.

---

[12] Originally introduced for reusable design solutions for architectural problems in the book "A Pattern Language: Towns, Buildings, Construction" [1] (archive.org/details/APatternLanguage) in 1977.

[13] List of design patterns like https://privacypatterns.org/categories/proxy/ or https://privacypatterns.eu/#/patterns/aggregation-gateway/.

6.4 Future Work

The concept presented here, and by many works [4, 5, 33] including Peekaboo [15], only protects one direction of communication: for privacy the concept is concerned with traffic from the IoT device to the cloud. Limiting this direction is also good for security reasons, e.g. blocking a malicious device from infecting other IoT devices or participating in a denial-of-service botnet by contacting victims over the Internet. The other direction of communication would be limiting the device's capability to receive arbitrary communication from the cloud: re-writing incoming messages could help against attacks based on maliciously crafted incoming packets. It would also allow the user to be asked for consent before allowing an update to be sent to the device. Analysing the contents of firmware at a hub, e.g. to identify the validity of it, is also possible if we extend the pipelines in this direction. The hub could quite easily check if it is a known firmware image if trusted lists exist. Checking the firmware locally is a harder problem due to the binary nature of firmware and due to the need to analyse the functionality of the software implementation, e.g. by static analysis; this could be done by the hub or by a cloud service.

Finally, we briefly discussed in Sect. 5.4 the obstacles of integrating existing devices. Future work could investigate the degree of difficulty to build an actually usable (i.e. user friendly) integration when setting up existing commercial-off-the shelf devices. This could include building a Wi-Fi setup that would support auto discovery in a restricted network. The proposed concept could be extended to include definition and manifest files for IoT devices, which would be out of scope for this paper. Similar to Peekaboo (see Fig. 1) this manifest file could pre-define a communication and filter pipeline. This should reduce the configuration effort for the user and help to reach people who are not that technically experienced as a target group. Besides the pure definition of such a standard, one could also provide some predefined pipelines for the most popular IoT devices, depending on the restriction desired. In addition, a collaboration platform could be designed for users to adapt and share their own definitions, so that, with the help of contributors, even niche or later published products could also benefit from manifest files.

Acknowledgments. The work of Pöhls and Spielvogel was funded by the Bavarian Ministry of Science and Arts (Germany) under the ForDaySec.de project.

References

1. Alexander, C., Ishikawa, S., Silverstein, M.: A Pattern Language: Towns, Buildings, Construction. Oxford University Press (1977). ISBN 0-19-501919-9
2. Anker Technology (UK) Ltd. About us (2022). https://uk.eufy.com/pages/about-us. Accessed 17 Dec 2023
3. Anthi, E., Ahmad, S., Rana, O., Theodorakopoulos, G., Burnap, P.: EclipseIoT: a secure and adaptive hub for the Internet of Things. Comput. Secur. **78**, 477–490 (2018). ISSN 0167-4048

4. Chi, H., Zeng, Q., Du, X., Luo, L.: PFirewall: semantics-aware customizable data flow control for smart home privacy protection. In: 28th Annual Network and Distributed System Security Symposium (NDSS) (2021). https://doi.org/10.48550/arXiv.2101.10522

5. Davies, N., Taft, N., Satyanarayanan, M., Clinch, S., Amos, B.: Privacy mediators: helping IoT cross the chasm. In: Proceedings of the 17th International Workshop on Mobile Computing Systems and Applications, HotMobile 2016, pp. 39–44. Association for Computing Machinery, New York, NY, USA (2016). ISBN 9781450341455

6. Diaz, M.: Eufy's security cameras send data to the cloud without consent, and that's not the worst part (2022). https://www.zdnet.com/article/eufys-security-cameras-send-data-to-the-cloud-without-consent-and-thats-not-the-worst-part. Accessed 17 Dec 2023

7. Ergen, S.C.: ZigBee/IEEE 802.15.4 summary (2004). http://pages.cs.wisc.edu/~suman/courses/707/papers/zigbee.pdf. Accessed 20 Jan 2024

8. EU Article 29 Data Protection Working Party (WP 223). Opinion 8/2014 on the Recent Developments on the Internet of Things (2014)

9. European Parliament and the Council of the European Union. Regulation (EU) 2016/679 of the European Parliament and of the Council of 27 April 2016 on the protection of natural persons with regard to the processing of personal data and on the free movement of such data, and repealing Directive 95/46/EC (General Data Protection Regulation). Official Journal, OJ L 119 of 4.5.2016, 1–88 (2016)

10. Fernandes, E., Paupore, J., Rahmati, A., Simionato, D., Conti, M., Prakash, A.: FlowFence: practical data protection for emerging IoT application frameworks. In: 25th USENIX Security Symposium, pp. 531–548. USENIX Association (2016). ISBN 978-1-931971-32-4

11. Home Assistant Project. Zigbee home automation (2017). https://www.home-assistant.io/integrations/zha/. Accessed 14 Sep 2023

12. Home Assistant Project. Z-Wave (2021). https://www.home-assistant.io/integrations/zwave_js/. Accessed 14 Sep 2023

13. Hong, J., Levy, A., Riliskis, L., Levis, P.: Don't talk unless i say so! securing the internet of things with default-off networking. In: 2018 IEEE/ACM Third International Conference on Internet of Things Design and Implementation (IoTDI), pp. 117–128 (2018)

14. Jin, H., et al.: Exploring the needs of users for supporting privacy-protective behaviors in smart homes. In: Proceedings of the 2022 CHI Conference on Human Factors in Computing Systems. ACM (2022)

15. Jin, H., Liu, G., Hwang, D., Kumar, S. Agarwal, Y. Hong, J.I.: Peekaboo: a hub-based approach to enable transparency in data processing within smart homes. In: 2022 IEEE Symposium on Security and Privacy (SP), pp. 303–320 (2022)

16. Kazim, M., Zhu, S.Y.: A survey on top security threats in cloud computing. Int. J. Adv. Comput. Sci. Appl. **6**(3), 109–113 (2015)

17. Kim, D., Patidar, P., Zhang, H., Anilkumar, A., Agarwal, Y.: Self-serviced IoT: practical and private IoT computation offloading with full user control. CoRR (2022). https://doi.org/10.48550/arXiv.2205.04405

18. Lasquety-Reyes, J.: Smart home - revenue forecast in the world from 2017 to 2025 (in million U.S. dollars) (2021). https://www.statista.com/forecasts/887554/revenue-in-the-smart-home-market-in-the-world. Accessed 25 Nov 2022

19. Mell, P., Grance, T.: The NIST definition of cloud computing (2011)

20. Moore, P.: Tweet by Paul Moore on twitter (2022). https://twitter.com/Paul_Reviews/status/1596169974091071493. Accessed 17 Dec 2023

21. Moore, P.: Eufy leaking your "private" images/faces and names... to the cloud (2022). https://www.youtube.com/watch?v=qOjiCbxP5Lc. Accessed 17 Dec 2022
22. Moore, P.: Eufy doorbell - another privacy failure... (2022). https://www.youtube.com/watch?v=etpbq_HH79c. Accessed 17 Dec 2022
23. OpenJS Foundation. Node-RED (2023). https://nodered.org/. Accessed 13 Jan 2024
24. OpenJS Foundation. Node-RED HTTP Endpoint (2023). https://cookbook.nodered.org/http/create-an-http-endpoint. Accessed 11 Jan 2024
25. OpenJS Foundation. Node-RED Connect to MQTT (2023). https://cookbook.nodered.org/mqtt/connect-to-broker. Accessed 11 Jan 2024
26. OpenJS Foundation. Node-RED Palette of standard nodes (2023). https://nodered.org/docs/user-guide/editor/palette/. Accessed 11 Jan 2024
27. Schumacher, M., Fernandez-Buglioni, E., Hybertson, D., Buschmann, F., Sommerlad, P.: Security Patterns - Integrating Security and Systems Engineering. John Wiley & Sons, Ltd., West Sussex, England (2006)
28. SEC Consult Unternehmensberatung GmbH. Tweet (2022). https://twitter.com/sec_consult/status/1595771113694527488. Accessed 17 Dec 2023
29. Spielvogel, K., Pöhls, H.C., Posegga, J.: TLS beyond the broker: enforcing fine-grained security and trust in publish/subscribe environments for IoT. In: Roman, R., Zhou, J. (eds.) STM 2021. LNCS, vol. 13075, pp. 145–162. Springer, Cham (2021). https://doi.org/10.1007/978-3-030-91859-0_8
30. Tawalbeh, L., Muheidat, F., Tawalbeh, M., Quwaider, M.: IoT privacy and security: challenges and solutions. Appl. Sci. **10**(12), 4102 (2020). https://doi.org/10.3390/app10124102
31. Total.js LLC. Flow visual programming interface (2023). https://www.totaljs.com/flow/. Accessed 13 Jan 2024
32. Z-Wave Alliance. Learn - Z-Wave (2023). https://www.z-wave.com/learn. Accessed 20 Jan 2024
33. Zavalyshyn, I., Duarte, N.O., Santos, N.: HomePad: a privacy-aware smart hub for home environments. In: 2018 IEEE/ACM Symposium on Edge Computing (SEC), pp. 58–73 (2018)
34. Zavalyshyn, I., Legay, A., Rath, A., Rivière, E.: SoK: privacy-enhancing smart home hubs. Proc. Priv. Enhancing Technol. **2022**(4), 24–43 (2022)
35. Zheng, S., Apthorpe, N., Chetty, M., Feamster, N.: User perceptions of smart home IoT privacy. Proc. ACM Hum. Comput. Interact. **2**(User perceptions of smart home IoT privacy), 1–20 (2018)

Combining Cryptography and Discrete-Event Systems to Study Sensor and Actuator Cyberattacks

Ahmed Khoumsi[1](✉), Mohammed Erradi[2], and Fahd Adni[3]

[1] Department of Electrical and Computer Engineering, University of Sherbrooke, Sherbrooke, Canada
ahmed.khoumsi@usherbrooke.ca
[2] ENSIAS, Rabat, Morocco
[3] Henceforth, Rabat, Morocco
f.adni@henceforth.ma

Abstract. We consider cyber-physical systems equipped with sensors and actuators controlled or monitored by software and communication capabilities. Such use of communication makes sensors and actuators possibly vulnerable to cyberattacks (more briefly: *attacks*). We consider two approaches to study sensor and actuator attacks. The *cryptographic* approach is to design each sensor and actuator to be invulnerable to attacks, regardless of the system in which it is deployed. The *discrete-event system* (DES)-based approach is to study the detection of sensor and actuator attacks by observing the behavior of the whole system, without adding any mechanism to sensors and actuators to make them invulnerable. In this paper, we introduce and compare the two approaches and suggest an efficient way to combine them. A concrete case study is presented.

Keywords: Cyber-physical elements · Sensor attacks · Actuator attacks · (in)vulnerable sensor · (in)vulnerable actuator · Asymmetric cryptography · Digital signature · Defense · Attacker · Discrete-event system (DES) · Supervisory control of DES · Diagnosis of DES

1 Introduction

Controlling or monitoring sensors and actuators by software and communication capabilities makes such sensors and actuators possibly vulnerable to *cyberattacks* (or more briefly: *attacks*). As a cyber-physical element, a sensor consists of physical and software resources to capture physical information and code it into digital form, before possibly applying software processing. An example of sensor is a surveillance camera that captures images and digitizes them into jpeg files which are then filtered to keep only regions of interest. Let *observer* be any entity that reads digital information provided by a sensor. A sensor is attacked by corrupting (e.g. modifying or erasing) its digital information before it is accessible to an observer (see Fig. 1(a)). Concretely, an attacker may modify or hide correct

© IFIP International Federation for Information Processing 2024
Published by Springer Nature Switzerland AG 2024
S. Bouzefrane and D. Sauveron (Eds.): WISTP 2024, LNCS 14625, pp. 33–48, 2024.
https://doi.org/10.1007/978-3-031-60391-4_3

information, or create nonexisting information. Moreover, an attacker can even completely replace the sensor.

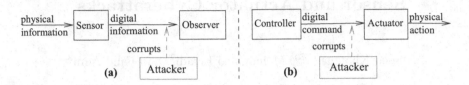

Fig. 1. (a) Sensor attack; (b) Actuator attack

As a cyber-physical element, an actuator consists of software and physical resources to receive commands in digital form before applying software and physical processing to convert the commands into physical actions. An example of actuator is a motor which receives a digital command to turn a wheel, verifies and if necessary corrects the command before generating the corresponding torque to turn the wheel. Let *controller* be any entity from which an actuator receives digital commands. An actuator is attacked by corrupting (e.g., modifying or erasing) digital commands intended for it (see Fig. 1(b)). Concretely, an attacker may modify or erase a command destined to an actuator. Moreover, an attacker can even completely replace a controller.

We consider two approaches to study sensors and actuators attacks. The first approach is *cryptographic* and aims to make each sensor and actuator invulnerable to attacks by design, regardless of the system in which it is deployed. The second approach uses *discrete-event systems* (DES) and aims to detect attacks by *observing* or *restricting* the behavior of the whole *system under study* (SUS), without adding any specific mechanism to sensors and actuators to make them invulnerable. The monitoring of the whole SUS is for example also used in [26], where the SUS's state is reconstructed from corrupted sensor measurements. However, the authors of [26] only consider sensors (and no actuators) and only observe (and do not restrict) the SUS's behavior.

We will show that the cryptographic and DES-based approaches are complementary and we will suggest an efficient way to combine them. The combination is applied whenever there exist undetectable attacks with the DES-based approach, and its principle is: 1) we identify the sensors and actuators whose vulnerability reduces attack detectability by the DES-based approach; 2) we update the SUS by making its identified sensors and actuators invulnerable using cryptography techniques; and 3) we apply the DES-based approach to detect attacks in the updated SUS. Our motivation is to only apply cryptography (which is quite expensive) to detect attacks which are undetectable with the DES-based approach.

This is the organization of the paper: Sects. 2 and 3 present the approaches of the two communities, respectively. Sect. 2 is primarily addressed to DES community as it introduces the cryptographic approach and illustrates it by a basic cryptographic solution. Sect. 3 is primarily addressed to cryptography community as it introduces the DES-based approach and illustrates it by a DES-based solution. In Sect. 4, we compare the two approaches and then suggest a way to combine them efficiently. A concrete case study is presented in Sect. 5. Finally, Sect. 6 concludes the paper.

2   Cryptographic Approach

The cryptographic approach is to design each sensor and actuator to be invulnerable to attacks, regardless of the system in which it is deployed. Several cryptographic solutions have been developed to design invulnerable sensors and actuators [3,4,6,7,24,30]. To illustrate how cryptography can be applied for our purpose, we will use *asymmetric cryptography* which is based on the use of *public* and *private* keys [27]. We use a *digital signature* system that allows to determine whether an information from a sensor or a command intended to an actuator has been *corrupted*. Interestingly, the presented digital signature system can be easily adapted to obtain an *encryption* system which allows to keep *secret* any information from a sensor or command intended to an actuator [27].

2.1   Design of an Invulnerable Sensor

A sensor is said to be *vulnerable* if the digital information it provides to an observer might be corrupted by an attacker (see Fig. 1(a)), while the sensor does not provide the observer with any means of distinguishing between corrupted and uncorrupted information. The suggested solution to make a sensor invulnerable requires to modify the behaviors of the sensor and the observer. The sensor has a *public* key and a *private* key which are used as illustrated in Fig. 2. After having digitized physical information, the sensor signs the digital information obtained. The (digital) signature is generated from the digital information and the sensor's private key. Then, the sensor makes the digital information and its signature accessible to an observer. Before accepting the digital information provided by the sensor, the observer authenticates it using the sensor's signature and public key. Authentication allows the observer to identify the sensor that produced the information and to verify that this information has not been intercepted and corrupted by an attacker. The information is accepted *iff* it is uncorrupted.

2.2   Design of an Invulnerable Actuator

An actuator is said to be *vulnerable* if the digital commands it receives from a controller might have been corrupted by an attacker (see Fig. 1(b)), while the actuator has no way of distinguishing between corrupted and uncorrupted commands. Using an approach similar to the one used in Sect. 2.1 for sensors, we obtain a cryptographic solution to make an actuator invulnerable to attacks. The controller has a *private* key and a *public* key which are used as illustrated in Fig. 3. Before providing a digital command to an actuator, the controller signs it. Signature is generated from the digital command and the controller's

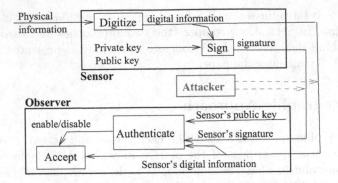

Fig. 2. Cryptographic design of an invulnerable sensor.

private key. Then, the controller makes the digital command and its signature accessible to an actuator. Before accepting the digital command provided by the controller, the actuator authenticates it using the controller's signature and public key. Authentication allows the actuator to identify the controller that issued the command and to verify that it is authorized to send commands to it. Authentication also allows the actuator to verify that the command has not been intercepted and corrupted by an attacker. The digital command is converted into a physical action *iff* authentication is successful.

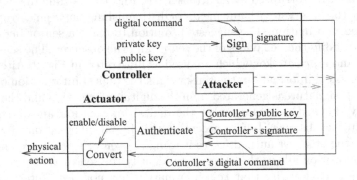

Fig. 3. Cryptographic design of an invulnerable actuator.

3   DES-Based Approach

Contrary to the cryptographic approach of Sect. 2 which is *local* to each sensor and actuator, the DES-based approach is *global*, that is, its objective is to detect attacks by considering the *system under study* (SUS) as a whole [1,2,8,12–22,28, 29,31–34,36]. As we will see, the global approach assumes to have a DES-based model which specifies how the SUS behaves in the absence of attack and how attacks affect such SUS. Such model is generally given as one or more *finite state automata* (or briefly: *automata*) that specify the set of possible event sequences that can be executed by the SUS. The basic idea is that from the knowledge of how the SUS behaves and how attacks affect it, the objective is to develop methods to detect attacks by *observing* (or monitoring) the SUS's behavior using techniques inspired from *diagnosis* of DES [25, 35].

Two perspectives are considered: a *defense*'s perspective whose objective is that *all* attacks are *detectable*, and an *attacker*'s perspective whose objective is that *all* its attacks are *undetectable*. A defense's strategy is therefore to *restrict* the behavior of the SUS to avoid situations where undetectable attacks are possible. Conversely, an attacker's strategy is to *restrict* its attacks so that they are undetectable. *Restriction* strategies in both perspectives use techniques inspired from *supervisory control* of DES [9–11, 23].

We have seen that two actions are required in studying attacks: *observing* and *restricting* the SUS behavior. What makes the problem difficult to study is that not all actions of the SUS are observable and controllable by a defense or attacker of SUS. To clarify the DES approach, in the remaining part of this section, we introduce the method of [8] as an illustrative example. We will present and explain the intuitive meaning of several automata, but without detailing how they are formally computed. The computations of all these automata are explained in [8] and use basic techniques from automata theory [5] and supervisor control and diagnosis of DES.

3.1 Model of the Attack-Free SUS

We consider the automaton of Fig. 4(a) which models a SUS in the absence of attack, where 0 is the initial state and 4 is an undesirable state (with x inside it). The events which can (resp. cannot) be *disabled* (i.e. prevented) by the defense are qualified as *controllable* (resp. *uncontrollable*) and indicated by arcs with (resp. without) a tick. The events which can (resp. cannot) be *observed* by the defense are qualified as *observable* (resp. *unobservable*) and indicated by solid (resp. dashed) arcs. So the set of controllable events is $\{\sigma, \rho\}$, and the set of observable events is $\{a, b, c, d\}$. Since ρ is controllable and c is uncontrollable, the solution to avoid the undesirable state 4 is to disable the occurrence of ρ. Otherwise, if state 3 is reached by the occurrence of ρ, uncontrollability of c implies that there is no means to avoid state 4. Disablement of ρ is represented by a red cross (x) in Fig. 4(a). Techniques of supervisory control of DES [10, 23] can be used to *automatically* determine which controllable events must be disabled to avoid undesirable states.

3.2 Model of the SUSUnder Attack

We consider the same SUS but under possible attacks, where ρ is the only *vulnerable actuator event* (i.e. event corresponding to an action realized by a vulnerable actuator) and b is the only *vulnerable sensor event* (i.e. event corresponding to digital information received from a vulnerable sensor). The SUS that was modeled by the automaton of Fig. 4(a) in the absence of attack, is now modeled by

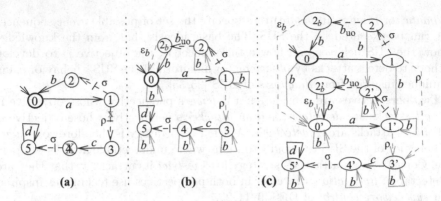

Fig. 4. SUS models: (a) without attack; (b,c) under attack.

the automaton of Fig. 4(b) in the presence of an attacker, where the transitions corresponding to attacks are in blue. Vulnerability of the actuator event ρ is modeled by the fact that now ρ is not controllable by the defense (hence the arc of ρ is now without a tick). Concretely, the attacker can force ρ so that the defense cannot disable its occurrence, which is called *Actuator Enablement* (AE) attack in [13]. Hence the defense cannot avoid to reach the undesirable state 4.

To model vulnerability of the sensor event b, its occurrence is now modeled in two steps as follows: in the first step, we have b_{uo} which represents an unobservable occurrence of b; and in the second step, we have the choice between b and ε_b. b represents the fact that the environment is informed of the occurrence of b, and ε_b represents the fact that the attacker hides from the environment that b has occurred. So in Fig. 4(b): b_{uo} means the actual occurrence of b; ε_b means that the attacker hides an actual occurrence of b, which is called *Sensor Erasure* (SE) attack in [13]. When b is immediately preceded by b_{uo} (i.e. there is no event between b_{uo} and b), then b means that the SUS *correctly* informs its environment that b has occurred. When b is not immediately preceded by b_{uo} (which is the case with any selfloop b), then b means that the attacker *falsely* informs the SUS's environment (e.g. a user of the SUS) that b has occurred, which is called *Sensor Insertion* (SI) attack in [13].

The SUS model of Fig. 4(b) does not distinguish the states reached in the *absence* of attack from the states reached in the *presence* of attack. Moreover, there is no state that is reached uniquely in the absence of attack. Indeed, states $0, 1, 2, 2_b$ can be reached: in the *absence* of attack (by an event sequence without a blue transition) and in the *presence* of attack (by an event sequence with one or more blue transitions). As an example, state 2 is reached (from the initial state 0) by $a\sigma$ and $bab\sigma b$. So another model of the SUS is generated whose each state is reached only in the *absence* of attack or only in the *presence* of attack, which is represented in Fig. 4(c). The states reached only in the absence of attack are $0, 1, 2, 2_b$, while all the other states (with an apostrophe) are reached only in the presence of attack.

3.3   Attack Detection

Let *defense* denote an entity that monitors the SUS to detect attacks. The defense, however, only has *partial* observation of SUS's behavior, so the only means of surveillance is by detecting the observable events. In our example, the set of events that are observable by the defense is $\{a, b, c, d\}$. To study attack detection, it is relevant to generate a model of the SUS under attack as it is *observed* by a defense, that is, a model which specifies *all* event sequences that can be *observed* by the defense. Such model is the automaton of Fig. 5 which is obtained by applying a *projection* (or *mask*) operator to the automaton of Fig. 4(c). Note that the automaton of Fig. 5 does not contain the unobservable events $\sigma, \rho, b_{\mathrm{uo}}, \varepsilon_b$, which is normal since this automaton models the SUS as it is *observed* by the defense. Also note that in the automaton of Fig. 5, each state r is labeled by one or more states $\{q_1, q_2, \cdots, \}$ of the automaton of Fig. 4(c). This means that when the defense observes an event sequence that leads to r, then the defense knows that the SUS is in one of the states $q_1, q_2, \cdots$ that label r, without knowing which one exactly. For example, the state $\{1, 2, 2_b, 0', 3'\}$ is reached after the observation of a. The defense is unsure whether the SUS is in state 1, 2, 2_b, 0' or 3', because a is observed after the execution of any of the following event sequences: a (it leads to 1), $a\sigma$ (it leads to 2), $a\sigma b_{\mathrm{uo}}$ (it leads to 2_b), $a\sigma b_{\mathrm{uo}}\varepsilon_b$ (it leads to 0'), and $a\rho$ (it leads to 3').

In Fig. 5, we represent states with three colors as follows: green $\bigcirc$ (resp. red $\bigcirc$) states are labeled *uniquely* by states reached in the *absence* (resp. *presence*) of attack, and black states ($\bigcirc$) are labeled by *both* states reached in the *presence* and in the *absence* of attack. Therefore, the defense detects the *absence* (resp. *presence*) of attack when it observes an event sequence leading to a $\bigcirc$ (resp. $\bigcirc$) state. And the defense is *unsure* whether an attack has occurred when it observes an event sequence leading to a $\bigcirc$ state.

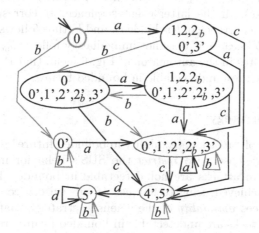

Fig. 5. SUS model for attack detection.

3.4   Attack Detectability in Bounded Future

Let us present how to verify attack *detectability* in bounded future, that is, whether the occurrence of any attack is detected after a bounded time. For that purpose, we need to model the SUS (all of its behavior, not just its observable behavior) by an automaton (represented in Fig. 6) which distinguishes the following four categories of states: 1) states where the defense is *certain* that *no* attack has occurred (green circle ◯), 2) states where the defense is *certain* that *an* attack has occurred (red circles ◯), 3) states reached when *no* attack has occurred but the defense is *unsure* of it (black circles filled with green ◉), and 4) states reached when *an* attack has occurred but the defense is *unsure* of it (black circles filled with red ●). The automaton of Fig. 6 is the *synchronous product* of the automata of Figs. 4(c) and 5. (Ignore the red crosses (x) for now, they will be used later for another purpose.) Therefore, absence (resp. presence) of attack is detected when the SUS has executed an event sequence that leads to a ◯ (resp. ◯) state in the automaton of Fig. 6.

Without loss of generality, we assume that the SUS does not remain indefinitely in the same state. This implies that the defense never remains unsure forever after an attack has occurred, *iff* there exists *no* **cycle of** ● states in the automaton of Fig. 6. In other words, the absence of **cycle of** ● states means that *all* attacks are detectable in a bounded future. Note that the absence of **cycle of** ● states means that any sequence of ● states (that represents a situation where an attack has occurred but the defense is unsure of it) has a bounded length (which means that the defense is unsure during a bounded time) and leads to a ◯ state (which means an attack detection). Since the automaton of Fig. 6 contains **cycles of** ● states, we deduce that there exist attacks that are not detectable in bounded future. Intuitively, no attack is detected at the observation of a trace $abab\cdots$, because such observation may for example correspond to the execution of $a\sigma b_{uo}ba\sigma b_{uo}b\cdots$ (absence of attack) or $a\sigma b_{uo}\varepsilon_b ba\sigma b_{uo}b\cdots$ (presence of attacks). In the latter event sequence, ε_b corresponds to an SE attack of b (actual occurrence of b is hidden), and b (that follows ε_b) corresponds to an SI attack of b because it does not immediately follows b_{uo}. So, concretely, the **cycles of** ● states in the automaton of Fig. 6 mean that there exist SE and SI attacks of b which are undetectable in bounded future.

3.5   Defense's Strategy

When the property of "attack detectability in bounded future" is not guaranteed, a strategy of the defense is to *restrict* the SUS's behavior in order to avoid the situations where attacks are not detectable in bounded future. This can be automatically achieved using techniques of supervisory control of DES [10, 23], which guarantees *optimality* of the defense's strategy, that is, *all and only* situations where attacks are undetectable in bounded future are avoided. Let us illustrate such defense's strategy in our example. As we have noted at the end of Sect. 3.4, the **cycles of** ● states in the automaton of Fig. 6 are due to the existence of SE and SI attacks of b which are undetectable in bounded future.

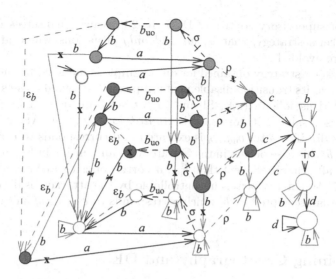

Fig. 6. SUS model to verify attack detectability.

Each of these **cycles of ●** states contains the event σ, hence the cycle can be cut by *disabling* (i.e. preventing) σ (and hence guaranteing attack detectability in bounded future of all SE and SI attacks of b). Since σ is controllable and invulnerable, the defense is able to disable it. This solution is concretely obtained by *disabling* σ whenever the defense is unsure whether an attack has occurred or not. The most restrictive solution is to disable σ from the beginning. A less restrictive solution is to disable σ after the observation of a given number of alternations of a and b. Intuitively, the defense is unsure on whether an attack has occurred when it observes an alternation of a and b starting with a (i.e. $abab\cdots$) while σ is enabled. When σ is disabled, this alternation can continue only if the SUS is attacked. Such disablement of σ means that to ensure attack detectability in bounded future, the defense has to *restrict* the behavior of the SUS even in the absence of attack. Note that the defense also detects an attack when it observes something other than an alternation of a and b starting with a. In particular, an AE attack of ρ is detected by the observation of c (since the absence of a loop between ρ and c implies that the observable c follows ρ after a bounded time).

3.6   Attacker's Strategy

The *defense*'s objective in Sect. 3.5 is to detect *every* attack in bounded future. We consider now the following *attacker*'s objective: the defense detects *no* attack, even after an unbounded future. In Sect. 3.4, we have seen that the defense detects an attack when the SUS executes an event sequence leading to a ○ state of the automaton of Fig. 6. So a strategy of the attacker is to *restrict* its attacks so that *no* ○ state is reached in the automaton of Fig. 6. This can be achieved using techniques of supervisory control of DES [10,23], which guarantees *optimality* of the attacker's strategy, that is, *all and only* situations where attacks are detectable are avoided.

The attacker's strategy obtained for our example is modeled by the automaton of Fig. 6 and its transition disablements (represented by red crosses x), which are interpreted as follows (AE, SI and SE attacks are defined in Sect. 3.2): 1) When ρ is disabled, it corresponds to *not executing* an AE attack of ρ. 2) When b is disabled after b_{uo}, ε_b is executed and corresponds to *executing* an SE attack of b; this case occurs in the ● state with an x inside in Fig. 6. 3) When b is disabled after another event than b_{uo}, it corresponds to *not executing* an SI attack of b. 4) When a (which is uncontrollable by the attacker) is disabled, this means that a is preempted by b, which corresponds to *executing* an SI attack of b.

4   Combining Cryptography and DES

4.1   Advantages and Disadvantages of Cryptography

Advantage: no model of the SUS is required, as attack detectability is studied *locally* to each sensor and actuator, *regardless* of the system where the sensor or actuator is deployed. *Disadvantage*: the required *equipment* can be costly and complex, or sometimes even physically impossible (e.g. if more space than available is needed).

4.2   Advantages and Disadvantages of the DESApproach

Advantage: there is more *insight* of the SUS, which can always help in a design process. Indeed, from a better understanding of the global SUS, the DES-based approach allows to develop attack detection strategies even with vulnerable sensors and actuators. *Disadvantage*: limiting the SUS's behavior is sometimes unsatisfactory. For example, in Sect. 3.5 we have seen that to be able to detect *all* attacks, the event σ must be disabled, even in the absence of attacks. Such solution is unsatisfactory if event σ corresponds to an essential action in the SUS.

4.3   About Having a Good Knowledge of the SUS

The cryptographic approach does not require having a good understanding of the whole SUS. On the contrary, the DES-based approach requires a good knowledge and modeling of the SUS and its attacks. Such need for modeling could be seen: as an *advantage* from the designer's viewpoint since it allows a good understanding of the SUS and its attacks; and as a *disadvantage* by the client who must pay for the design costs.

4.4   Our Suggested Combination Approach

We suggest an efficient way to combine cryptographic and DES-based approaches. For each component (i.e., sensor or actuator), let its *vulnerability* indicate whether it is *vulnerable* (V) or *invulnerable* (I). If we have in total N components, let their *global vulnerability* (GV) be the N-tuple which indicates the vulnerability of each component. There exist therefore 2^N possible values of GV.

Definition 1. *A GV gv is said to be* satisfactory *w.r.t. a given condition Cond, if the DES-based approach can detect in bounded future* all *attacks of the sensors and actuators that are vulnerable in gv, while respecting Cond.*

Note that $gv_I = (I, I, \cdots, I)$ is satisfactory whatever *Cond*, since it implies that the DES-based approach has no attack to detect. For simplicity of our explanations, we consider uniquely the following condition: the SUS's behavior is not restricted. That is, we will use the following specific definition:

Definition 2. *We consider that a GV gv is* satisfactory, *if the DES-based approach can detect in bounded future* all *attacks of the sensors and actuators that are vulnerable in gv, without restricting the SUS's behavior.*

So, as we have seen in Sect. 3.4, a *gv* is *satisfactory iff* the automaton to verify attack detectability of the vulnerable sensors and actuators (such as the automaton of Fig. 6) has *no* **cycle of** ● states. Def. 2 is not restrictive, as the procedure we will present is applicable for the general Def. 1.

For our example of Sect. 3, the GV (V, V) (i.e., b and ρ are vulnerable) is *not satisfactory*, because we have seen in Sect. 3.5 that to guarantee that *all* attacks are detectable in bounded future, the defense must *restrict* the SUS's behavior by disabling σ, in order to cut *all* **cycles of** ● states in the automaton of Fig. 6.

We only consider the defense viewpoint as she has the possibility to influence the design of the SUS and decide on the vulnerability of its sensors and actuators. Also, we consider that to each component is associated a cost to make it invulnerable using cryptography. So we can deduce the cost associated to each GV by adding the costs of its invulnerable components. The idea of our proposition is to find the least costly *satisfactory* GV, to which we can then apply the DES-based approach. Concretely, the objective is to find the least costly vulnerability configuration *gv* such that the DES-based approach can detect in bounded future all attacks of the vulnerable sensors and actuators *without restricting the SUS's behavior* (or "while respecting *Cond*", if we consider any other condition *Cond*). Note that when the costs associated to all components are equal, the objective becomes to find a satisfactory GV with as many vulnerable components as possible. The motivation is to save the design and equipment cost of making any sensor or actuator invulnerable using cryptography, if it does not improve attack detectability by the DES-based approach. We suggest the following four-step solution:

Step 1: the set of GVs is sorted in increasing cost. If several GVs have the same cost, their relative order is selected arbitrarily. Obviously, the least and most costly GVs are $gv_V = (V, V, \cdots, V)$ and $gv_I = (I, I, \cdots, I)$, respectively.

Step 2: we proceed iteratively with the sorted list of GVs, hence starting with $gv_V = (V, V, \cdots, V)$. Each iteration consists in verifying whether a GV is satisfactory. We continue to iterate until we find a satisfactory GV. In the worst case, the found satisfactory GV is gv_I, that is, all sensors and actuators should be made invulnerable using cryptography.

Step 3: we update the SUS by applying cryptography to make invulnerable every sensor and actuator which is I in the GV found in Step 2.

Step 4: the DES-based method is applied to the updated SUS.

Let us illustrate our method with the example of Sect. 3 with the pair (b, ρ), where b is a vulnerable sensor event and ρ is a vulnerable actuator event. We assume that it is more costly to make b invulnerable than to make ρ invulnerable. Hence the GVs are sorted as follows: (V, V), (V, I), (I, V), (I, I). As seen in Sect. 3.5, (V, V) is not satisfactory since it requires to disable σ to make *all* attacks detectable in bounded future. Next, we find that (V, I) is not satisfactory and (I, V) is satisfactory. Concretely, vulnerability of ρ poses no problem for attack detection (as already explained, an AE attack of ρ is simply detected with the observation of c), while b must be invulnerable to avoid situations where attacks of b are not detectable in bounded future without restricting the SUS's behavior. Hence in step 3, ρ remains vulnerable while b is made invulnerable using a cryptographic solution. Then in step 4, the DES-based approach can be applied to the updated SUS in order to detect attacks of ρ.

5 Case Study

We consider a tank of an air compression system which is controlled by a control unit (CU) and equipped by the following sensors and actuators:

Sensors: a pressure sensor S_p and a temperature sensor S_t.
Actuators: a feeding valve V_f, a relief valve V_r, a product valve V_p, and a pump P.

CU is informed by S_p of the pressure value p, and by S_t of the temperature value t. CU sends open/close commands to V_f, V_r and V_p, and start/stop commands to P. We can describe the basic system's behavior by a 3-state and 4-transition automaton:

States:
- a normal (N) state when $p \in [p_{min}, p_{max}]$ and $t \in [t_{min}, t_{max}]$, for some specified $p_{min}, p_{max}, t_{min}, t_{max}$;
- an under-pressure (UP) state when $p < p_{min}$ or $t < t_{min}$; and
- an over-pressure (OP) state when $p > p_{max}$ or $t > t_{max}$.

Transitions: N→UP, UP→N, N→OP, and OP→N.

CU's behavior for keeping the tank as much as possible in state N is as follows:

- if CU detects N→UP, it closes V_r and V_p, opens V_f and starts P;
- if CU detects UP→N, it stops P and closes V_f;

- if CU detects N→OP, it closes V_f and V_p and opens V_r; and
- if CU detects OP→N, it closes V_r.

We call *anomaly* any consequence of an attack, so that attack detection is transformed into *anomaly detection*. Let us determine which sensors and actuators must be invulnerable to detect each of the following four anomalies we have identified:

Anomaly of inconsistent sensors (A_{is}): values of p or t do not respect laws of thermodynamics (LT). A_{is} is caused by a *sensor attack* (information from S_p or S_t *modified*). CU deduces A_{is} from the non-respect of LT, with *no need for invulnerable components*.

Anomaly of silent sensor (A_{ss}): a sensor does not provide information for more than a given delay δ_{ss}. A_{ss} is caused by a *sensor attack* (information from S_p or S_t *erased*). CU deduces A_{ss} when it has not received any information from a sensor for more than δ_{ss}, with *no need for invulnerable components*.

Anomaly of critical pressure (A_{cp}): the system remains (or seems to remain) in state UP or OP for more than a given delay. A_{cp} may be caused: by a *sensor attack*, where the system is in state N but CU believes it is in state UP or OP because an attacker has *modified* information from S_p or S_t; or by an *actuator attack*, where the system remains in UP or OP because an attacker has *modified* or *erased* commands sent to actuator(s). CU can deduce A_{cp} if *either sensors or actuators are invulnerable* (i.e. no need that both sensors and actuators are invulnerable). If S_p and S_t are invulnerable, CU receives correct values of p and t, so that UP or OP is real and CU deduces that such persistent UP or OP is due to an *actuator attack* (commands *modified* or *erased*). On the other hand, if all actuators are invulnerable, CU deduces that A_{cp} is not due to *modified* commands for actuators, so that A_{cp} is due to a *sensor attack* (information *modified*) or an *actuator attack* (commands *erased*).

Anomaly of silent CU (A_{scu}): no command from CU is received by an actuator for more than a given delay δ_{scu}. A_{scu} is caused by an *actuator attack* (commands *erased*). *If an actuator is invulnerable*, it deduces A_{scu} when it has not received any command from CU for more than δ_{scu}.

To recapitulate:

- detecting A_{is} and A_{ss} is achievable with no need for invulnerable components;
- detecting A_{cp} is achievable if either sensors or actuators are invulnerable;
- detecting A_{scu} is achievable if the actuators are invulnerable.

We deduce that if the actuators are invulnerable, the four anomalies are detectable, without necessity for the sensors to be invulnerable.

So the 3-state and 4-transition automaton that models the basic system's behavior is completed with the following *anomalous* states and transitions:

- Four anomalous states are respectively reached with occurrences of the four anomalies and are therefore named A_{is}, A_{ss}, A_{cp} and A_{scu}.
- 11 anomalous transitions N→A_{is}, UP→A_{is}, OP→A_{is}, N→A_{ss}, UP→A_{ss}, OP→A_{ss}, UP→A_{cp}, OP→A_{cp}, N→A_{scu}, UP→A_{scu}, and OP→A_{scu}.

CU deduces an anomaly (and hence an attack) when it detects any transition $* \to A_{is}$, $* \to A_{ss}$ or $* \to A_{cp}$, and an invulnerable actuator deduces an attack when it detects any transition $* \to A_{scu}$.

6   Conclusion

6.1   Contributions

We have presented and analyzed two main approaches to study sensor and actuator cyberattacks: the *cryptographic* approach and the *discrete-event system*-based approach. We considered both defense and attacker viewpoints. After comparing the two approaches and highlighting their complementarity, we suggested a solution to combine them efficiently and illustrated our solution with a concrete case study.

6.2   Future Work

We plan to improve our combination solution to support two more complex cases: 1) the *intelligent* part of the system (in addition to sensors and actuators) is vulnerable to attacks; and 2) technical problems not due to attacks must be as much as possible distinguished from attacks.

We also plan to explore the integration of artificial intelligence and machine learning in combining cryptography and discrete event systems, in order to develop more efficient solutions for both defense and attacker perspectives.

References

1. Carvalho, L., Wu, Y., Kwong, R., Lafortune, S.: Detection and prevention of actuator enablement attacks in supervisory control systems. In: 13th International Workshop on Discrete Event Systems (WODES), pp. 298–305. IEEE, Xi'an, China (2016)
2. Carvalho, L., Wu, Y., Kwong, R., Lafortune, S.: Detection and mitigation of classes of attacks in supervisory control. Automatica **97**, 121–133 (2018)
3. Cheon, J., et al.: Toward a secure drone system: flying with real-time homomorphic authenticated encryption. IEEE Access **6**, 24325–24339 (2018)
4. Essa, A., Al-Shoura, T., Nabulsi, A.A., Al-Ali, A.R., Aloul, F.: Cyber Physical Sensors System Security: Threats, Vulnerabilities, and Solutions. In: Proceedings of the 2nd International Conference on Smart Grid and Smart Cities (ICSGSC), pp. 62–67. IEEE, Kuala Lumpur, Malaysia (2018)
5. Hopcroft, J., Motwani, R., Ullman, J.: Introduction to Automata Theory, Languages, and Computation. Addison-Wesley, Boston, MA, USA (June (2006)
6. Kang, J.W., Joo, I.Y., Dae-Hynn, C.: False data injection attacks on contingency analysis: attack strategies and impact assessment. IEEE Access **6**, 8841–8851 (2018)
7. Kanjee, M.R., Liu, H.: Authentication and key relay in medical cyber-physical systems. Secur. Commun. Netw. **9**, 874–885 (2016)

8. Khoumsi, A.: Sensor and actuator attacks of cyber-physical systems: a study based on supervisory control of discrete event systems. In: Proceedings of the 8th International Conference on Systems and Control (ICSC), pp. 176–182. IEEE, Marrakesh, Morocco (2019)

9. Khoumsi, A.: Decentralized architectures for supervisory control of discrete event systems. In: García, J. (ed.) Encyclopedia of Electrical and Electronic Power Engineering, pp. 661–673. Elsevier, Oxford (2023). https://doi.org/10.1016/B978-0-12-821204-2.00050-7, https://www.sciencedirect.com/science/article/pii/B9780128212042000507

10. Khoumsi, A.: Supervisory control of discrete event systems under total and partial observation. In: García, J. (ed.) Encyclopedia of Electrical and Electronic Power Engineering, pp. 649–660. Elsevier, Oxford (2023). https://doi.org/10.1016/B978-0-12-821204-2.00081-7, https://www.sciencedirect.com/science/article/pii/B9780128212042000817

11. Khoumsi, A.: Supervisory control of real-time discrete event systems. In: García, J. (ed.) Encyclopedia of Electrical and Electronic Power Engineering, pp. 674–687. Elsevier, Oxford (2023). https://doi.org/10.1016/B978-0-12-821204-2.00051-9, https://www.sciencedirect.com/science/article/pii/B9780128212042000519

12. Lima, P., Alves, M., Carvalho, L., Moreira, M.: Security against network attacks in supervisory control systems. In: 20th IFAC World Congress, pp. 12333–12338. Elsevier, Toulouse, France (2017)

13. Lima, P., Carvalho, L., Moreira, M.: Detecteable and undetectable network attack security of cyber-physical systems. In: 10th International Workshop on Discrete Event Systems (WODES), pp. 179–185. Elsevier, Sorrento Coast, Italy (2018)

14. Lin, L., Su, R.: Synthesis of covert actuator and sensor attackers as supervisor synthesis. IFAC-PapersOnLine $53(4)$, 1–6 (2020). https://doi.org/10.1016/j.ifacol.2021.04.047

15. Lin, L., Su, R.: Synthesis of covert actuator and sensor attackers for free. Discrete Event Dyn. Syst. 30, 561–577 (2020). https://doi.org/10.1007/s10626-020-00312-2

16. Lin, L., Su, R.: Synthesis of covert actuator and sensor attackers. Automatica 130, 109714 (2021). https://doi.org/10.1016/j.automatica.2021.109714

17. Lin, L., Thuijsman, S., Zhu, Y., Ware, S., Su, R., Reniers, M.: Synthesis of successful actuator attackers on supervisors. In: 2019 American Control Conference (ACC) (2019)

18. Meira-Goes, R., Kang, E., Kwong, H., Lafortune, S.: Stealthy deception attacks for cyber-physical systems. In: Conference on Decision and Control (CDC), pp. 4224–4230. IEEE, Melbourne, Australia (2017)

19. Meira-Goes, R., Kang, E., Kwong, H., Lafortune, S.: Synthesis of sensor deception attacks at the supervisory layer of cyber-physical systems. Automatica 121, 109172 (2020)

20. Meira-Góes, R., Lafortune, S., Marchand, H.: Synthesis of supervisors robust against sensor deception attacks. IEEE Trans. Autom. Control $66(10)$, 4990–4997 (2021). https://doi.org/10.1109/TAC.2021.3051459

21. Meira-Goes, R., Marchand, H., Lafortune, S.: Towards resilient supervisors against sensor deception attacks. In: Conference on Decision and Control (CDC), pp. 5144–5149. IEEE, Nice, France (2019)

22. Paoli, A., Sartini, M., Lafortune, S.: Active fault tolerant control of discrete-event systems using online diagnostics. Automatica $47(4)$, 639–649 (2011)

23. Ramadge, P.J., Wonham, W.M.: The control of discrete event systems. Proc. IEEE 77, 81–98 (1989)

24. Rehman, S.U., Sowerby, K., Coghill, C.: Analysis of impersonation attacks on systems using RF fingerprinting and low-end receivers. J. Comput. Syst. Sci. **80**(3), 591–601 (2018)
25. Sampath, M., Sengupta, R., Lafortune, S., Sinnamohidden, K., Teneketzis, D.: Diagnosability of discrete event systems. IEEE Trans. Autom. Control **40**, 1555–1575 (1995)
26. Shoukry, Y., Tabuada, P.: Event-triggered state observers for sparse sensor noise/attacks. IEEE Trans. Autom. Control **61**(8), 2079–2091 (2016). https://doi.org/10.1109/TAC.2015.2492159
27. Stallings, W.: Cryptography and Network Security: Principles and Practice. Pearson, Harlow, England (2017)
28. Su, R.: Supervisor synthesis to thwart cyber attack with bounded sensor reading alterations. Automatica **94**, 35–44 (2018)
29. Tai, R., Lin, L., Su, R.: Synthesis of optimal covert sensor-actuator attackers for discrete-event systems. Automatica **151**, 110910 (2023). https://doi.org/10.1016/j.automatica.2023.110910
30. Tang, H., Yang, Q., Long, K.: A network coding and DES based dynamic encription scheme for moving target defense. IEEE Access **6**, 26059–26068 (2018)
31. Thorsley, D., Teneketzis, D.: Intrusion detection in controlled discrete event systems. In: 45th IEEE Conference on Decision and Control, pp. 6047–6054. IEEE, San Diego, CA, USA (2006)
32. Wakaiki, M., Tabuada, P., Hespanha, J.: Supervisory control of discrete-event systems under attacks. Dyn. Games Appl. **9**, 965–983 (2019)
33. Wang, Y., Bozkurt, A., Pajic, M.: Attack resilient supervisory control of discrete-event systems. In: Conference on Decision and Control (CDC), pp. 2015–2020. IEEE, Nice, France (2019)
34. Wang, Y., Bozkurt, A., Smith, N., Pajic, M.: Attack-resilient supervisory control of discrete-event systems: a finite-state transducer approach. IEEE Open J. Control Syst. **2**, 208–220 (2023)
35. Wang, Y., Yoo, T., Lafortune, S.: Diagnosis of discrete event systems using decentralized architectures. Discrete Event Dyn. Syst. Theory Pract. **17**(2), 233–263 (2007)
36. Zhu, Y., Lin, L., Su, R.: Supervisor obfuscation against actuator enablement attack. In: European Control Conference (ECC), pp. 1760–1765. IEEE, Naples, Italy (2019)

Towards Interconnected Quantum Networks: A Requirements Analysis

Swantje Kastrup[(⊠)] and Nils gentschen Felde

Universität der Bundeswehr München, Neubiberg, Germany
swantje.kastrup@unibw.de

Abstract. Most of nowadays quantum key distribution (QKD) networks rely on trusted nodes. While trusted nodes allow for overcoming range limitations of QKD, their use hinders building interconnected networks as trust in every node has to be granted in such networks. In this paper, we focus on the requirements to enable interconnected QKD networks and sketch a way towards an interconnected multi-vendor/multi-provider QKD research network.

Keywords: QKD · networks · multi-provider · interconnection · requirements

1 Introduction

Quantum computers capable of breaking classical cryptography are expected to be available in the next 20 years when trying to err on the safe side [3]. Therefore, classical cryptographic algorithms and systems should be replaced by quantum-safe alternatives to not only ensure protection from Q-day on, but to also prevent "store now, decrypt later" attacks. There are two primarily discussed solutions to protect the privacy of messages from attackers with quantum computers: post quantum cryptography (PQC) and quantum key distribution (QKD). While the use of PQC algorithms is considered a good solution for short term security (e. g., for authentication processes), it is not sure whether it is also suited for long-term security (e. g., for message encryption) as new algorithms or attacks might be developed that break their security. In contrast QKD can, in theory, provide information theoretic security and is therefore studied in testbeds around the globe. But the use of QKD currently has several limitations. First, the security of each QKD protocol depends on the security of the implementation of the algorithm and the used hardware. At the time of writing, no certified QKD devices exist. Furthermore, in order to exchange a quantum key, the parties have to be connected through a quantum channel. Due to attenuation and loss a direct peer-to-peer channel is range restricted [6]. So, in order to cover arbitrary long distances, repeaters are needed. Recently an entanglement swapping with storage of quantum information could be demonstrated across two 25 km-long fibers [15]. The authors calculate that a repeater chain covering 800 km could be feasible using their technology. But even 800 km are still not enough to provide global

© IFIP International Federation for Information Processing 2024
Published by Springer Nature Switzerland AG 2024
S. Bouzefrane and D. Sauveron (Eds.): WISTP 2024, LNCS 14625, pp. 49–63, 2024.
https://doi.org/10.1007/978-3-031-60391-4_4

QKD coverage. This is why current quantum networks make use of so-called trusted nodes. Trusted nodes have the task to relay messages (or often encryption keys) within quantum key distribution networks (QKDNs). They ensure that the messages are hop-by-hop QKD-encrypted, but the use of trusted nodes results in loss of security and confidentiality as every relaying node can access the message in plaintext. The use of trusted nodes further prohibits building interconnected QKDNs, comparable to the internet infrastructure, because trust in every node of such a network cannot be assumed.

Contribution and Structure of the Paper

This is why this paper takes a closer look at the requirements that have to be fulfilled in order to build dynamic and scalable QKDNs with multiple node owners (Sect. 3). We will extend existing requirement catalogues so that a support of interconnected QKDNs can be considered in the future. We will further review existing protocols and results from experimental QKDNs to give an overview of existing solutions for some of the new requirements in Subsect. 3.4 and provide a list of open research questions in Subsect. 4.3. The paper concludes with an overview of our own infrastructure setup in the greater Munich area (MuQuaNet, a QKD research network in Munich, see Sect. 4) and gives an outlook on the methodology and future steps in order to tackle the challenges identified earlier.

2 Related Work

Between 2004 and 2024 many quantum testbeds have been deployed in order to evaluate different quantum technologies or network architectures. Cao et al. compared many of those which were deployed until 2021 in [4]. Their comparison shows that most networks consist of 2 to 11 nodes, with only China having networks that exceed this by far with over 150 connected nodes for the network connecting the Micius satellite with Beijing, Jinan, Hefei, and Shanghai networks [5]. While the Chinese networks are the only ones that can be considered as large-scale, most of the nodes in the networks are end-user nodes that are connected to an optical switch in a star topology. Only some of the nodes act as trusted relay nodes: the backbone of the network consists of a line of 32 of them [5]. Since 2019 the EuroQCI initiative aims to build a pan-European QKDN. A first demonstration was given by connecting three nodes situated in different countries [20].

While many QKDNs, such as the EuroQCI demonstration, focus on QKD technology and physical details, we would like to focus our literature review on some networks where also network design and message or key relaying is considered as this will be the focus of our requirements analysis later on.

The DARPA Quantum Network [7] consits of three nodes. Quantum keys are integrated in IPsec and when two nodes that are not directly connected want to communicate, a random key is generated and shared between the communication partners encrypting it with QKD keys hop-by-hop. The SECOQC network also works by relaying key material hop-by-hop [18]. Furthermore Rass et al. introduce in [19] the idea of using multi-path key relaying in order to increase the networks resilience against attackers taking over trusted nodes. Using this model, a key is split into n shares, which are sent along n distinct paths, where no node except from source and target is part of more than one part. As long as an attacker does not control more than $n - 1$ nodes on different paths in the network, a message will be protected. The SwissQuantum network addresses the problem that QKD keys might not be available due to low keyrates and that end user devices might be connected to the QKDN though a classical channel [26]. They therefore use classical encryption in addition to QKD. Newer works, like [12], consider using PQC additionally, as classical encryption is not expected to be sufficient. Like the other networks, SwissQuantum network relays generated random keys using one-time pad (OTP) encryption. Relayed keys are used in encryptors and IPsec. The Madrid Quantum Network is different from the previously described networks, as it is implemented as an SDN [8]. Here, a centralized controller manages the relay of keys in the network.

All those networks have in common that they do not require inter-domain communication and that they assume that all nodes can be trusted as they are all owned by one or more organizations that agreed in advance to trust each other. There is literature on inter-domain communication and trusted node problems as well. Wang et al. discuss in [28] how keys can be relayed across domain borders. However, they do not discuss the challenges that different domains might provide different quality of service, or that the relaying nodes of the other network are unknown and therefore might not be trustworthy. Another paper on large-scale QKDNs discusses interfaces between trusted nodes that are responsible for key relaying and therefore implement a key management [13]. James et al. propose protocols to standardize these interfaces for SDN-controlled QKDNs. With their work the scaling for networks owned by one provider is achieved, but interconnected networks are not supported.

3 Requirements Analysis

As the literature review showed, there are many approaches to build quantum networks but all operate on a low scale or with only one provider. In order to identify the requirements to build interconnected networks consisting of multiple participants/providers that all control their own hardware, we identified three use cases we believe to be representative of the many scenarios of QKDN usage.

3.1 Use Cases

All use cases considered for the analysis will be described through user stories. This way methods of the field of requirements engineering can be used to identify the functionality needed to build an interconnected quantum network.

The first use case is a civil application, that was also identified by Cao et al. in [4]. The second use case addresses a more specialized application by looking at military networks. Military networks need to match high security standards and pose strong requirements on availability and reliance. Addressing two use cases with different requirements will ensure that the requirements identified in this paper will be applicable to a wider range of possible network users.

Civil Use Case. This first use case addresses communication with end users in a civil environment. For an respresentative example we address the financial sector as it has high security requirements.

One of the most critical parts in online banking for end users is the risk of credential disclosure. With classical encryption being broken, it would be easy for an attacker to spy on credentials and by this get access to the customer's account. To address this problem we formulate the user story in Table 1 which we will use as the base for our requirements analysis.

End users are unlikely to have QKD devices available in the near future. This refers to the so-called last-mile problem. Even though there had been experiments on mobile QKD devices (see [27]) the technology is currently less mature than quantum repeaters. So, even if future QKDNs will include repeaters, the last-mile problem will still have to be addressed.

As long as the user has no direct access to QKD, PQC will be needed to encrypt the communication with the bank's server. Nevertheless, the additional use of QKD can further increase security. Please note that considering the last-mile problem when identifying requirements for network design will allow for legacy application support in the long term.

Table 1. User story for civil use case.

As	bank customer
I would like to	access my online bank account secured by QKD
in order to	avoid my credentials being stolen

Military Use Case. As discussed in Sect. 2, current QKDNs are all deployed by either one provider or at least one group of interest, where everyone considers the other providers nodes as secure for message transmission even though they could read their message. Salmanian et al. state in [21] that such an assumption might not be suitable for military networks. In their work on tactical MANETs they consider Communities of Interest (CoI) among the members of a military alliance. For messages sent within these CoIs they propose additional asymmetric encryption to ensure that these messages can only be read by members of the same CoI. This contrasts the trusted node model of current QKDNs that mandates trusting every node of the network. Using the trusted node model it is impossible for members of a military alliance to use the same QKD infrastructure both for country internal or CoI-internal communication and for communication with allies. As an example, consider Fig. 1: If Alice wants to send a message to Bob with whom she is in the white CoI, she needs the guarantee, that the message is not routed along nodes that are only part of the black CoI.

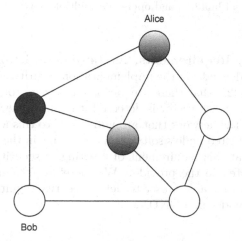

Fig. 1. Example of a network with two CoIs (colored black and white). Shaded nodes are members of both CoIs.

A naive approach to separate internal communication from allies would be to use firewalls to prevent messages from leaving one's own infrastructure. This approach could also be extended to CoIs, but does not scale well with dynamically changing CoIs. Additionnaly, all CoIs have to be preconfigured in the network and cannot be defined by a user. This may be sufficient for this military use case where the number of CoIs is limited and all CoIs are known ahead of time, but when building a QKDN that may be used by anyone, users may want to define arbitray CoIs.

We captured the special requirements of the military use case in the two user stories shown in Tables 2 and 3. We believe that similar requirements could also arise in a corporate context.

Table 2. User story for military use case – encryption.

As	a country being part of a military alliance
I would like to	communicate QKD-encrypted with my partners
in order to	protect sensitive information from unauthorized access

Table 3. User story for military use case – network architecture.

As	the military of a country
I would like to	have a shared QKD network that can be used by multiple CoIs
in order to	avoid building and operating multiple networks

Changing Security Requirements. As stated in the introduction, the security of QKD always depends on the implementation security of a QKD protocol. Satoh et al. show in [22] that there are various attack vectors to quantum networks. In case a new attack vector is detected it might be necessary to immediately avoid nodes of the network that are vulnerable to this attack. Also known vulnerabilities of a trusted node's software might result in the need to avoid this node. We believe that this requirement of reacting to security breaches should not be solely entrusted to the provider. We therefore formulate an additional user story in Table 4 to enable a user to define security requirements that allow for the exclusion of nodes in a QKDN.

Table 4. User story for changing security requirements.

As	a user
I would like to	exclude nodes of a QKDN based on security parameters
in order to	avoid insecure nodes

3.2   Deriving Requirements

Based on the three use cases we identified in Subsect. 3.1 we can now derive functionalities of an interconnected QKDN. We will start with the main requirements following directly from the user stories and will then identify further functionality that is needed to fulfill these. For the analysis we will focus on network functionality. We assume peer-to-peer QKD connections are available between some but not all nodes of the network (i.e. not a fully connected mesh).

Send QKD Encrypted Message. The use cases in Tables 1 and 2 are based on the initial need to send a message QKD encrypted. To accomplish this, the following three requirements have to be met in order to connect to the network.

Define an Encryption Entity. A user who wants to have his message encrypted is not necessarily part of the QKDN. Therefore it has to be decided whether the user's devices should be responsible for encryption and the QKDN only provides keys to the user, or whether the user sends his message to an access point which is then in charge of encrypting the message.

Connect to Access Point. The access point is a service that has several purposes. It is mainly needed for access control because QKDNs only have limited bandwidth. Unauthorized access could result in a lack of key material for authorized users and has to be prevented. Furthermore, quality of service (QoS) requirements have to be negotiated with the user before routing. Mehic et al. discuss in [16] how QoS requirements can be fulfilled by a QKDN.

Additionally, for interconnected networks the access point has to know which requirements can be fulfilled across the network. In case of multiple autonomous systems operated by different providers, this might include negotiating contracts between the providers in advance.

Find Most Secure Classical Path to Access Point. In order to use the QKDN it might be necessary to first find a classical path to an access point (see last-mile-problem in Sect. 3.1). Even though it is not the task of the QKDN to support the routing to its access points, we would like to mention it here, because this connection is the most vulnerable in the network and the route should therefore be chosen carefully.

Isolate CoI-Internal Communication in Interconnected Infrastructure. Before addressing routing which is needed to send a message to its destination, we will take a closer look at requirements following from the military use case introduced in Table 3.

Exclude TNs Outside of CoI. The need of an interconnected network results in the requirement to define among which trusted nodes of the network a message may be routed. Otherwise sensitive information might be disclosed.

Define CoI for Message. In order to exclude trusted nodes outside a CoI, CoIs first have to be defined. This can be done either in advance (i. e. a set of pre-configured CoIs is distributed to all users which might use the network) or by requesting available CoIs from the network. After that, a message has to be related to a CoI. Otherwise the relaying nodes won't be able to route the message appropriately.

Exclude Connections Based on Security Requirements. The need to exclude nodes based on security requirements introduced with the user story in Table 4 is a generalization of the need to exclude nodes given a CoI discussed before. As mentioned in Sect. 3.1 various security parametes can result in the need to exclude a trusted node. It can be due to vulnerabilities in the node's hard- and software or in its operating system. Also a missing certification might require a user to exclude a node. In contrast to existing recommendations like ITU-T Y.3800 [9] in an interconnected QKDN this decision cannot be made for routing in general affecting all users of the network because security assumptions and requirements might vary from user to user. This is particularly relevant when excluding nodes based on geolocation, provider, or CoI as for the military scenario. As another example, German users might want to exclude nodes offering only OTP encrypted key relay because the federal office of information security of Germany recommends using AES encryption instead of OTP [2].

Define Security Requirements for Message. In order to exclude nodes based on the user's needs, there has to be a language to specify which requirements apply for a message. This requirement again is a generalization of the requirement to define a CoI for a message introduced by the military use case. As the requirements might vary from message to message, they either have to be transferred with the message, or in advance so that a matching path can be prepared.

Get Available Security Parameters. As the list of possible security parameters that could be relevant for a network is long and not all nodes in a network might offer the same information about themselves, there has to be a way for the user to request which parameters are available. Only then he is able to define his security requirements properly. The QKDN could either offer a separate service providing the security parameters or the access point could also offer this information.

Route Message to Decryption Entity. Routing in QKDNs can be realised in various ways, as the user's message itself has to be routed to the target and quantum keys have to be used for encryption, which might themselves have to be relayed. This results in three possible routing architectures (compare also [9]): First, the message is peer-to-peer-relayed through the QKDN and quantum keys are used between each two peers. This way no extra routing of key material is necessary. Second, before the message is sent, an encryption key is relayed between the encryption/decryption entities. The message is then encrypted and sent somewhere through the classical network to the decryption entity. The latter variant has the advantage that the route taken by the key material can be controlled afterwards and if it is considered insecure, the key can be discarded without having the risk of message content disclosure. Both architectures can be combined, resulting in the third possible routing architecture.

A network consisting of different participants/providers can be organized in different ways. For example with MANETs each node can be seen autonomous. Routing works because all participants agreed to use the same routing algorithm and offer uniform interfaces. In other networks, providers own administrative domains for which they define the internal routing protocol (e. g., OSPF). Routing between domains is ensured by using other protocols (e. g., BGP). With the requirement of a routing mechanism that connects all participants we want to ensure that none of these designs is excluded. Whatever routing design is chosen in the end, it is necessary that the routing algorithm supports the exclusion of nodes across the network based on the security requirements of a message as we discussed previously.

Resolve Decryption Entity. Before routing, the target's decryption entity has to be resolved in order to identify the routing target. Resolving the entity can imply the mapping of a decryption entity's identifier to an address, but it can also imply the process of identifying the decryption entity responsible for a given communication target.

Consider QoS Requirements. During the routing process, not only the security requirements of the message have to be considered, but also the QoS requirements negotiated with the access point.

Authenticate TNs with Neighbors. To avoid man-in-the-middle attacks, all nodes in the network have to authenticate their neighbors.

Get Proof that the Route Fulfilled Given Restrictions. Finally, in case of key relay instead of direct message routing, delivering a proof-of-transit of the path chosen in the QKDN allows to verify that no routing restrictions were violated. If the chosen path violates the routing restrictions the relayed key can be discarded. This way message disclosure due to configuration errors can be prevented. Nevertheless, this proof does not give any guarantee that the trusted nodes were not controlled by an attacker.

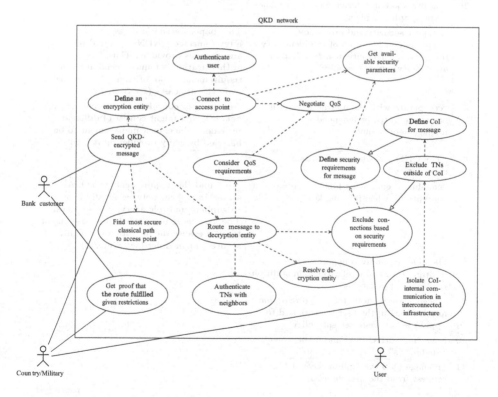

Fig. 2. Requirements derived from the use cases defined in Subsect. 3.1.

3.3   Catalogue of Requirements

All requirements identified in Subsect. 3.2 are summarized in form of a use case diagram in Fig. 2. In this section we summarize the main requirements of ITU recommendations ITU-T Y.3800 [9] and show which requirements will have to be modified (Table 5) or added (Table 6) in order to support interconnected QKDNs.

Table 5. Catalogue of Requirements according to [9].

no	requirement	comment
1	"supply a requested IT-secure key within the security assumptions to a cryptographic application subject to agreed service availability and reliability specifications of the QKDN"	
2	"interface between the user network and the QKDN to supply keys in an appropriate key format to various applications"	Please note, in our scenario we focus on an encryption entity which is to fetch/receive cryptographic material from the QKDN.
3	"supply a key in a format selected by the cryptographic application"	
4	"support security and protection, including consideration of confidentiality, integrity, authenticity, non-repudiation, availability and traceability"	This paper's scenario bases on interconnected QKDNs operated by autonomous providers. Thus, authentication is found crucial and a new requirement "proof-of-transit" is derived from the use cases (see Sect. 3.2).
5	"co-operate with the user network either in an integrated or independent management manner"	Our analysis considers an interconnected network that might consist of different providers. We expect management to be handled by every provider on its own.
6	"The QKDN has key management capabilities"	
7	"capable of employing highly secure encryption" when relaying keys	We found this requirement crucial. As stated in [10] the network should be able to support multiple encryption schemes. The user must be enabled to choose one of them, because the definition of "highly secure" might differ (see Sect. 3.2).
8	"be able to supply common keys for multiple terminal applications, in addition to P-to-P applications"	
9	"receive key requests from cryptographic applications in the user network and to apply the key management policy"	
10	have "network control and management capabilities"	
11	"manage QoS taking into account the request from the user network"	

continued

Table 5. continued

no	requirement	comment
12	"automatically authenticate and operate QKD nodes that are rebooted"	This requirement can be extended by our more general requirement of authenticating trusted nodes (see Sect. 3.2) because authentication is not only relevant when rebooting nodes, but also when new nodes join the network.
13	"use an authenticated channel for classical communication"	
14	"use optical fibre channels or direct free space optical channels for quantum channel networking"	In our scenario, we will not focus on technical specifics of the underlying OKD network. Thus, this requirement is not handled in our use case diagramm

Table 6. Additional requirements for interconnected QKDNs derived within this section.

no	requirement
15	Resolve decryption entities
16	Provide available security attributes
17	Provide an interface so that users can specify security requirements
18	Exclude trusted nodes based on security requirements
19	Provide a proof that security requirements were considered during routing

3.4 Gap Analysis

After identifying the requirements to build interconnected QKDNs, we can now analyze which of the new requirements are fulfilled by current QKDNs, which are addressed in literature, and where further research is required.

All quantum networks considered in Sect. 2 decided that the network should only relay keys. The keys are either provided to the user or often included in IPsec. For all networks the user is directly connected to the trusted node and no further classical routing is considered. Even though, we believe that the last-mile problem should be addressed in future work, because currently the option of moving clients connecting to different access points is not considered.

Furthermore, to our knowledge there is currently no framework available that allows for requesting security attributes and defining routing restrictions based on them in large-scale networks. The current routing strategies tend towards using multi-path routing in order to protect traffic against attackers ([19,24]). However, multi-path routing is not sufficient to support interconnected QKDNs for several reasons. The first reason is, that all nodes are still assumed to be trustworthy in general apart from a limited amount of attacked nodes. The second reason is, that there might not be multiple paths available in the network. In such a network, a sender has to decide, whether he wants to use QKD anyways or not. The knowledge about the security attributes of a path could help him with this decision. And finally, multi-path key relay increases network traffic and key consumption. An interconnected network is likely to have more users than an isolated network for a restricted group of participants. Therefore it will have to offer high key rates in order to be able to support multi-pathing.

Also the idea by Rass et al. to only store encrypted keys on intermediate nodes, as an alternative solution to multi-path routing, requires initial trust in the node that the encryption is done correctly [23]. Solutions (e. g. [14]) on how to exclude nodes during routing exist for classical networks, but they suffer the problem of only scaling for small networks. Here, further research is needed. Regarding requirement 19, solutions how the traversed nodes can be traced exist (e. g. [19] for multi-path QKD, [1] for progammable networks and [25] for multi-domain networks).

4 Closing the Gap: Towards Interconnected QKDNs

In Subsect. 3.4 we identified several gaps in current QKDN development which we address in our research project MuQuaNet. In the following section we will describe our QKD testbed and why it is suited to study the problems of interconnected QKDNs. We will further describe our current research and identify research questions that should be addressed in the future.

4.1 MuQuaNet QKD-Testbed – Overview and Architecture

The Munich Quantum Network is a QKD-testbed in the greater Munich area which aims to connect univiersities, the Bundeswehr (German army), other German authorities and private companies. Figure 3 shows the planned infrastructure of 10 trusted nodes, which is currently set up. The network uses QKD hardware from different suppliers, including self-developed free-space QKD devices. All partners participating in the MuQuaNet have in common that they have different and very high security requirements for network traffic entering/leaving

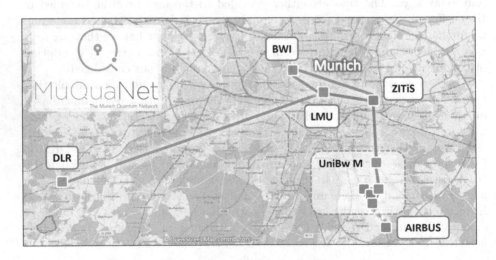

Fig. 3. Overview of the MuQuaNet infrastructure.

their private networks. Therefore, one solution we consider is treating every node belonging to one organization as an independent QKDN. This results in six QKDNs that have to be interconnected.

4.2 Addressing Nowadays' Deficits of QKDNs: Ongoing Conceptual and Implementation Work

For the MuQuaNet we decided to use the QKD infrastructure for key relay only. Messages are encypted with relayed keys and sent along a classical network route. In order to realize key relay, we decided to follow ITU-T reccomendations 3800-3803 ([9–12]) with our implementation. Just like James et al. in [13] we use REST based interfaces between the trusted nodes. But in contrast to their work, we decided not to build an SDN, but to build a distributed network that allows partner affilliations to stay as autonomous as possible. For this, we specify interfaces a key management has to offer in order to connect to other independent nodes. From our point of view, this also implies adding support of neighbor discovery, like ARP, and the use of existing routing protocols, like OSPF. In the long term this will enable us to easily extend our network by new end users and trusted nodes.

Furthermore, MuQuaNet will offer both a key supply service and a message relay service, where the access point of the network is responsible for encrypting the message, i. e. is the encryption entity. For this, we currently develop a specification language that allows for requesting available network services and their selection.

4.3 Future Work and Outreach

In order to use QKD at a large-scale as soon as possible, we identify the following research questions that should be adressed in the future. How can moving users find their nearest QKDN access point in the network? How can security parameters of a network be detected and how can they be presented to the user? How can routing consider given security requirements? The challenge with the latter two questions arises with growing networks. Protocols like IntServ for QoS signaling have scaling problems in large scale networks [17]. Here new solutions have to be developed in order to enable interconnected QKDNs.

5 Conclusion

Trusted node QKDNs suffer the drawback that using them always requires trust in the infrastructure and their providers. This research targets the vision of interconnected QKDNs and avoiding the setup and operation of parallel (QKD-) infrastructures on a large scale. The requirements analysis of this paper identifies additional funcitionalities that have to be supported in order allow for shared network usage. The most important are the exclusion of trusted nodes based on security parameters and the availabity of such parameters across a multi-vendor and multi-provider network. If the use of QKD should not depend on the successful development of quantum repeaters, for which it is unknown how long it will take until large-scale operation is possible, we believe that reasearch must not focus on simple key realying, but rather consider alternative security measures while making use of as many QKD-features as possible in order to enhance the actual level of security.

Acknowledgement. This research paper of project MuQuaNet is funded by dtec.bw – Digitalization and Technology Research Center of the Bundeswehr. dtec.bw is funded by the European Union – NextGenerationEU.

References

1. Borges, E.S., Bonella, V.B., Santos, A.J.D., Menegueti, G.T., Dominicini, C.K., Martinello, M.: In-situ proof-of-transit for path-aware programmable networks. In: 2023 IEEE 9th International Conference on Network Softwarization (NetSoft), pp. 170–177 (2023). https://doi.org/10.1109/NetSoft57336.2023.10175482
2. Bundesamt für Sicherheit in der Informationstechnik: Kryptografie quantensicher gestalten (German) (2021). https://www.bsi.bund.de/SharedDocs/Downloads/DE/BSI/Publikationen/Broschueren/Kryptografie-quantensicher-gestalten.html
3. Bundesamt für Sicherheit in der Informationstechnik: Status of quantum computer development (Entwicklungsstand Quantencomputer Version 2.0) (2023). https://www.bsi.bund.de/SharedDocs/Downloads/DE/BSI/Publikationen/Studien/Quantencomputer/Entwicklungstand_QC_V_2_0.html
4. Cao, Y., Zhao, Y., Wang, Q., Zhang, J., Ng, S.X., Hanzo, L.: The evolution of quantum key distribution networks: On the road to the Qinternet. IEEE Commun. Surv. Tutorials **24**(2), 839–894 (2022). https://doi.org/10.1109/COMST.2022.3144219
5. Chen, Y.A., et al.: An integrated space-to-ground quantum communication network over 4,600 kilometres. Nature **589**(7841), 214–219 (2021)
6. Dianati, M., Alléaume, R., Gagnaire, M., Shen, X.: Architecture and protocols of the future European quantum key distribution network. Secur. Commun. Netw. **1**(1), 57–74 (2008)
7. Elliott, C.: The darpa quantum network. In: Quantum Communications and Cryptography, pp. 91–110. CRC Press (2018)
8. García Cid, M.I., Ortiz Martín, L., Martín Ayuso, V.: Madrid quantum network: a first step to quantum internet. In: Proceedings of the 16th International Conference on Availability, Reliability and Security. ARES 2021, Association for Computing Machinery, New York, NY, USA (2021). https://doi.org/10.1145/3465481.3470056
9. ITU: Overview on networks supporting quantum key distribution, recommendation ITU-T Y.3800 (2019)
10. ITU: Functional requirements for quantum key distribution networks, recommendation ITU-T Y.3801 (2020)
11. ITU: Quantum key distribution networks - functional architecture, recommendation ITU-T Y.3802 (2020)
12. ITU: Quantum key distribution networks - key management, recommendation ITU-T Y.3803 (2020)
13. James, P., Laschet, S., Ramacher, S., Torresetti, L.: Key management systems for large-scale quantum key distribution networks. In: Proceedings of the 18th International Conference on Availability, Reliability and Security. ARES 2023, Association for Computing Machinery, New York, NY, USA (2023). https://doi.org/10.1145/3600160.3605050

14. Kapadia, A., Naldurg, P., Campbell, R.: Routing with confidence: supporting discretionary routing requirements in policy based networks. In: Proceedings. Fifth IEEE International Workshop on Policies for Distributed Systems and Networks, 2004. POLICY 2004, pp. 45–54 (2004). https://doi.org/10.1109/POLICY.2004.1309149

15. Krutyanskiy, V., et al.: Telecom-wavelength quantum repeater node based on a trapped-ion processor. Phys. Rev. Lett. **130**(21), 213601 (2023)

16. Mehic, M., Rass, S., Fazio, P., Voznak, M.: Quantum Key Distribution Networks: A Quality of Service Perspective. Springer (2022). https://doi.org/10.1007/978-3-031-06608-5

17. Menth, M.: A scalable protocol architecture for end-to-end signaling and resource reservation in IP networks. In: de Souza, J.M., da Fonseca, N.L., de Souza e Silva, E.A. (eds.) Teletraffic Engineering in the Internet Era, Teletraffic Science and Engineering, vol. 4, pp. 211–222. Elsevier (2001). https://doi.org/10.1016/S1388-3437(01)80123-2, https://www.sciencedirect.com/science/article/pii/S1388343701801232

18. Peev, M., et al.: The SECOQC quantum key distribution network in Vienna. New J. Phys. **11**(7), 075001 (2009)

19. Rass, S., Sfaxi, M.A., Ghernaouti-Hélie, S., Kyamakya, K.: Secure message relay over networks with QKD-links. In: Second International Conference on Quantum, Nano and Micro Technologies (ICQNM 2008), pp. 10–15. IEEE (2008)

20. Ribezzo, D., et al.: Deploying an inter-European quantum network. Adv. Quantum Technol. **6**(2), 2200061 (2023)

21. Salmanian, M., Brown, J.D., Watson, S., Song, R., Tang, H., Simmelink, D.: An architecture for secure interoperability between coalition tactical MANETs. In: MILCOM 2015 - 2015 IEEE Military Communications Conference, pp. 37–42 (2015). https://doi.org/10.1109/MILCOM.2015.7357415

22. Satoh, T., Nagayama, S., Suzuki, S., Matsuo, T., Hajdušek, M., Meter, R.V.: Attacking the quantum internet. IEEE Trans. Quantum Eng. **2**, 1–17 (2021). https://doi.org/10.1109/TQE.2021.3094983

23. Schartner, P., Rass, S.: How to overcome the 'trusted node model' in quantum cryptography. In: 2009 International Conference on Computational Science and Engineering. vol. 3, pp. 259–262 (2009). https://doi.org/10.1109/CSE.2009.171

24. Schatz., D., Altheide., F., Koerfgen., H., Rossberg., M., Schaefer., G.: Virtual private networks in the quantum era: a security in depth approach. In: Proceedings of the 20th International Conference on Security and Cryptography - SECRYPT, pp. 486–494. INSTICC, SciTePress (2023). https://doi.org/10.5220/0012121800003555

25. Sprintson, A., Yannuzzi, M., Orda, A., Masip-Bruin, X.: Reliable routing with QoS guarantees for multi-domain IP/MPLS networks. In: IEEE INFOCOM 2007 - 26th IEEE International Conference on Computer Communications, pp. 1820–1828 (2007). https://doi.org/10.1109/INFCOM.2007.212

26. Stucki, D., et al.: Long-term performance of the Swissquantum quantum key distribution network in a field environment. New J. Phys. **13**(12), 123001 (2011). https://doi.org/10.1088/1367-2630/13/12/123001

27. Vest, G., et al.: Quantum key distribution with a hand-held sender unit. Phys. Rev. Appl. **18**, 024067 (2022). https://doi.org/10.1103/PhysRevApplied.18.024067

28. Wang, Q., Yu, X., Zhu, Q., Zhao, Y., Zhang, J.: Quantum key pool construction and key distribution scheme in multi-domain QKD optical networks (QKD-on). In: 4th Optics Young Scientist Summit (OYSS 2020), vol. 11781, pp. 509–512. SPIE (2021)

A Similarity Approach
for the Classification of Mitigations
in Public Cybersecurity Repositories
into NIST-SP 800-53 Catalog

Ahmed Elmarkez[1,2,3]($\boxtimes$) ⓘ, Soraya Mesli-Kesraoui[3] ⓘ, Flavio Oquendo[1] ⓘ,
Pascal Berruet[2] ⓘ, and Djamal Kesraoui[3] ⓘ

[1] IRISA - Université Bretagne Sud, Vannes, France
[2] LAB-STICC - Université Bretagne Sud, Lorient, France
[3] Segula Engineering, Lanester, France
ahmed.elmarkez@segula.fr
https://www.segulatechnologies.com/

Abstract. By 2025, it is projected that cybercrimes will escalate to
an alarming annual figure of 10.5 trillion USD. To counter this growing threat, cybersecurity repositories such as CVE, CWE, CAPEC, and
Mitre Att&ck serve as crucial platforms for the exchange of threat intelligence and mitigations. These repositories play a pivotal role in the
prevention of cyber threats. Yet, mitigations in these repositories are
manually described by various experts, lacking standardized rules and
often failing to reference widely accepted catalogs like NIST SP800-53.

To enhance the effectiveness and usability of mitigations within security repositories, this paper proposes an automatic classification method
for repository mitigations, categorizing them into NIST SP800-53 classes.
This classification relies on similarity approaches and introduces a novel
algorithm aimed at refining and optimizing the accuracy of the classification results.

Keywords: Mitigation · Security pattern · NIST SP800-53 · CAPEC ·
Mitre Att&ck · Classification · Similarity · TF-IDF · Doc2Vec · BERT

1 Introduction

Cybersecurity Ventures estimates global cybercrime costs to grow by 15 percent
per year, reaching 10.5 trillion USD annually by 2025, up from 3 trillion USD
in 2015 [13]. In addition, 48% of companies reported a cyberattack in 2022, up
from 43% in 2021 [2]. To counter these threats, companies undertake a cyber
risk assessment, which is one of the most common cybersecurity activities used
in 2022 [1]. That (such as EBIOS RM [3], ISO 27005 [7], ISO 31000 [5]) is a
technique for identifying and assessing risks and threats to a system or organization. Subsequently, for each identified risk, security measures or mitigations are

ⓒ IFIP International Federation for Information Processing 2024
Published by Springer Nature Switzerland AG 2024
S. Bouzefrane and D. Sauveron (Eds.): WISTP 2024, LNCS 14625, pp. 64–79, 2024.
https://doi.org/10.1007/978-3-031-60391-4_5

defined to address these risks. A mitigation (security measure, countermeasure, or security pattern) is the technical and contextual application of a desirable property, structure, or behavior of software that aims to reduce the likelihood and impact of a threat [23]. Mitigations are often classified in a common catalog like NIST SP800-53 [12] or ISO 27002 [6] to facilitate their implementation and deployment.

In practice, cybersecurity analysts often use cybersecurity repositories like CVE[1], CWE[2], CAPEC[3], and Mitre Att&ck[4] which share threat intelligence and mitigations to prevent those threats [8]. The main purpose of these repositories is to support system designers and developers in their threat identification and treatment. For that, these repositories provide a list of mitigations.

However, mitigations in these security repositories are written manually and do not refer to commonly used catalogs. It is then the responsibility of analysts to link the textual mitigations, proposed in the security repository, with their corresponding security measure from the common catalog, which can be tedious and a source of error. Also, the level of detail of mitigation in these repositories tends to be inconsistent, especially in CAPEC and CWE. For example, one of the prescribed mitigations for CAPEC 42 (MIME Conversion) calls for disabling "the 7 to 8 bit conversion by removing the F=9 flag from all Mailer specifications in the sendmail.cf file". This level of detail may lead CAPEC adopters to believe that they are not concerned with MIME Conversion attacks if they implement a Microsoft Exchange server rather than a Sendmail-based email server. Such a mistake could lead to increased attack exposure and a false sense of security [10]. Hence, to increase the effectiveness and consistency, it would be beneficial to abstract this level of detail of mitigation by classifying them into more abstract classes. In addition, mitigations in repositories can have different points of view. For example, both CAPEC-126 and CAPEC-79 (Fig. 1) have an information input validation mitigation, but this mitigation is written from different points of view (the first is presented as a design mitigation and the second as a test mitigation). Regrouping to the same group will simultaneously create a manageable and serviceable list of accepted mitigation strategies [11].

Several studies have classified mitigations and security patterns manually [9,10,14,18,25]. However, the large number of mitigations in security repositories (for example, 1200 mitigations in CAPEC) and the regular updating of these repositories (CAPEC version 3.9, CWE version 4.11, and Mitre atta&ck version 13) can make manual classification tedious, source of error and, above all, very consuming in time and resources. On the other hand, the automatic classification of mitigations in repositories may improve efficiency by speeding up the classification process and ensuring a consistent and standardized approach, eliminating inconsistencies and errors that can arise from human subjectivity.

Similarity classification is one of the automatic classification approaches that has been widely used and has demonstrated its usefulness in the automatic

---

[1] https://cve.mitre.org/.
[2] https://cwe.mitre.org/.
[3] https://CAPEC.mitre.org/.
[4] https://attack.mitre.org/.

classification of cybersecurity data [15,17,26]. This technique is based on word processing techniques to transform a text into a vector. A similarity calculation is then performed to identify similar data according to the distance between their vectors.

The general purpose of this work is to automatically classify mitigations from repositories to NIST SP800-53 catalog using similarity-based approaches. To sum up, this paper presents two contributions:

- An automatic classification approach to classify mitigations from repositories to the NIST SP800-53 using three existing similarity-based techniques: TF-IDF, Doc2Vec and BERT.
- A novel algorithm proposition, overcoming the limitations of the existing techniques and improving results.

The remainder of the paper is structured as follows: Sect. 2 presents relevant works and background. In Sect. 3 we describe the research method for this work. Section 4 proposes the automatic classification methodology and its evaluation. In Sect. 5, we present our novel algorithm to improve previous section results. The threats to the validity of our work are presented in Sect. 6. We conclude and present our future works in Sect. 7.

2   State of the Art

2.1   Security Knowledge Repositories

Sharing threat knowledge can be of the utmost importance to prevent attacks and malicious actions on a system. Cybersecurity information sharing is currently carried out through repositories (CVE, CAPEC, CWE, Mitre ATT&Ck). The purpose of each repository is to disclose information on one or more aspects of security like vulnerability, attack, etc.

CVE (Common Vulnerabilities and Exposures) provides a reference method for publicly known information-security vulnerabilities and exposures. The mission of its Program is to identify, define, and catalog publicly disclosed cybersecurity vulnerabilities.

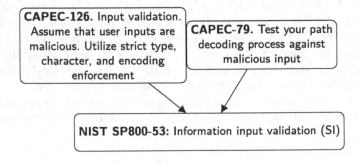

Fig. 1. Motivation example

The CAPEC (Common Attack Pattern Enumeration and Classification) repository provides a publicly available catalog of common attack patterns. Attack Patterns are the description of the common attributes and approaches employed by adversaries to exploit known weaknesses in cyber-enabled capabilities. Attack patterns help those developing applications, or administrating cyber-enabled capabilities, to better understand the specific elements of an attack and how to stop them from succeeding.

The CWE (Common Weakness Enumeration) is a community-developed list of common software and hardware weakness types that have security ramifications. Targeted at both the development and security practitioner communities, the main goal of CWE is to stop vulnerabilities at the source by educating software and hardware architects, designers, programmers, and acquirers on how to eliminate the most common mistakes before products are delivered.

Mitre Att&ck (adversarial Tactics, Techniques, and Common Knowledge) is a globally accessible knowledge repository of adversary tactics and techniques based on real-world observations. The ATT&CK knowledge repository is used as a foundation for the development of specific threat models and methodologies in the private sector, in government, and in the cybersecurity product and service community.

2.2 NIST SP800-53

NIST SP800-53 [12] is a comprehensive set of security controls designed to guide and enhance the security of organizations and systems. This standard provides a detailed catalog of security controls and mitigations organized into 20 control families or classes such as Access control (AC), Awareness and Training (AT), Configuration and Management (CM), etc. Each control family is uniquely identified by a two-character code (e.g., SI for System Integrity). The implementation of security and privacy controls may encompass policy elements, oversight, supervision, manual processes, and automated mechanisms, which are executed by systems or carried out by individuals.

2.3 Related Work

Several studies have tried to classify security mitigations (also called security patterns) [9,10,14,18,25]. The authors in [9] conducted a literature survey on publications describing security patterns and manually classified a set of 360 security patterns based on the application domain. The authors of [18] had collected and classified security and privacy design patterns based on a generic architecture, which improves and facilitates the selection process and assists automotive software and engineers in adopting and using security solutions and technologies available on the market. Moreover, in [14] the authors proposed to classify mitigations where the nodes are the system boundaries and the leaves are the STRIDE threats. Works of [10] had tried to classify the CAPEC mitigations into the abstract classes of NIST 800-53 [12] to improve their usability, manageability, and serviceability.

However, all the mentioned studies had classified the mitigations manually, and given the growing number of security mitigations, this is not practical. In addition, even if the authors in [25] proposed a semi-automatic classification, they didn't base their classification on a common catalog like NIST 800-53, unlike our study. Indeed, they hierarchically cluster the mitigations to a given number of clusters for the first time. Then, they assign a security principle to each group by analyzing the group's mitigation.

On the other hand, the literature reports applications of the similarity techniques in the cybersecurity domain to analyze data topics and to define similarities between them. The work in [15] proposed a method to automatically link CAPECs to CVEs using three similarity techniques: TF-IDF, USE, and Sentence-BERT. Moreover, they experimentally confirm that TF-IDF is the best technique. The works of [21] sought to automatically link CVE to CAPEC by using Doc2Vec technique to link textual descriptions of CVE documents and CAPEC documents. The cosine similarity metric was then used to have their correlation evaluated. TF-IDF was used in [26] as a similarity technique to link CAPEC data to CWE ones. The K-Means algorithm [17] was also used to group CAPEC entries into generic labels. However, none of the mentioned studies tried to classify the mitigations in the cybersecurity repositories using a similarity-based approach.

3   Research Approach

For the automatic classification of repositories mitigations, we have proposed a two-phased approach. The first phase (**Automatic classification of mitigations**) proposes a solution to classify the mitigations of security repositories into NIST SP800-53 catalog. We applied, tested, and evaluated three techniques using a similarity approach (Sect. 4). Based on the analysis of the existing techniques results, **a novel algorithm (second phase) was proposed**. In this phase, we consider the limitations resulting from the second phase to create an algorithm that improves the results of the existing techniques. The proposed algorithm was evaluated using the same metrics and datasets.

4   Automatic Classification of Mitigations

The steps of the automatic classification approach of mitigations from repositories into NIST SP800-53 (Fig. 2) are detailed in the following subsections.

4.1   Text Processing

The text extracted from NIST SP800-53 classes and security repositories undergoes a cleaning process, which involves converting all words to lowercase, removing punctuation and stop words, lemmatization (returning to the root word), and stemming (e.g., "ing" and "ed"). To facilitate automatic classification, we

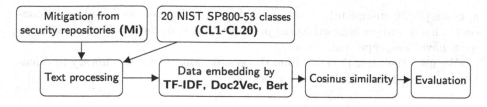

Fig. 2. Classification methodology steps

developed a Python code using the *"nltk"* library for these tasks. It is important to note that for *BERT* inputs, we omit the removal of stop words, lemmatization, and stemming. This model is trained to comprehend and analyze sentences in context, as discussed in more detail in Subsect. 4.2. Following this step, we create a list for each mitigation, containing the specific mitigation and the descriptions of the 20 classes from NIST SP800-53.

4.2 Data Embedding

This step involves converting data into vectors through the application of three methods: TF-IDF, DOC2VEC, and BERT. The selection of these vectorization techniques is grounded in two considerations. Initially, our objective was to opt for techniques employing diverse approaches for calculating sentence vectors. TF-IDF represents a non-contextual method, whereas BERT and Doc2Vec are contextual techniques that consider the entire context of the words. Secondly, we chose these techniques from among the most widely utilized methods in the literature and for text vectorization.

TF-IDF. This algorithm [20] assesses the significance of a term, denoted as t contained in a document d, concerning a given collection or corpus of documents (denoted as N). This evaluation (formula 1) is conducted by multiplying the term's frequency $tf(t, d)$, where $n_{t,d}$ represents the occurrence of t in d) and the inverse frequency of the term $idf(t)$ across documents. Notably, this approach does not consider the contextual use of the word; it solely focuses on calculating its frequency.

$$tf(t, d) = \frac{n_{t,d}}{\sum_{s \in d} n_{s,d}} \qquad idf(t) = \log \frac{N}{|\{d_j : t \in d_j\}|} \qquad (1)$$

We used Python to implement TF-IDF and *"TfidfVectorizer"* from the *"sklearn.feature_extraction.text"* library to calculate our TF-IDF document vectors.

DOC2VEC. Based on Word2Vec technique, this contextual approach involves transforming a word into a vector, considering the context in which the word appears [16]. Consequently, a word may have varying vectors based on its context. This technique is based on the principle that two words with close contexts must have close representations.

We used the *Doc2Vec* class from the *gensim.models.doc2vec* library to calculate our DOC2VEC documents vectors.

BERT. This contextual technique [24] uses unsupervised learning to learn a text and then assign a vector to a word. To fine-tune the BERT model to the cybersecurity domain, we chose to follow the TSDAE approach [27]. This approach involves introducing noise into the input sequences by deleting or swapping tokens (e.g., words). These damaged sentences are encoded by the transformer model into sentence vectors. Another decoder network then attempts to reconstruct the original input from the damaged sentence encoding [4,27]. We used the data from the CVE repository as inputs for the TSDAE approach.

4.3 Cosine Similarity

After data embedding, we use the outputted vectors to calculate the cosine similarity[5] between each repository's mitigation and the 20 NIST SP800-53 classes. It gives a useful measure of how similar two documents are likely to be, in terms of their subject, and independently of the length of the documents. Given two n-dimensional vectors of attributes, the cosine similarity is calculated using the formula 2 and it will range from 0 (no similarity) to 1 (same documents). We used the *cosine_similarity* from the *sklearn.metrics.pairwise* library to calculate cosine similarity between two documents.

$$cos(\boldsymbol{p}, \boldsymbol{q}) = \frac{p_1 q_1 + p_2 q_2 + ... + p_n q_n}{\sqrt{p_1^2 + p_2^2 + ... + p_n^2}\sqrt{q_1^2 + q_2^2 + ... + q_n^2}} = \frac{\boldsymbol{pq}}{|\boldsymbol{p}||\boldsymbol{q}|} \tag{2}$$

The outputted similarities are then sorted, and we obtain, for every mitigation, a sorted list of NIST SP800-53 classes.

4.4 Evaluation Method

To evaluate the three techniques (TF-IDF, Doc2Vec, BERT), we address these two research questions.

- **RQ1.** Which of the techniques is more accurate and efficient?
- **RQ2.** How do those parameters (accuracy and efficiency) change according to the used repository?

To address RQ1, we employed two metrics to evaluate the performance of the used techniques: the recall@n metric for assessing accuracy and the total execution time to evaluate efficiency. The recall@n metric pertains to the top-n accurately classified mitigations relative to the total number of mitigations.

---

[5] https://www.itl.nist.gov/div898/software/dataplot/refman2/auxillar/cosdist.htm.

Here, by rank n, we refer to the first n classes returned by the algorithm. Its calculation is defined by the formula 3 [22].

$$Recall@n = \frac{\text{n first well classified mitigations}}{\text{total mitigations number}} \tag{3}$$

To address RQ2, we use three repositories of mitigations: Mitre Att&ck ICS, CAPEC (extracted from [19]), and Defend. The Mitre Att&ck ICS repository contains 42 mitigations related to NIST SP800-53. In [19], a set of 24 CAPECs is associated with NIST SP800-53 security controls, and in Defend, 42 mitigations are linked to NIST SP800-53. It's important to note that no other identified data sources establish a direct link between CAPEC or CWE mitigations and NIST SP800-53.

For NIST SP800-53, we concatenate the descriptions of the security controls of the same class to construct its overall description. In the case of Mitre Att&ck ICS, we consider both the mitigation's name and description. Regarding CAPEC data, we consider the concatenation of all CAPEC mitigations, since in the dataset the CAPECs are linked to NIST SP800-53 based on their descriptions rather than their mitigations. For Mitre Defend, we concatenate the name and definition of the mitigations.

In the validation step, if a mitigation is associated with more than one class, the automatic classification is considered as accurate if at least one of these classes is assigned to the mitigation in the corresponding dataset.

4.5   Results and Discussion

RQ1. On the Mitre Att&ck ICS data, our analysis reveals a recall (recall@3) of 90% for TF-IDF, 74% for Doc2Vec, and 67% for BERT, as depicted in Fig. 3. Notably, TF-IDF achieves a swift recall@n of 100% at rank 11, outpacing Doc2Vec (rank 13) and BERT (rank 19). On the CAPEC data, we observe a recall at rank 3 of 83% for TF-IDF, 58% for Doc2Vec, and 67% for BERT. Interestingly, TF-IDF attains a 100% recall at an early stage (rank 7), in contrast to the slower convergence of Doc2Vec (rank 17) and BERT (rank 20). Examining the Mitre Defend data (Fig. 4), TF-IDF emerges as the most robust, achieving a recall@3 of 79%, while Doc2Vec and BERT attain 71% and 64%, respectively. The results show that Doc2Vec converges at rank 13, whereas TF-IDF converges at rank 16, and BERT at rank 20.

Regarding execution time, the results indicate that TF-IDF outperforms Doc2Vec and BERT (Fig. 5). TF-IDF is on average 45 times faster than Doc2Vec and 75 times faster than BERT. This discrepancy is attributed to the simplicity of mathematical instructions and operations employed by TF-IDF, in contrast to the more complex ones used by Doc2Vec and BERT.

RQ2. The three techniques have better accuracy for Mitre Att&ck ICS data. After analyzing the mitigations of this repository, we find that the vocabulary used is very similar to the NIST SP800-53 which justifies these results. For the

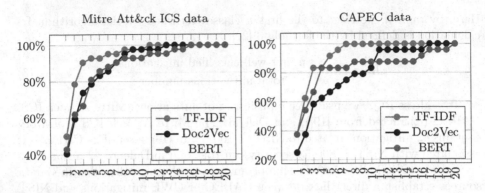

Fig. 3. Recall@n of TF-IDF, DOC2VEC and BERT on: a) Mitre Att&ck data; b) CAPEC data

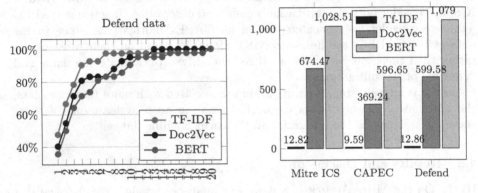

Fig. 4. Recall@n of TF-IDF, DOC2VEC and BERT on Defend data

Fig. 5. Computation time for TF-IDF, Doc2Vec and Bert on: a) Mitre Att&ck ICS data; b) CAPEC data; c) Mitre Defend data

execution timing (Fig. 5), logically bigger the repositories are, the longer the execution timing is.

Discussion. These findings indicate that non-contextual techniques such as TF-IDF yield superior outcomes in both computation time and classification accuracy compared to contextual approaches like Doc2Vec and BERT. Specifically, when considering recall@3, the classification accuracy of TF-IDF is consistently 15.6% higher on average than that of Doc2Vec and BERT. In light of these results, it can be concluded that non-contextual methods, exemplified by TF-IDF, excel at automatically classifying mitigations. The underwhelming performance of contextual techniques can be attributed to the varying terminologies employed in the repositories, with CAPEC mitigations utilizing a more technical language than NIST SP800-53. Conversely, the success of non-contextual techniques can be attributed to the keywords defining standardized NIST SP800-53 mitigations, facilitating the linkage of mitigations to their corresponding classes.

However, upon scrutinizing the inaccurate classifications using TF-IDF (Table 1), it becomes evident that certain mitigations, such as Mitre Att&ck ICS M0938, were misclassified due to the prominence of words like "block" which correlates more strongly with the SC class than other classes. A similar pattern is observed with M0934, where the presence of the word "block" influenced the classification erroneously. In contrast, accurately classified mitigations like M0954, M0817, and M0917 (Table 1) are well-classified from the first rank, benefiting from descriptions that contain terms specific to their respective classes. For example, M0954 includes "configuration" a term specific to the CM class, M0817 involves "supply chain" and "supplier" linked to the SR class, and M0917 features terms such as "train", "user interaction", "spearphishing" and "social engineering" aligning with the AT class.

Table 1. Examples of an inaccurate/accurate classifications

ID	Name	Description	NIST SP800-53 class	Rank 3 classes attributed by the TF-IDF	Accuracy
M0938	Execution Prevention	Block execution of code on a system through application control, and/or script blocking.	SI	SC, CM, SA	inaccurate
M0934	Limit Hardware Installation	Block users or groups from installing or using unapproved hardware on systems, including USB devices.	MP	SC, CM, AC	inaccurate
M0954	Software Configuration	Implement configuration changes to software (other than the operating system) to mitigate security risks associated with how the software operates.	CM	CM, SA, SI	accurate
M0817	Supply Chain Management	Implement a supply chain management program, including policies and procedures to ensure all devices and components originate from a trusted supplier and are tested to verify their integrity.	SR	SR, PM, SA	accurate
M0917	User Training	Train users to be aware of access or manipulation attempts by an adversary to reduce the risk of successful spearphishing, social engineering, and other techniques that involve user interaction.	AT	AT, AC, IA	accurate

5   Novel Algorithm Proposal

To overcome the problem of TF-IDF, we propose a novel algorithm that increases the value of the keywords in their classes in order to differentiate them.

5.1   Algorithm Implementation

The main idea of this algorithm is to define a set of keywords characterizing each of the NIST SP800-53 classes (formula 4, Algorithm 1). Then, given a mitigation

M, the calculation of the occurrence of its words in every *class i* of NIST SP800-53 is performed *Occ(w,c)*. If one of the words matches a keyword in the NIST SP800-53 class, then the occurrence of that word in that class is boosted by adding an integer to it N. This boost gives more value to the class keywords present in mitigation.

$$Score(M, classi) = \sum_{j=1}^{lenght(M)} (\texttt{Occ(word j,classe i) + N}) \qquad (4)$$

$$N = \begin{cases} Interger > 0 & \text{if the word j is a keyword} \\ 0 & \text{otherwise} \end{cases}$$

For each NIST SP800-53 class, we identified a set of keywords that characterize it. For this, we applied TF-IDF and took the most recurrent keywords returned.

5.2   Evaluation Method

To assess the performance of our proposed algorithm and compare it with the TF-IDF, we address the following questions.

- **RQ3.** How does the proposed algorithm perform compared to TF-IDF in terms of computation time and accuracy?
- **RQ4.** What is the impact of the number of keywords used and the boost value on the performance of the keyword counting algorithm?

To address RQ3, we conduct a comparison of performance in terms of recall@n and computation time between our proposed algorithm and the TF-IDF. For RQ4, we assess the recall@3 of our algorithm across a range of keyword numbers from 1 to 201 and boost values ranging from 1 to 201 with a step of 5. These evaluations are performed using the three validation datasets mentioned earlier. It's important to note that recall@3 is used as an example to streamline calculations, and the results obtained can be generalized to all recall@n.

5.3   Results and Discussion

RQ3. In terms of accuracy, the results (see Figs. 6 and 7) show that the use of keywords can improve recall@n. The proposed algorithm performs better than TF-IDF. Indeed, in the third rank, our algorithm performs on average 7% better than TF-IDF. These results are explained by the fact that TF-IDF takes into account the logarithm of the inverse of the frequency of the class containing a given word, which decreases the score of the word if it belongs to several classes. Whereas our algorithm does the opposite. It increases the values of the keyword in the class where it appears the most and then decreases its values in other classes.

Regarding computation time, our keyword algorithm takes slightly longer than TF-IDF (Fig. 8). This is attributed to our keyword-counting algorithm relying on TF-IDF for the determination of keywords to be utilized. The process of identifying keywords introduces a slight delay compared to TF-IDF.

Algorithm 1. The proposed algorithm

ourAlgorithm(mitigations, classes, keywordsLists, boost)
scoresList ← []
for i ← 1, $length(mitigations)$ do
    corpus ← []
    scores ← []
    insert(corpus,textProcess(mitigations[i]))
    for j ← 1, 20 do
        insert(corpus,textProcess(classes[j]))
        insert(scores,0)
    end for
    vectors ← countVectorize(corpus)
    for j ← 2, 21 do
        for $word \in corpus[1]$ do
            if word in keywords[j] then
                scores[j-1]+ = $boost$
            end if
            scores[j-1]+ = vectors[j][word]
        end for
    end for
    insert(scoresList,scores)
end for
Return scoresList

RQ4. When calculating the recall@3 for a number of keywords ranging from 1 to 201 and a boost value ranging from 1 to 201 with a step of 5, we observe, for Mitre Att&ck data, that the optimal value of boost is between 76–96 with an optimal number of keywords equals to 21. On the other hand, for the CAPEC data, the optimal values correspond to a boost between 106 and 161 with a keyword number between 126 and 131, also a boost between 86 and 161 with a keyword number equals 156, and finally, a boost between 106 and 161 with a keywords number equals to 151. Finally, for Defend data, the optimal values are: number of keywords equals to 21 and a boost equals to 61. Overall, we conclude that the recall@3 is influenced by both the boost factor and the number of keyword values. Furthermore, the optimal values for these two parameters vary across different datasets based on the used terminologies. This underscores the importance of refining the keyword list to establish a carefully selected common set of keywords that can effectively work across diverse datasets.

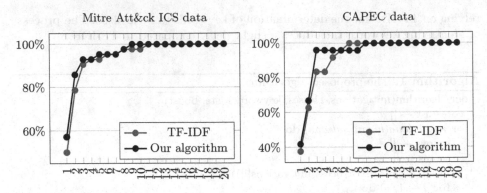

Fig. 6. Recall@n of TF-IDF and the proposed algorithm on: a) Mitre Att&ck ICS data; b) CAPEC data

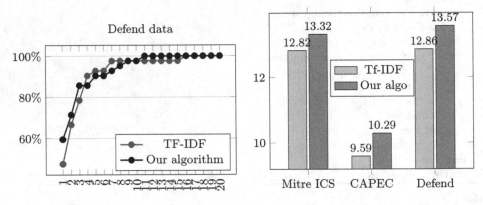

Fig. 7. Recall@n of TF-IDF and the proposed algorithm on Defend data

Fig. 8. Computation time for TF-IDF and the proposed algorithm on: a) Mitre Att&ck ICS data; b) CAPEC data c)Mitre Defend data

6   Threats to Validity

This section outlines potential threats that could undermine our approach and discusses how we addressed them.

One potential threat is the risk of not using appropriate metrics for interpreting results, constituting a construct threat. To mitigate this risk, we consistently employed metrics that have been previously utilized in similar works. Our choice of well-established metrics such as recall@n and run time enabled a meaningful comparison of the classification techniques. Notably, recall@n has been employed in a comparable context to assess the performance of similarity approaches in classifying data from other cybersecurity repositories [15].

Internal threats, concerning the consistency of conclusions about causes and effects, are addressed by acknowledging the limited number of experimental data.

While our experiments drew from reliable sources such as security repositories and scientific papers, the availability of only three datasets directly linked to NIST SP800-53 poses a potential limitation. The first and third datasets (Mitre Att&ck ICS and Mitre Defend) originate from widely used public cybersecurity repositories, while the second dataset is extracted from a peer-reviewed article [19].

External threats pertain to the generalization of our experiment results to other repositories, such as CWE and CAPEC. To mitigate this threat, given the lack of direct links between CWE or CAPEC repositories and NIST SP800-53, we employed three distinct datasets in our validation. The differences in vocabulary and mitigation granularity between these datasets helped us address this threat.

7   Conclusion and Future Work

In this work, a methodology for the automatic classification of mitigations in cybersecurity repositories has been proposed. A similarity approach was adopted to automatically classify mitigations in public repositories to the NIST SP800-53 classes. Three text processing techniques were tested: TF-IDF, Doc2Vec, and BERT. The conducted experimentation on a set of CAPEC, Mitre Att&ck, and Mitre Defend mitigations showed that the non-contextual like TF-IDF technique performs better than the contextual techniques such as Doc2Vec and BERT. Next, after analyzing the results, we proposed a novel algorithm that uses keywords to better classify the mitigations. This algorithm based on TF-IDF ameliorates the classification results by 7% on average in three different repositories.

As discussed, different publications addressed the classification of mitigations in public repositories, e.g. [9,10,14,18,25]. Yet, they used manual classification which is limited given the large number of today's mitigations and the regular updating of security repositories. It is now solved by the solution that we presented in this paper. In fact, for the first time, using the presented solution, it is possible to classify automatically a large number of mitigations according to the NIST SP800-53 classification scheme. That also improves the manageability and the serviceability of mitigations in these repositories by regrouping similar ones to the same class.

In future work, we will continue to improve the keyword lists of our novel algorithm and apply it to other cybersecurity repositories' mitigations.

References

1. Cyber Security Breaches Survey (2022). https://www.gov.uk/government/statistics/cyber-security-breaches-survey-2022/cyber-security-breaches-survey-2022
2. The Hiscox Cyber Readiness Report (2022). https://www.hiscox.co.uk/cyberreadiness
3. La méthode EBIOS Risk Manager | ANSSI. https://cyber.gouv.fr/la-methode-ebios-risk-manager

4. Unsupervised Training for Sentence Transformers. https://www.pinecone.io/learn/unsupervised-training-sentence-transformers/
5. ISO - ISO 31000 - Management du risque (2021). https://www.iso.org/fr/iso-31000-risk-management.html
6. ISO/IEC 27002:2022. https://www.iso.org/fr/standard/75652.html
7. ISO/IEC 27005:2022. https://www.iso.org/fr/standard/80585.html
8. Ahmed, M., Panda, S., Xenakis, C., Panaousis, E.: MITRE ATT&CK-driven cyber risk assessment. In: Proceedings of the 17th International Conference on Availability, Reliability and Security, pp. 1–10. ARES 2022, Association for Computing Machinery, New York, NY, USA (2022). https://doi.org/10.1145/3538969.3544420
9. Bunke, M., Koschke, R., Sohr, K.: Application-Domain Classification for Security Patterns. In: International Conferences on Pervasive Patterns and Applications (PATTERNS), pp. 138–143 (2011)
10. Engebretson, P., Pauli, J., Streff, K.: Abstracting parent mitigations from the capec attack pattern dictionary. In: Proceedings of the 2008 International Conference on Security & Management, SAM 2008, Las Vegas, Nevada, USA, July 14-17, pp. 245–250 (2008)
11. Engebretson, P.H.: A hierarchical approach for useable and consistent CAPEC-based attack patterns. Masters Theses, Doctoral Dissertations (2009)
12. Force, J.T.: Security and Privacy Controls for Information Systems and Organizations. Tech. Rep. NIST Special Publication (SP) 800-53 Rev. 5, National Institute of Standards and Technology (2020). https://doi.org/10.6028/NIST.SP.800-53r5, https://csrc.nist.gov/publications/detail/sp/800-53/rev-5/final
13. Freeze, D.: Cybercrime to cost the world $10.5 trillion annually by 2025 (2018). https://cybersecurityventures.com/cybercrime-damages-6-trillion-by-2021/
14. Hafiz, M., Adamczyk, P., Johnson, R.E.: Organizing security patterns. IEEE Softw. **24**(4), 52–60 (2007). https://doi.org/10.1109/MS.2007.114
15. Kanakogi, K., et al.: Tracing CVE vulnerability information to CAPEC attack patterns using natural language processing techniques. Information **12**(8), 298 (2021). https://doi.org/10.3390/info12080298
16. Le, Q., Mikolov, T.: Distributed representations of sentences and documents. In: International Conference on Machine Learning, pp. 1188–1196. PMLR (2014)
17. Likas, A., Vlassis, N., Verbeek, J.J.: The global k-means clustering algorithm. Pattern Recogn. **36**(2), 451–461 (2003). https://doi.org/10.1016/S0031-3203(02)00060-2
18. Marko, N., Vasenev, A., Striecks, C.: Collecting and classifying security and privacy design patterns for connected vehicles: SECREDAS approach. In: Casimiro, A., Ortmeier, F., Schoitsch, E., Bitsch, F., Ferreira, P. (eds.) SAFECOMP 2020. LNCS, vol. 12235, pp. 36–53. Springer, Cham (2020). https://doi.org/10.1007/978-3-030-55583-2_3
19. Meng, B., et al.: VERDICT: a language and framework for engineering cyber resilient and safe system. Systems **9**(1), 18 (2021). https://doi.org/10.3390/systems9010018, https://www.mdpi.com/2079-8954/9/1/18
20. Miller, D.R., Leek, T., Schwartz, R.M.: A hidden markov model information retrieval system. In: Proceedings of the 22nd Annual International ACM SIGIR Conference on Research and Development in Information Retrieval, pp. 214–221 (1999)
21. Navarro, J., et al.: HuMa: a multi-layer framework for threat analysis in a heterogeneous log environment. In: Imine, A., Fernandez, J.M., Marion, J.-Y., Logrippo, L., Garcia-Alfaro, J. (eds.) FPS 2017. LNCS, vol. 10723, pp. 144–159. Springer, Cham (2018). https://doi.org/10.1007/978-3-319-75650-9_10

22. Nguyen, A.T., Nguyen, T.T., Nguyen, T.N., Lo, D., Sun, C.: Duplicate bug report detection with a combination of information retrieval and topic modeling. In: Proceedings of the 27th IEEE/ACM International Conference on Automated Software Engineering, pp. 70–79 (2012)
23. Regainia, L., Salva, S.: A Methodology of security pattern classification and of attack-defense tree generation. In: 3rd International Conference on Information Systems Security and Privacy pp. 136–146 (2017). https://doi.org/10.5220/0006198301360146
24. Reimers, N., Gurevych, I.: Sentence-BERT: sentence embeddings using siamese BERT-networks. arXiv preprint arXiv:1908.10084 (2019)
25. Salva, S., Regainia, L.: A catalogue associating security patterns and attack steps to design secure applications. J. Comput. Secur. 27, 49 (2019). https://doi.org/10.3233/JCS-171063
26. Touloumis, K., Michalitsi-Psarrou, A., Kapsalis, P., Georgiadou, A., Askounis, D.: Vulnerabilities manager, a platform for linking vulnerability data sources. In: 2021 IEEE International Conference on Big Data (Big Data), pp. 2178–2184 (2021). https://doi.org/10.1109/BigData52589.2021.9672026
27. Wang, K., Reimers, N., Gurevych, I.: TSDAE: using transformer-based sequential denoising auto-encoder for unsupervised sentence embedding learning. arXiv:2104.06979 [cs] (2021)

Top Cyber Threats: The Rise
of Ransomware

Amir Djenna[1]([✉]), Mohamed Belaoued[2], and Nourdine Lifa[1]

[1] Constantine2 University, Constantine 25000, Algeria
{amir.djenna,nourdine.lifa}@univ-constantine2.dz
[2] Lab-I*, UR 4474, Université de Reims Champagne-Ardenne, Reims, France
mohamed.belaoued@caplogy.fr

Abstract. Ransomware stands out as a particularly malicious type of cyberattack, wielding the potential to inflict severe financial, operational, and reputational harm. The insidious nature of ransomware, with their ability to encrypt or exfiltrate sensitive data, demands a paradigm shift in cybersecurity strategies. Further, the ability to predict and forecast such malware is paramount for bolstering overall cybersecurity resilience. In this paper, we provide a comprehensive overview of the evolution of ransomware, detailing key characteristics and specifications of zero-day ransomware, along with limitations in static and dynamic analyses, with the goal of identifying effective defense strategies. Despite substantial advancements, enduring challenges and notable research gaps persist, necessitating ongoing innovation in cybersecurity. Furthermore, this study serves as a valuable resource for cybersecurity professionals and researchers, shedding light on key trends, challenges, limitations, and potential avenues for future research in the realm of ransomware forecasting.

Keywords: Cybersecurity · Malware · Ransomware · Artificial Intelligence

1 Introduction

With the growing reliance on digital infrastructure and the exponential growth of networks, cybersecurity has become a critical concern for individuals, businesses and governments. Among the various cyber threats, ransomware attacks have become one of the most devastating and widespread forms of malicious activity. Joseph Popp is credited with creating the inaugural ransomware in 1989 [1]. His ransomware attack, named AIDS or PC Cyborg, involved the distribution of floppy disks containing malicious scripts to various AIDS researchers [1]. According to Sophos survey [2], The incidence of ransomware attacks surged from 37 percent in 2020 to 66 percent in 2021. In recent years, the proliferation of ransomware attacks has emerged as a formidable challenge, posing a significant threat to the confidentiality, integrity, and availability of digital assets across

© IFIP International Federation for Information Processing 2024
Published by Springer Nature Switzerland AG 2024
S. Bouzefrane and D. Sauveron (Eds.): WISTP 2024, LNCS 14625, pp. 80–95, 2024.
https://doi.org/10.1007/978-3-031-60391-4_6

various sectors. The insidious nature of ransomware, with its ability to encrypt or exfiltrate sensitive data, demands a paradigm shift in cybersecurity strategies. CryptoLocker, CryptoWall, and Locky operate as ransomware-as-a-service (RaaS), with CryptoWall, in particular, accumulating over 320 million dollars in revenue throughout its existence [3]. According to the latest 2023 ransomware statistics report [4], there were 623.3 million ransomware attacks globally in 2021, 93% of ransomware is Windows-based executables, and Ransomware was the most common attack type for the manufacturing industry in 2021. The ransomware business model has grown exponentially in the last decade [5] and it is projected to cost more than 10 Trillion USD by 2025 [6]. The rise of zero-day ransomware characterized by its ability to exploit previously unknown vulnerabilities, presents a significant challenge for conventional cybersecurity approaches. In addition, the current state-of-the-art in unknown ransomware detection often falls short due to the limitations of static and dynamic analysis methods. That which requires a comprehensive understanding of its evolution, characteristics, and the limitations of existing analysis methods. Therefore, we aim to contribute to the development of robust defense mechanisms, thereby fortifying the collective cybersecurity posture. In this study, we present a background on the most notable ransomware and their impact. We establish a foundational understanding of zero-day ransomware. We analyse the main adopted approaches, existing limitations and research gaps related to static and dynamic analysis of zero-day ransomware. We provide strategic recommendations as future research directions. This insight is instrumental in guiding future research endeavors. The remaining sections of the paper are organized as follows: Sect. 2 presents notable ransomware incidents worldwide. Section 3 provides the key characteristics of advanced ransomware. Section 4 illustrates the life cycle of a typical ransomware. Section 5 outlines the specifications of zero-day ransomware. Section 6 explores the main adopted approaches for ransomware detection, highlighting their advantages and disadvantages, and discusses the limitations associated with both static and dynamic analysis. Finally, Sect. 7 concludes this study.

2   Notable Ransomware and Their Impact

There has been a pronounced proliferation of ransomware propagation on a global scale. Table 1 illustrates notable ransomware incidents that have occurred in the past decade:

Moreover, the predictions are alarming, the cost of ransomware cyberattacks is estimated to be more than 265 billion USD by 2031 [18]. In the realm of cybersecurity, ransomware constitutes a form of online attack orchestrated by cybercriminals or state-sponsored groups. The perpetrators seek a financial ransom as a condition for relinquishing their control over encrypted or pilfered data. The most file types targeted by ransomware encryption include Microsoft Office files (.doc, .docx, .xls, .xlsz, .ppt, .pptx, .rtf); Open Office files (.odt, .ods, .odp); Text files (.txt, .RTF); Mail files (.pst); Compressed files (.rar, .zip, .7z); Image files (.JPG, .PNG, .JPEG); Database files (.sql, .dba, .mdb, .odb,

Table 1. Notable ransomware incidents worldwide.

Ransomware	Type	Description	Targeted Company	Monetary Impact
CryptoLocker [7] 2013–2014	Trojan	One of the first widespread ransomware, demanding payment in Bitcoin.	Various, primarily Windows users	3 Million USD
WannaCry [9] 2017	Vulnerability in SMB protocol	Exploited Windows vulnerabilities, affected organizations globally.	Multiple (global attack); Microsoft Windows users	4 Billion USD
NotPetya [10] 2017	A wiper exploiting an SMB vulnerability	Initially disguised as ransomware, it was later revealed to be a wiper	Various, severely impacted Maersk and Merck	10 Billion USD
Locky [11] 2016–2018	Phishing emails distributing a macro	Delivered by email with an attached Microsoft Word document that contains malicious macros	Various (predominantly healthcare providers) in multiple countries	1 Billion USD
Ryuk [12] 2018-Present	TrickBot infection	Known for targeting enterprises and demanding high ransoms	Healthcare and municipalities	From 15 to 500 Bitcoin
GandCrab [13] 2018–2019	Phishing, exploit kits	Utilized a ransomware-as-a-service (RaaS) model, declared retirement in 2019	Businesses and individuals	2 Billion USD
REvil [14] 2019–2021	Zero-Day	Known for attacking large enterprises and demanding high ransoms	Kaseya and downstream customers, JBS	70 Million USD
DoppelPaymer [15] 2019-Present	Spear-phishing, unpatched vulnerabilities	Used a fairly sophisticated routine, starting off with network infiltration via malicious spam emails containing spear-phishing links designed to lure unsuspecting users into executing malicious code	City of Torrance, CA; University hospital	40 Million EUR
SamSam [16] 2016–2018	JBoss vulnerability	Used vulnerabilities to gain access to a victim's network by executing brute-force tactics, including the Remote Desktop Protocol (RDP)	Municipalities, hospitals and institutions	>6 Million USD
ColonialPipeline [17] 2021	Phishing, remote system exploitation	DarkSide ransomware impacted critical infrastructure	Colonial Pipeline	4.4 Million USD

.db3, .sqllite); Key files (.pem, .crt); Adobe PDF files. Ransomware can targets files, folders, memory, screen, database, master boot record, IoT, Cloud, Cyber Physical Systems, and other systems as extortion-based cyberthreat [8]. When ransomware specifically targets healthcare institutions or critical infrastructures, where human lives are at stake, it is classified as killware. One of the most popular ransomware is WannaCry [19]. WannaCry was first launched in May 2017, it affected more than 150 countries, leaving devastating effects on more than 100,000 companies. Using the EternalBlue exploit toolkit, WannaCry exploits the SMB vulnerability in Microsoft Windows and employs the AES algorithm for encrypting data files. This crypto ransomware caused over 1 billion dollars of damage in one week, making it one of the top cyber-tragedies of all times. According to ENISA [20], Fig. 1 illustrates a comparison of incident numbers across various sectors. The graph indicates that ransomware exhibits a trend of indiscriminate targeting affecting all sectors.

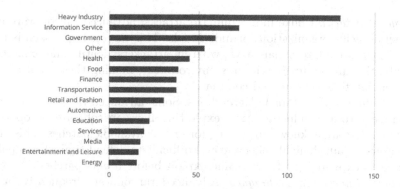

Fig. 1. Repartition of ransomware incidents across various sectors.

3   Key Characteristics of Advanced Ransomware

Furthermore, advanced ransomware unlike conventional ransomware exhibit a heightened level of sophistication due to the rapid growth of its attacks and the creation of new variants capable of bypassing anti-viruses and anti-malwares measures [21]. This class of ransomware goes beyond mere encryption, demonstrating adaptability, stealth, and the capability to exploit zero-day vulnerabilities. The key characteristics of advanced ransomware are depicted in the Fig. 2:

– *Evasion Techniques*, Advanced ransomware employs sophisticated evasion tactics to circumvent traditional security protocols. This may include polymorphic code, which dynamically alters its appearance to evade signature-based detection, or the use of encryption algorithms to conceal its malicious payload during transit. WannaCry employed evasion techniques to propagate rapidly across networks and avoid detection.

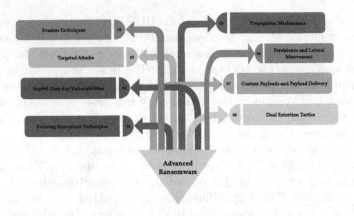

Fig. 2. The key characteristics of advanced ransomware.

– *Targeted Attacks*, Unlike indiscriminate attacks, advanced ransomware often targets specific organizations or individuals. This targeted approach is facilitated by thorough reconnaissance, wherein attackers identify and exploit vulnerabilities unique to the victim's environment, making these attacks more challenging to anticipate and counter.

– *Exploitation of Zero-Day Vulnerabilities*, Some advanced ransomware strains leverage zero-day vulnerabilities, exploiting flaws in software or operating systems that are unknown to the vendor or lack available patches. This allows attackers to launch highly effective and difficult-to-defend-against campaigns. NotPetya exploited the EternalBlue exploit before it gets patched.

– *Evolving Encryption Techniques*, Advanced ransomware frequently utilizes advanced encryption algorithms, making it exceptionally challenging, if not impossible, to decrypt files without the corresponding key. The use of asymmetric cryptography and strong encryption standards contributes to the ransomware's efficacy in rendering data inaccessible.

– *Propagation Mechanisms*, Modern ransomware often exhibits multiple means of propagation, incorporating both traditional methods like phishing emails and exploiting network vulnerabilities, as well as innovative techniques such as leveraging compromised legitimate websites or using malicious advertisements to deliver payloads.

– *Persistence and Lateral Movement*, Advanced ransomware is adept at maintaining persistence within a compromised network. It can employ techniques for lateral movement, moving stealthily within a system, escalating privileges, and strategically selecting critical assets for encryption or exfiltration. WannaCry and NotPetya used lateral movement and persistence techniques.

– *Custom Payloads and Payload Delivery*, To avoid detection, advanced ransomware may utilize custom payloads tailored to specific targets. The delivery mechanisms often involve social engineering tactics, exploiting human vulnerabilities to encourage users to execute the malicious payload inadvertently.

– *Dual Extortion Tactics*, A distinctive feature of advanced ransomware is the dual extortion strategy. In addition to encrypting files, attackers may threaten to expose sensitive data if the ransom is not paid. This dual threat adds an extra layer of pressure on victims, especially in sectors where data confidentiality is paramount. DoppelPaymer is a double extortion ransomware, and REvil is a quadruple extortion ransomware.

4   Life Cycle of a Typical Ransomware

understanding the ransomware lifecycle is essential for developing effective strategies to prevent, detect, and respond to such attacks. This includes a combination of technical defenses, user education, and incident response planning. Basically, the traditional core actions that ransomware can carry out are LEDS (Lock, Encrypt, Delete, and Steal). However, the predominant phases of advanced ransomware involve several stages, from the initial infection to potential recovery or containment efforts. Figure 3 depicts an in-depth breakdown of the typical ransomware lifecycle:

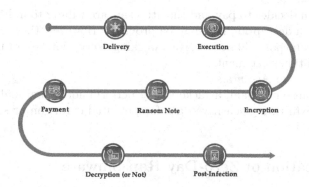

Fig. 3. Ransomware lifecycle.

a. *Delivery*

Phishing ransomware often begins with a phishing attack, where attackers send deceptive emails containing malicious links or attachments. Clicking on these links or opening infected attachments initiates the infection. Malicious Websites, users may unknowingly download ransomware by visiting compromised websites. Drive-by downloads occur when the malware is automatically downloaded and executed without the user's knowledge. Exploiting Vulnerabilities, ransomware can exploit vulnerabilities in software, operating systems, or network devices. Failure to apply security patches and updates can leave systems susceptible to exploitation.

b. *Execution*

Once the malicious payload is delivered, the ransomware is executed on the victim's system. This often involves the activation of a dropper, a small program that installs the ransomware on the target machine.

c. *Encryption*

The ransomware uses strong encryption algorithms to lock files on the victim's system. Some sophisticated variants may encrypt entire hard drives. The encryption process is rapid, making it difficult for the victim to interrupt the attack.

d. *Ransom Note*

After encryption, a ransom note is displayed on the victim's screen. This note informs the victim that their files are encrypted and provides instructions on how to pay the ransom. It may include details such as the ransom amount, the cryptocurrency wallet address, and a deadline for payment.

e. *Payment*

The victim is instructed to pay the ransom, often in cryptocurrency like Bitcoin to receive the decryption key. Attackers may use Tor or other anonymizing services to facilitate communication and payment.

f. *Decryption (or Not)*

If the victim decides to pay and the attackers are willing to uphold their end of the bargain, a decryption key may be provided. However, there are instances where victims who paid did not receive a working decryption key, or the attackers demanded additional payments.

g. *Post-Infection Activities*

After the ransom is paid, attackers may perform additional malicious activities, such as exfiltrating sensitive data for potential extortion or selling on the dark web.

5   Specification of Zero-Day Ransomware

Unknown ransomware or zero-day ransomware refers to a type of ransomware that exploits vulnerabilities in software or systems for which no patch or fix is currently available. It takes advantage of a "zero-day" vulnerability, meaning that attackers exploit a security flaw on the same day (or before) the vulnerability becomes publicly known. The Table 4 summarizes the specifications of zero-day ransomware.

6   Ransomware Detection and Analysis

Various machine and deep learning models have been devised for the detection of ransomware, encompassing architectures like Convolutional Neural Networks [23], Long Short-Term Memory [24], Extreme Learning Machine [25], Multi-Layer Perceptron [26], Recurrent Neural Network [27], and hybrid deep learning [28] approaches. Additionally, research endeavors have delved into alternative ransomware detection techniques grounded in behavioral analysis [29] [30]

Table 2. A summary of related works on ransomware detection.

Approaches	Strenghts	Weaknesses
Behavior-Based Detection [23] [24] [25] [26] [27]	- Identifies previously unseen ransomware based on behavior.	- May generate false positives if legitimate activities exhibit similar behaviors
Machine Learning-Based Approaches [37] [38] [39] [40] [41]	- Enables the development of models that can generalize patterns.	- Requires labeled datasets for training; may struggle with previously unseen ransomware behaviors
Deep Learning Architectures [42] [43] [44] [45] [46]	- Capable of learning intricate patterns, improving accuracy	- Requires significant computational resources and extensive labeled datasets
Dynamic Analysis and Sandboxing [47] [48] [49] [50] [51]	- Allows observation of ransomware behavior in a controlled environment	- Sophisticated ransomware may detect sandboxing environments and alter behavior
Threat Intelligence Integration [52] [53] [54] [55]	- Enhances real-time detection of emerging ransomware threats	- Relies on availability and accuracy of threat intelligence feeds
Honeypots and Deception Technologies [56] [57] [58] [59] [60]	- Provides a controlled environment to study ransomware behaviors	- Implementation complexity; risk of false positives
Anomaly Detection [61] [62] [63] [64] [65]	- Identifies deviations from normal behavior indicative of ransomware	- May generate false alarms in dynamic and complex IT environments
Hybrid Approaches [66] [67] [68] [69] [70]	- Combines multiple techniques for a comprehensive detection system	- May increase complexity and resource requirements
Blockchain for Ransomware Prevention [71] [72] [73] [74] [75]	- Offers potential for secure and decentralized storage	- Implementation challenges; scalability issues; requires widespread adoption

[31] [32] [33]. Some investigations have explored innovative methods, including Voting Ransomware Detection [34], and the application of Xception Convolutional Neural Network on portable executable headers [35]. Moreover, strategies such as content-based detection and employing backup solid-state drives [36] have been examined as proactive measures for ransomware defense. Table 2 summarizes various approaches to ransomware detection, along with their respective advantages and disadvantages:

Tables 3 explores the limitations associated with both ransomware static analysis and dynamic analysis, providing insights into their respective challenges in combating ransomware threats.

Challenges and future directions

The question that arises is: Does a given defensive posture reliably defeat the ransomware cyber attacks? In fact, traditional protection approaches still expose critical infrastructure to advanced ransomware cyber attacks notably via Command & Control and RAT (Remote Access Trojan). In addition, advanced ransomware exploit zero-day vulnerabilities and permissions. Thus, the identification and mitigation of zero-day vulnerabilities stand as pivotal challenges. As an illustrative case, the "CVE-2023–28252" (Common Vulnerabilities and Exposure) represents a recent zero-day vulnerability that is exploitable on all versions of Microsoft Windows, including Windows 11. This vulnerability is designed to escalate privileges and access the Common Log File System (CLFS) for unauthorised modification. Consequently, it enables an attacker to gain access, take control, and execute ransomware malicious code. The Nokoyama ransomware serves as an instance of the exploitation of this vulnerability within Microsoft Windows servers. Indeed, cyber-ransomware actors mainly use a set of tech-

Table 3. Static and Dynamic ransomware analysis limitations.

Static Analysis	Description	Limitations
Signature Dependency	-Often relies on signature-based detection, where known patterns of ransomware are identified.	-It is ineffective against new or polymorphic variants of ransomware that can alter their code to evade signature detection
Limited Visibility into Runtime Behavior	-Examines the code without executing it, providing limited insight into the actual runtime behavior of the ransomware.	-It may miss sophisticated ransomware that exhibits malicious behavior only during execution
Inability to detect packed or Obfuscated Code	-Ransomware often uses packing or obfuscation techniques to hide its true intent and evade static analysis.	-Struggles to analyze such packed or obfuscated code, reducing its effectiveness in identifying ransomware
False Positives	-May generate false positives, flagging legitimate files as malicious due to similarities with known ransomware signatures.	-This can lead to unnecessary alerts and hamper the efficiency of security systems
Dynamic Analysis	Description	Limitations
Evasion Techniques	-Ransomware actors employ evasion techniques to detect if their code is running in a sandbox.	-May fail to detect ransomware that alters its behavior or remains dormant until it reaches a real target system
Resource-Intensive	-Involves running the ransomware in a controlled environment, which can be resource-intensive	-This may not be feasible in real-time or in high-traffic environments, limiting the scalability of dynamic analysis
Limited visibility into persistence mechanisms	-May not fully reveal the persistence mechanisms employed by ransomware such as registry modifications or file system changes	-Understanding the full extent of how ransomware maintains a presence on a system may be challenging
Encrypted communications	-Ransomware may encrypt its communications with command and control servers, making it harder to analyze the network traffic during dynamic analysis.	-This can impede the detection of ransomware activities that involve communication with external servers
Complex behavior analysis	-Some ransomware exhibits complex behavior that may require sophisticated analysis techniques, surpassing the capabilities of traditional dynamic analysis	-Advanced ransomware may evade detection by mimicking normal user behavior, making it difficult for dynamic analysis to differentiate malicious actions

niques and tactics to perform a dramatic ransomware attacks such as: Data Encrypted for impact; Obfuscated {changing the form, changing the size, hiding malicious data, removing indicators of compromise}; Masquerading {masquerading file extensions, names, file locations, file signatures}; Command and Scripting Interpreter; Process Injection. Besides, zero-day ransomware can be categorised into two main categories: targeted zero-day ransomware and non-targeted zero-day ransomware. Targeted zero-day ransomware is directed at specific high-value entities, including government institutions, large corporations, and key personnel with elevated access to critical systems, confidential data, or substantial financial resources. Non-targeted zero-day ransomware, on the other hand, is typically launched against a large number of users utilising vulnerable systems, such as operating systems, firmware, browsers, and even Internet of Things (IoT) devices. The primary objective is to compromise these systems and leverage them to build extensive botnets such as the scenario of the famous WannaCry incident. This case underscores the pressing need for proactive measures and innovative solutions to address the evolving landscape of zero-day threats within the cybersecurity paradigm.

Table 4. Specifications of zero-day ransomware.

Num	Specification	Description
1	Exploits unpatched vulnerabilities	Zero-day ransomware targets software or systems with vulnerabilities that are not yet known to the vendor or the public. This gives attackers an advantage because there is no available fix or patch to address the vulnerability
2	Stealthy and silent	Zero-day ransomware often operates silently and stealthily to avoid detection. It may use advanced evasion techniques to bypass traditional security measures
3	Advanced techniques	Zero-day ransomware may employ advanced techniques, including polymorphic code (changing its code structure to evade signature-based detection) and encryption to hide its malicious activities
4	Rapid spread	Since there is no patch available to fix the exploited vulnerability, zero-day ransomware can spread quickly. Cybercriminals may target multiple organizations simultaneously, taking advantage of the window of opportunity before security experts can respond
5	Targeted attacks	Zero-day ransomware is often used in targeted attacks against specific organizations or individuals. At-tackers may conduct reconnaissance to identify valuable targets and then craft tailored attacks to maximize the impact
6	High value and high stakes	Zero-day vulnerabilities are valuable commodities in the cybercriminal underground. The use of zero-day ransomware implies a high level of sophistication and suggests that the attackers are well-resourced and motivated
7	Lack of pre-existing signatures	Traditional antivirus solutions rely on signature-based detection, which involves identifying known patterns of malicious code. Since zero-day ransomware exploits previously unknown vulnerabilities, there are no pre-existing signatures for detection
8	Limited time of defense	Organizations have limited time to defend against zero-day ransomware attacks before a patch is developed and deployed. This underscores the importance of proactive security measures and rapid incident response
9	Potential for large-scale impact	Due to their ability to spread rapidly and exploit vulnerabilities that may be present in widely used software, zero-day ransomware attacks have the potential for large-scale impact, affecting numerous organizations and individuals
10	Requires rapid response	Detecting and responding to zero-day ransomware requires a rapid and coordinated response. Organizations need to employ advanced threat detection and response capabilities to identify and mitigate such attacks

While machine learning has proven effective in many cybersecurity applications, including malware detection, it does have limitations, especially when it comes to dealing with zero-day ransomware. Here are a few examples that highlight the challenges and limitations of machine learning in this context: ML models rely on historical data for training, but zero-day threats, by definition, have no historical records. ML models struggle to generalise well to unknown patterns or behaviours. Without sufficient data on zero-day ransomware, models might lack the contextual information needed to effectively identify emerging threats. Polymorphic ransomware is designed to change its code structure regularly, making it difficult for traditional-based ML models to detect. The lack of predefined signatures or patterns can hinder detection accuracy. ML models heavily depend on the features extracted during training. If crucial features are missed or if the feature set is inadequate, the model's effectiveness diminishes. Developing a comprehensive feature set for zero-day ransomware is challenging due to the evolving nature of threats. Unseen features might be crucial for detection, and the model's failure to capture them could lead to vulnerabilities. In the context of zero-day ransomware, where new and unseen patterns emerge, an overly cautious ML model might miss genuine threats. Cybercriminals use techniques to manipulate or trick ML models, known as adversarial attacks. They intentionally tweak inputs to deceive the ML model into making incorrect predictions. ML models, including those used for ransomware detection, are susceptible to adversarial attacks. The models might misclassify or fail to recognise subtle changes introduced by attackers, leading to false negatives or false positives.

These examples underscore the need for a multi-faceted cybersecurity approach that combines advanced AI techniques with other facets such as advanced threat intelligence and strong incident response capabilities to effectively counter zero-day ransomware threats. Furthermore, a multi-layered security approach that combines explainable AI with collaborative threat intelligence provides a more robust measures against evolving threats.

7   Conclusion

The rise of zero-day ransomware characterized by its ability to exploit previously unknown vulnerabilities, presents a significant challenge for conventional cybersecurity approaches. Intelligent solutions for cybersecurity represent a paradigm shift in the ongoing battle against ransomware. Embracing intelligent solutions is not merely a choice it is an imperative step toward a more resilient and proactive cybersecurity posture. The adaptive nature and predictive capabilities position them as indispensable tools for organizations seeking to fortify their defenses in an increasingly complex digital landscape. This study provided a comprehensive overview of the evolution of ransomware and prevailing attack patterns, aiming to pinpoint potent defense strategies. Moreover, the study helps cybersecurity professionals and researchers by illuminating key trends, challenges, limitations, and prospective avenues for future research in the zero-day ransomware forecasting.

References

1. The Strange History of Ransomware. https://medium.com/@alinasimone/the-bizarre-pre-internet-history-of-ransomware-bb480a652b4b Accessed 10 Oct 2023
2. S. Adam, The State of Ransomware 2022, Sophos News 2022. https://news.sophos.com/en-us/2022/04/27/the-state-of-ransomware-2022/ Accessed 10 Oct 2023
3. De Groot, J.: A History of Ransomware Attack: The Biggest andWorst Ransomware Attack of All Time. 2017, Https://digitalguardian.com/blog/history-ransomware-attacks-biggest-and-worst-ransomware-attacks-all-time. Accessed 10 Oct 2023
4. The Latest 2023 Ransomware Statistics. https://aag-it.com/the-latest-ransomware-statistics/ Accessed 10 Oct 2023
5. CISA 2021 Trends Show Increased Globalized Threat of Ransomware. https://www.cisa.gov/uscert/ncas/alerts/aa22-040a Accessed 26 Oct 2023
6. Cybercrime To Cost The World 10.5 Trillion USD Annually By 2025, Cybercrime Magazine. https://cybersecurityventures.com/cybercrime-damages-6-trillion-by-2021/ Accessed 26 Oct 2023
7. Cybercrime Magazine. https://cybersecurityventures.com/global-ransomware-damage-costs-predicted-to-reach-250-billion-usd-by-2031/#:~:text=The%20cost%20of%20cybercrime%20is,to%20exceed%20%20%241.75%20trillion%20USD, last accessed 2023/10/26
8. Keshavarzi, M., Ghaffary, H.R.: A dedicated and separated attack chain for ransomware offenses as the most infamous cyber extortion. Comput. Sci. Rev. **36**, 100233 (2020)
9. WannaCry: All you need to know. https://www.kaspersky.com/resource-center/threats/ransomware-wannacry Accessed 27 Oct 2023
10. ENISA's Report on the Threat Landscape for Ransomware Attacks. https://www.enisa.europa.eu/publications/enisa-threat-landscape-for-ransomware-attacks Accessed 27 Oct 2023
11. Cryptolocker. https://me-en.kaspersky.com/resource-center/definitions/cryptolocker Accessed 27 Oct 2023
12. WannaCry. https://www.cisa.gov/sites/default/files/FactSheets/NCCIC%20ICS_FactSheet_WannaCry_Ransomware_S508C.pdf Accessed 27 Oct 2023
13. Petya and NotPetya. https://www.malwarebytes.com/petya-and-notpetya Accessed 27 Oct 2023
14. What is locky ransomware. https://www.cybertalk.org/what-is-locky-ransomware/Accessed 27 Oct 2023
15. Ryuk ransomware. https://www.cloudflare.com/learning/security/ransomware/ryuk-ransomware/ Accessed 27 Oct 2023
16. Behind scences grandcrabs operation. https://www.virusbulletin.com/virusbulletin/2020/01/behind-scenes-gandcrabs-operation/ Accessed 27 Oct 2023
17. REvil ransomware explained. https://www.csoonline.com/article/570101/revil-ransomware-explained-a-widespread-extortion-operation.html Accessed 27 Oct 2023
18. An overview of the doppelpaymer. https://www.trendmicro.com/en_za/research/21/a/an-overview-of-the-doppelpaymer-ransomware.html Accessed 27 Oct 2023
19. SamSam. https://symantec-enterprise-blogs.security.com/blogs/threat-intelligence/samsam-targeted-ransomware-attacks Accessed 27 Oct 2023

20. Colonial Pipeline explained. https://www.techtarget.com/whatis/feature/Colonial-Pipeline-hack-explained-Everything-you-need-to-know Accessed 27 Oct 2023
21. Djenna, A., Bouridane, A., Rubab, S., Marou, I.M.: Artificial intelligence-based malware detection, analysis, and mitigation. Symmetry **15**(3), 677 (2023)
22. Djenna, A., Barka, E., Benchikh, A., Khadir, K.: Unmasking cybercrime with artificial-intelligence-driven cybersecurity analytics. Sensors **23**(14), 6302 (2023)
23. Zhang, B., Xiao, W., Xiao, X., Sangaiah, A.K., Zhang, W., Zhang, J.: Ransomware classification using patch-based CNN and self-attention network on embedded n-grams of opcodes. Futur. Gener. Comput. Syst. **110**, 708–720 (2020)
24. Roy, K.C., Chen, Q.: Deepran: attention-based bilstm and CRF for ransomware early detection and classification. Inf. Syst. Front. **23**, 299–315 (2021)
25. Jahromi, A.N., Hashemi, S., Dehghantanha, A., Choo, K.K.R., Newton, K.H., D. E., Parizi, R. M.: An improved two-hidden-layer extreme learning machine for malware hunting. Comput. Secur. **89**, 101655 (2020)
26. Homayoun, S., Dehghantanha, A., Ahmadzadeh, M., Hashemi, S., Khayami, R.: An improved two-hidden-layer extreme learning machine for malware hunting. IEEE Trans. Emerg. Top. Comput. **8**, 341–351 (2017)
27. Jha, S., Prashar, D., Long, H.V., Taniar, D.: Recurrent neural network for detecting malware. Comput. Secur. **99**, 102037 (2020)
28. Al Razib, M., Javeed, D., Khan, M.T., Alkanhel, R., Muthanna, M.S.A.: Cyber threats detection in smart environments using SDN-enabled DNN-LSTM hybrid framework. IEEE Access **10**, 53015–53026 (2022)
29. Abbasi, M.S., Al-Sahaf, H., Mansoori, M., Welch, I.: Behavior-based ransomware classification: a particle swarm optimization wrapper-based approach for feature selection. Appl. Soft Comput. **121**, 108744 (2022)
30. Celdrán, A.H., Sánchez, P.M.S., Castillo, M.A., Bovet, G., Pérez, G.M., Stiller, B.: Intelligent and behavioral-based detection of malware in IoT spectrum sensors. Int. J. Inf. Secur. **22**, 541–561 (2023)
31. Sharma, P., Kapoor, S., Sharma, R.: Ransomware detection, prevention and protection in IoT devices using ML techniques based on dynamic analysis approach. Int. J. Syst. Assur. Eng. Manag. **14**, 287–296 (2023)
32. Gazzan, M., Sheldon, F.T.: Opportunities for early detection and prediction of ransomware attacks against industrial control systems. Future Internet **15**, 144 (2023)
33. De Gaspari, F., Hitaj, D., Pagnotta, G., De Carli, L., Mancini, L.V.: Evading behavioral classifiers: a comprehensive analysis on evading ransomware detection techniques. Neural Comput. Appl. **34**, 12077–12096 (2022)
34. Davies, S.R., Macfarlane, R., Buchanan, W.J.: Majority voting ransomware detection system. J. Inf. Secur. **14**, 264–293 (2023)
35. Moreira, C.C., Moreira, D.C., de Sales Jr, C.D.S.: Improving ransomware detection based on portable executable header using xception convolutional neural network. Comput. Secur. **130**, 103265 (2023)
36. Min, D., Ko, Y., Walker, R., Lee, J., Kim, Y.: A content-based ransomware detection and backup solid-state drive for ransomware defense. IEEE Trans. Comput. Aided Des. Integr. Circuits Syst. **41**, 2038–2051 (2021)
37. Cusack, G., Michel, O., Keller, E.: Machine learning-based detection of ransomware using SDN. In: 18th ACM International Workshop on Security in Software Defined Networks & Network Function Virtualization, Tempe, Arizona, USA (2018)

38. Almomani, I., AlKhayer, A., Ahmed, M.: An efficient machine learning-based app-roach for Android v. 11 ransomware detection. In: 1st IEEE International Confer-ence on Artificial Intelligence and Data Analytics (CAIDA), Riyadh, Saudi Arabia (2021)

39. Gera, T., Singh, J., Mehbodniya, A., Webber, J.L., Shabaz, M., Thakur, D.: Dom-inant feature selection and machine learning-based hybrid approach to analyze android ransomware. Secur. Commun. Network. **21**, 21–22 (2021)

40. Lee, K., Lee, S.Y., Yim, K.: Machine learning based file entropy analysis for ran-somware detection in backup systems. IEEE Access **7**, 110205–110215 (2019)

41. Almousa, M., Basavaraju, S., Anwar, M.: Api-based ransomware detection using machine learning-based threat detection models. In: 18th IEEE International Con-ference on Privacy, Security and Trust (PST), Auckland, New Zealand (2021)

42. Chaganti, R., Ravi, V., Pham, T.D.: Deep learning based cross architecture internet of things malware detection and classification. Comput. Secur. **120**, 102779 (2022)

43. Bello, I., et al.: Detecting ransomware attacks using intelligent algorithms: recent development and next direction from deep learning and big data perspectives. J. Ambient. Intell. Humaniz. Comput. **12**, 8699–8717 (2021)

44. Ravi, V., Pham, T.D., Alazab, M.: Attention-based multidimensional deep learn-ing approach for cross-architecture IoMT malware detection and classification in healthcare cyber-physical systems. IEEE Trans. Comput. Soc. Syst. **10**, 1597–1606 (2022)

45. Rathore, H., Agarwal, S., Sahay, S. K., Sewak, M.: Malware detection using machine learning and deep learning. In: 6th Big Data Analytics International Con-ference, BDA, Warangal, India (2018)

46. Messay-Kebede, T., Narayanan, B. N., Djaneye-Boundjou, O.: Combination of traditional and deep learning based architectures to overcome class imbalance and its application to malware classification. In: NAECON IEEE National Aerospace and Electronics Conference, Dayton, OH, USA (2018)

47. Jamalpur, S., Navya, Y. S., Raja, P., Tagore, G., Rao, G. R. K.: Dynamic malware analysis using cuckoo sandbox. In: 2st IEEE International Conference on Inventive Communication and Computational Technologies (ICICCT), Coimbatore, India (2018)

48. Hwang, J., Kim, J., Lee, S., Kim, K.: Two-stage ransomware detection using dynamic analysis and machine learning techniques. Wireless Pers. Commun. **112**, 2597–2609 (2020)

49. Subedi, K. P., Budhathoki, D. R., Dasgupta, D.: Forensic analysis of ransomware families using static and dynamic analysis. In: IEEE Security and Privacy Work-shops (SPW), San Francisco, CA, USA (2018)

50. da Costa, F.H., et al.: Exploring the use of static and dynamic analysis to improve the performance of the mining sandbox approach for android malware identifica-tion. J. Syst. Softw. **183**, 111092 (2022)

51. Kamal, A., et al.: A user-friendly model for ransomware analysis using sandboxing. Comput. Mater. Continua **67**, 1–14 (2021)

52. Rastogi, N., Dutta, S., Zaki, M. J., Gittens, A., Aggarwal, C.: Malont: an ontology for malware threat intelligence. In: International Workshop on Deployable Machine Learning for Security Defense, San Diego, CA, USA (2020)

53. Keim, Y., Mohapatra, A.K.: Cyber threat intelligence framework using advanced malware forensics. Int. J. Inf. Technol. **14**(2019), 1–10 (2019)

54. Piplai, A., Mittal, S., Abdelsalam, M., Gupta, M., Joshi, A., Finin, T.: Knowledge enrichment by fusing representations for malware threat intelligence and behavior.

In: IEEE International Conference on Intelligence and Security Informatics (ISI), Arlington, VA, USA (2020)

55. Aldauiji, F., Batarfi, O., Bayousef, M.: Utilizing cyber threat hunting techniques to find ransomware attacks: a survey of the state of the art. IEEE Access **10**, 61695–61706 (2022)

56. Moore, C.: Detecting ransomware with honeypot techniques. In: IEEE Cybersecurity and Cyberforensics Conference (CCC), Amman, Jordan (2016)

57. Chakkaravarthy, S.S., Sangeetha, D., Cruz, M.V., Vaidehi, V., Raman, B.: Design of intrusion detection honeypot using social leopard algorithm to detect IoT ransomware attacks. IEEE Access **8**, 169944–169956 (2020)

58. Matin, I.M.M., Rahardjo, B.: The use of honeypot in machine learning based on malware detection: a review. In: 8th IEEE International Conference on Cyber and IT Service Management (CITSM), Pangkal, Indonesia (2020)

59. Matin, I.M.M., Rahardjo, B.: TMalware detection using honeypot and machine learning. In: 7th IEEE International Conference on Cyber and IT Service Management (CITSM), Jakarta, Indonesia (2019)

60. Wang, B., Dou, Y., Sang, Y., Zhang, Y., Huang, J.: IoTCMal: towards a hybrid IoT honeypot for capturing and analyzing malware. In: IEEE International Conference on Communications (ICC), Dublin, Ireland (2020)

61. Woralert, C., Liu, C., Blasingame, Z.: HARD-lite: a lightweight hardware anomaly realtime detection framework targeting ransomware. IEEE Trans. Circuits Syst. I Regul. Pap. **70**, 1–12 (2023)

62. Sharma, P., Chaudhary, K., Khan, M. G.: The art-of-hyper-parameter optimization with desirable feature selection: optimizing for multiple objectives: ransomware anomaly detection. In: International Conference on Medical Imaging and Computer-Aided Diagnosis (MICAD) Medical Imaging and Computer-Aided Diagnosis, Birmingham, United Kingdom (2022)

63. Sharma, P., Kapoor, S., Sharma, R.: HARD-lite: ransomware detection, prevention and protection in IoT devices using ml techniques based on dynamic analysis approach. Int. J. Syst. Assur. Eng. Manage. **14**, 287–296 (2023)

64. Abusitta, A., de Carvalho, G.H., Wahab, O.A., Halabi, T., Fung, B.C., Al Mamoori, S.: Deep learning-enabled anomaly detection for IoT systems. Internet Things **21**, 100656 (2023)

65. Bhuvaneswari, R., Kumar, E.K., Padmasini, A., Varma, K.P.: Insider threat detection of ransomware using AutoML. CRC Press Artif. Intell. Blockchain Comput. Secur. **1**, 724–733 (2023)

66. Singh, A., Mushtaq, Z., Abosaq, H.A., Mursal, S.N.F., Irfan, M., Nowakowski, G.: Enhancing ransomware attack detection using transfer learning and deep learning ensemble models on cloud-encrypted data. Electronics **12**, 3899 (2023)

67. BN, C., SH, B.: Revolutionizing ransomware detection and criticality assessment: multiclass hybrid machine learning and semantic similarity-based end2end solution. Multimedia Tools and Applications, 1–34 (2023)

68. Smmarwar, S. K., Gupta, G. P., Kumar, S.: A hybrid feature selection approach-based android malware detection framework using machine learning techniques. In: Cyber Security, Privacy and Networking (ICSPN), Thailand (2022)

69. Khan Abbasi, M.H., Ullah, S., Ahmad, T., Buriro, A.: A real-time hybrid approach to combat in-browser cryptojacking malware. Appl. Sci. **13**, 2039 (2023)

70. Karbab, E.B., Debbabi, M., Derhab, A.: SwiftR: cross-platform ransomware fingerprinting using hierarchical neural networks on hybrid features. Expert Syst. Appl. **225**, 120017 (2023)

71. Gupta, S., Thakur, P., Biswas, K., Kumar, S., Singh, A.P.: Developing a blockchain-based and distributed database-oriented multi-malware detection engine. In: Maleh, Y., Shojafar, M., Alazab, M., Baddi, Y. (eds.) Machine Intelligence and Big Data Analytics for Cybersecurity Applications. SCI, vol. 919, pp. 249–275. Springer, Cham (2021). https://doi.org/10.1007/978-3-030-57024-8_11

72. Pletinckx, S., Trap, C., Doerr, C.: Malware coordination using the blockchain: an analysis of the cerber ransomware. In: IEEE Conference On Communications and Network Security (CNS), Privacy And Networking (ICSPN), Beijing, China, pp. 1–9 (2018)

73. Delgado-Mohatar, O., Sierra-Cámara, J.M., Anguiano, E.: Blockchain-based semi-autonomous ransomware. Futur. Gener. Comput. Syst. **112**, 589–603 (2020)

74. Akcora, C.G., Li, Y., Gel, Y.R., Kantarcioglu, M.: Bitcoinheist: topological data analysis for ransomware detection on the bitcoin blockchain. Futur. Gener. Comput. Syst. 1–15 (2019)

75. Gu, J., Sun, B., Du, X., Wang, J., Zhuang, Y., Wang, Z.: Consortium blockchain-based malware detection in mobile devices. IEEE Access **6**, 12118–12128 (2018)

Enhancing Security in Blockchain Enabled IoT Networks Empowered with zk-SNARKs and Physically Unclonable Functions

Pranav Unni[1]([✉]), Saumya Banerjee[2], and Samia Bouzefrane[3]

[1] Amity University, Haryana, India
pranavcosmos4@gmail.com
[2] Trasna Solutions, Munich, Germany
soumya.banerjee@trasna.io
[3] Conservatoire National des Arts et Métiers, Paris, France
samia.bouzefrane@lecnam.net

Abstract. In the realm of IoT and blockchain, security and privacy are paramount. This paper explores the fusion of Zero-Knowledge Succinct Non-Interactive Arguments of Knowledge (zk-SNARKs) and Physically Unclonable Functions (PUFs) to bolster the security of blockchain-enabled IoT networks.

By harnessing zk-SNARKs' ability to prove knowledge without revealing sensitive information and PUFs' unique device-based identity verification, we establish a robust framework for data protection and device authentication. We investigate the practical integration of these technologies into IoT ecosystems, addressing challenges and assessing their impact on scalability, efficiency, and security.

The research showcases a novel solution for enhancing data confidentiality, integrity, and authenticity within IoT networks while empowering devices to prove their identity without disclosing sensitive data. The proposed novel method has a behemoth advantage over conventional data breaches as PUF values are not in transit. It could also help in reducing memory usage and easy scalability. However, it may introduce risks like integration complexity and therefore it is expected to stay updated with evolving cryptographic standards.

Keywords: zk-SNARK · PUF · blockchain · IoT

1 Introduction

Blockchain technology and the Internet of Things (IoT) have individually revolutionized multiple sectors, from healthcare and manufacturing to finance and smart cities. However, as these technologies continue to intersect, issues surrounding security and privacy have emerged as significant barriers to their collective potential. While blockchain brings transparency and immutability to data management, and IoT contributes to the smart automation of various tasks, their merger exacerbates existing vulnerabilities, making

© IFIP International Federation for Information Processing 2024
Published by Springer Nature Switzerland AG 2024
S. Bouzefrane and D. Sauveron (Eds.): WISTP 2024, LNCS 14625, pp. 96–110, 2024.
https://doi.org/10.1007/978-3-031-60391-4_7

it crucial to develop comprehensive solutions that ensure both data integrity and user privacy. Previous works have focused on either blockchain or IoT security mechanisms in isolation, often lacking a unified approach that harnesses the strengths of both worlds. This paper breaks new ground by merging Zero-Knowledge Succinct Non-Interactive Arguments of Knowledge (zk-SNARKs) with Physically Unclonable Functions (PUFs) to construct a highly secure and privacy-preserving environment for blockchain-enabled IoT networks. We delve into the intricate challenges of integrating these two technologies and provide an in-depth analysis of their impact on system scalability, efficiency, and security. Through this innovative approach, we aim to set a new standard for safeguarding data and devices in increasingly complex IoT ecosystems.

2   State of the Art

The landscape of security and privacy in IoT and blockchain technologies has been explored extensively, yet several gaps persist, particularly concerning their intersection. This section aims to review prior works that inform the security framework we propose, highlighting areas that our research uniquely addresses.

Blockchain technology has proven itself as a robust solution for decentralizing data management and ensuring data integrity. Researchers have explored its applicability across sectors like healthcare, supply chain, and finance. However, blockchain's innate transparency can compromise user privacy, an issue that becomes even more pronounced when IoT devices are involved. Conversely, IoT brings the challenge of securing a multitude of interconnected devices with varying security protocols. These issues have been studied in isolation but rarely from the perspective of a unified IoT-blockchain ecosystem.

Zero-Knowledge Proofs, particularly zk-SNARKs, have emerged as powerful tools for maintaining user privacy on blockchain networks. They enable transactions to be validated without revealing the content of the transaction itself. Most existing studies focus on financial transactions, with little exploration of how zk-SNARKs can secure data transactions within an IoT network. PUFs have been traditionally used for hardware-based security, uniquely identifying each device through variations in its manufacturing process. They have been deployed for device authentication in various domains like embedded systems and mobile devices but have seldom been applied in the context of blockchain-enabled IoT networks. Conceptually, zk-SNARKs are zero-knowledge succinct non-interactive arguments of knowledge [1], that permits a prover to convince a verifier without any real interaction and relinquish the knowledge of a witness attesting to the validity of an NP relation. This will also exclude the broadcasting of any information about the witness. There are different plausible applications of ZK-SNARKS specially for private smart contracts [2]. In Spite of several possible advantages of ZK-SNARKS, zk-SNARKs still demonstrate substantial lacking on speed of convergence with respect to the large memory usage and gate keeping activities [3, 4]. While investigating the integrated roadmap of ZKP (as well as with ZK-SNARK) on embedded systems, ASIC ecosystem, we deeply inspired with the solution of ZPiE [5], which provides an API to design circuits, perform the setup phase, generate proofs and verify them. Of similar interest, a public blockchain-based lightweight anonymous authentication platform for low-power loT devices using zk-SNARKs is proposed. This lightweight anonymous authentication protocol is designed using the SHA256 hash function. The heavy proving processes of the zk-SNARK protocol are offloaded to a powerful loT machine [6]. Interested readers can also refer to the other relevant research articles, which emphasize the ZK-SNARKS and hardware integration [7, 8].

The paper aims to fill the existing research gap by proposing an integrated security framework that leverages the strengths of zk-SNARKs for data protection and PUFs for device authentication in blockchain-enabled loT networks. Our work offers a pioneering solution that comprehensively addresses the issues of data confidentiality, integrity, and authenticity while considering the practical challenges of scalability and efficiency.

The research is meticulously outlined through several key sections. The Methodology section elucidates the research techniques, tools, and algorithms employed to achieve the objectives. This is followed by the System Architecture section, which provides a detailed blueprint of the proposed security framework, making use of both zk-SNARKs and PUFs. In the Implementation section, the practical integration of these technologies into a blockchain-enabled loT network is explained. The Performance Evaluation section showcases metrics and analyses that attest to the efficiency, scalability, and security of the framework. Finally, the paper culminates in a Conclusion that synthesizes the key findings and their broader implications. For academic rigor, all cited works are comprehensively listed in the References section.

3 Methodology

The methodology employed in this paper represents the cornerstone of the innovative approach to enhancing security within blockchain-enabled loT networks. By seamlessly integrating Zero-Knowledge Succinct Non-Interactive Arguments of Knowledge (zk-SNARKs) with Physically Unclonable Functions (PUFs), this paper devises a comprehensive framework designed to safeguard against unauthorized access while simultaneously preserving sensitive device-specific information. This section provides an exhaustive exposition of each phase of the methodology, encompassing key aspects such as key generation, authentication procedures, zero knowledge proof generation, and verification. Additionally, this paper elucidates the manifold benefits of this integration, including heightened security and optimized resource utilization, to underline the significance and novelty of the research contributions. This methodology underpins the quest to establish a resilient and privacy-conscious foundation for blockchain-based loT networks, setting new standards for security and authentication paradigms in this rapidly evolving domain. Figure 1 shows a bird's eye view of the methodology the novel solution follows.

There are multiple phases involved in this section which are discussed in great detail in the corresponding subsections.

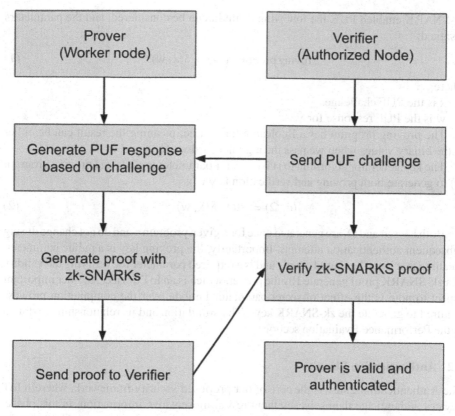

Fig. 1. Methodology for integrating zk-SNARK with PUF in a peer-to-peer IoT blockchain network.

3.1 Setup Phase

The setup phase in the integration of zk-SNARKs with Physically Unclonable Functions (PUFs) involves the generation and distribution of cryptographic keys, ensuring a robust foundation for secure authentication within blockchain-enabled IoT networks.

The first step in the setup phase revolves around the generation of cryptographic keys specific to zk-SNARKs. These keys consist of a proving key (σ) and a verification key (Ω). The process is initiated with the selection of a secret parameter, commonly denoted as lambda (λ). This secret parameter plays a pivotal role in ensuring the security of zk-SNARKs but must be guarded carefully since knowledge of λ can lead to the creation of fake zk-SNARK proofs, potentially rendering the security system useless. It is also researched that the key generation process can be initiated in-device using the device's fingerprint (PUF) [9].

The proving key and verification key is generated using the secret parameter lambda (λ) and the specific proving program (τ), denoted as $\delta(x, w)$, relevant to the authentication context, where x is the public input and w is the witness as seen in (1). The generation process is encapsulated within a key generator algorithm (α). In context of creating a zk-SNARK enabled PUF, the following formula can be considered, and the parameters assigned:

$$\text{Proving program } (\tau) \Rightarrow \delta(x, w) \tag{1}$$

where,

x is the PUF challenge.

w is the PUF response for x.

The proving program has a Boolean return value, meaning the result can be either of the binary values when we pass the argument values for x and w.

The key generator algorithm (α) takes secret parameter lambda and proving program (τ) to generate both proving and verification key (2):

$$(\sigma, \Omega) \Rightarrow \alpha(\lambda, \delta(x, w)) \tag{2}$$

Both keys, σ and Ω, are generated once for a given program τ and do not change during subsequent authentication attempts. Importantly, the proving key is a public parameter, meaning that it can be shared openly and is a required parameter for verifying the validity of a zk-SNARK proof generated by the prover, which is an IoT device. Another important aspect to note is the effect of secret parameter lambda over the computation prowess required to generate the zk-SNARK keys. The simulation and its relationship are drawn in the Performance Evaluation section.

3.2 Authentication Phase

The Authentication Phase is the core of our proposed security framework, wherein IoT devices authenticate themselves without revealing sensitive information. In this phase, when an IoT device seeks access to the blockchain network, the server initiates the process by sending a PUF challenge (χ) to the device. This challenge, represented as a public input (x), serves as a cryptographic puzzle that the IoT device needs to solve.

Upon receiving the PUF challenge (χ), the IoT device generates a unique PUF response (ρ) based on its inherent physical characteristics (3). The PUF response is computed using the PUF challenge (χ) and the device's individual PUF circuitry (K). This response (ρ) is device-specific and serves as a critical component in the subsequent proof generation:

$$\rho \Rightarrow K(\chi) \tag{3}$$

where

K is the PUF circuitry which determines the PUF response ρ based on the PUF challenge χ sent by the server (or another IoT device acting as an authorized node).

Building on the generated PUF response (ρ) and the public key (σ) distributed during the setup phase, the IoT device employs zk-SNARKs to construct a zk-proof (π). This proof (π) cryptographically attests that the device possesses the requisite PUF response (ρ) without divulging the actual response or any sensitive data. The zk-SNARK proof generation process (γ) is executed securely within the confines of the IoT device's environment (4):

$$\pi \Rightarrow \gamma(\rho, \sigma) \tag{4}$$

With the zk-SNARK proof (π) successfully generated, the IoT device transmits both the proof (π) and the original PUF challenge (χ) back to the server for verification. Crucially, the actual PUF response (ρ) remains confidential and is not transmitted during this phase.

3.3 Verification Phase

Upon receiving the zk-SNARK proof (π) and the PUF challenge (χ) from the IoT device, the server, along with any third-party verifier, undertakes zk-SNARK proof verification. This verification process entails using the verification key (Ω), the received PUF challenge (χ), and the zk-SNARK proof (π) to confirm the validity of the authentication attempt. Mathematically, the verification process is represented as seen in (5):

$$V(\Omega, \chi, \pi) \Rightarrow \{\text{Proof valid ? True: False}\} \qquad (5)$$

where,
   V is the verification algorithm that checks the validity of the zk-SNARK proof π.

3.4 Authorization Phase

Upon successful verification of the zk-SNARK proof (π), the server makes an access decision based on the authenticity of the IoT device. If the verification process returns "True," signifying the proof's validity, the IoT device is considered authenticated and authorized to access the blockchain network. Conversely, if the verification process returns "False," access is denied, ensuring that only legitimate and authorized devices are permitted entry.

This multi-phased approach to authentication, verification, and authorization provides a robust security framework for blockchain-enabled IoT networks. It ensures that only genuine IoT devices gain access while protecting sensitive PUF responses and device-specific information, ultimately advancing the security and privacy of such networks. The entire algorithm is summarized in algorithm 1.

Algorithm 1: PUF Authentication using zk-SNARK in IoT network

---

Input: IoT Device (D), Server (S), Public Key (σ), Verification Key (Ω), PUF Challenge(χ), IoT Network Array (N), zk-Proof generation function (γ), Verification algorithm (V)

Output: Access Granted or Denied for D to enter N

Process:
  Authentication Phase:
    1: D receives χ from S.
    2: PUF Response of D (ρ) ← D::generatePUFresponse(χ)
    3: zk-Proof generated by D (π) ← γ(ρ, σ)
    4: D transmits (π, χ) to S
  Verification Phase:
    5: S receives (π, χ)
    6: bool isVerified ← V(Ω, π, χ)
    7: **if** isVerified:
    8:      D::accessGranted ← **True**
    9: **else:**
    10:     D::accessGranted ← **False**
    11: **end if**
  Authorization Phase:
    12: **if** D::accessGranted:
    13:   N.append(D)
    14:   D granted access to network N
    15: **else:**
    16:   D denied access to network N
    17: **end if**

---

4   System Architecture

The System Architecture section of this paper delves into the structural design and components of our proposed security framework, which integrates Zero-Knowledge Succinct Non-Interactive Arguments of Knowledge (zk-SNARKs) with Physically Unclonable Functions (PUFs) to fortify the security of blockchain-enabled Internet of Things (IoT) networks. This section provides a comprehensive insight into the architectural blueprint of our system, elucidating the key components, their interactions, and their roles in ensuring robust security and efficient functionality.

4.1   Overview of System Components

At the heart of our system architecture lies a dynamic interplay of various components, each contributing to the overall security and efficiency of the blockchain-enabled IoT network. The fundamental components include:

IoT Devices: IoT devices form the foundation of our architecture. These sensor nodes, actuators, and smart devices are dispersed throughout the network and serve as the endpoints for data collection, communication, and authentication. Each IoT device possesses a unique Physically Unclonable Function (PUF), which acts as a secure identifier.

Server or Authorized Node: The server, often referred to as the verifier, serves as the central authority responsible for managing access to the blockchain network. It plays a pivotal role in the generation and distribution of zk-SNARK keys, as detailed in the setup phase. Additionally, the server initiates and oversees the authentication and verification processes. Networks aiming at complete decentralization may aim at replacing servers with an authorized node which is an IoT Device. The selection of the authorized node is done using generic consensus mechanism like HDPoA [10].

Blockchain Network: The blockchain network functions as the distributed ledger that records all transactions and activities within the IoT ecosystem. It is composed of a network of nodes, including validator nodes and worker nodes (IoT devices), responsible for reaching consensus and maintaining the integrity of the blockchain.

zk-SNARK Module: The zk-SNARK module encompasses the zk-SNARK key generation, proof generation, and verification processes. It interacts closely with both the server and the IoT devices, facilitating the creation and validation of zk-SNARK proofs.

Secure Communication Channels: Secure communication channels establish connections between IoT devices, the server, and the blockchain network. These channels ensure the confidentiality and integrity of data exchanged during authentication and transaction processes.

4.2 Architectural Workflow

The architectural workflow illustrates how these components collaborate to ensure secure authentication and data protection within the blockchain-enabled IoT network:

Key Generation and Distribution: During the setup phase, as detailed in the methodology section, the server generates and distributes the zk-SNARK proving and verification keys (σ, Ω) to the IoT devices. These keys form the foundation for secure authentication.

Authentication: In the authentication phase, IoT devices receive PUF challenges from the server. They generate PUF responses and construct zk-SNARK proofs (π) to validate their authenticity without revealing sensitive information. The proofs are then submitted to the server for verification.

Verification: The server, armed with the verification key (Ω), evaluates the zk-SNARK proofs (π) and confirms the legitimacy of the authentication attempts. Valid IoT devices gain access to the blockchain network, while invalid attempts are denied.

Authorization and Blockchain Interaction: Authorized IoT devices are granted access to the blockchain network, where they can participate in data transactions and smart contract execution. The blockchain network employs consensus mechanisms to validate and record these transactions securely.

A detailed view of the system architecture can be understood from Fig. 2.

5 Implementation

The Implementation section is a pivotal phase in the realization of our research objectives, transforming the theoretical constructs of our security framework into a practical and operational system. In this section, we provide a comprehensive account of how we concretely applied the integrated technologies of Zero-Knowledge Succinct Non-Interactive Arguments of Knowledge (zk-SNARKs) and Physically Unclonable Functions (PUFs) within a blockchain-enabled Internet of Things (IoT) network. We explore the technical intricacies, key components, and methodologies that underpin the actualization of this innovative security architecture.

5.1 Integration of zk-SNARK and PUF Technologies

Integration with Existing IoT Infrastructure: The implementation begins with the seamless integration of the zk-SNARK and PUF technologies into the existing IoT infrastructure. This integration is carried out through a series of crucial steps:

- Interaction with IoT Devices: We established secure channels for communication between IoT devices and the server to facilitate the exchange of PUF challenges and responses while preserving data confidentiality and integrity.
- Integration with Server: The server, serving as the verifier, incorporates the zk-SNARK module, including the key generation, proof generation, and verification processes. This integration is essential for managing authentication requests and validating zk-SNARK proofs. In the case of peer-to-peer blockchain network, the server is yet another IoT device which has a higher privilege (an authorized node).
- Distribution of Proving Key: As outlined in the setup phase, the proving key (σ) is distributed to IoT devices securely, ensuring they can access and utilize it for proof generation.

5.2 Harnessing PUF Capabilities

The integration of PUF technology plays a pivotal role in device identification without compromising security. Our implementation ensures the following:

- PUF Challenge-Response Mechanism: IoT devices, equipped with PUF circuitry, actively respond to PUF challenges issued by the server during authentication. The PUF response remains confidential and unique to each device.
- Secure PUF Communication: Implementation includes robust encryption and cryptographic protocols to secure the challenge-response exchanges between IoT devices and the server, safeguarding the confidentiality and integrity of PUF communications.

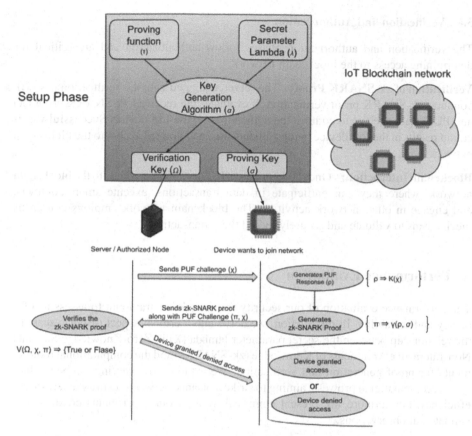

Fig. 2. System Architecture showing the integration of zk-SNARK and PUF

5.3 Authentication Workflow

The heart of our implementation is the authentication workflow, where IoT devices prove their identity without revealing sensitive information. This authentication process unfolds as follows:

PUF Challenge and Response: The server initiates authentication by dispatching a PUF challenge (χ) to the IoT device. The IoT device's PUF circuitry generates a device-specific PUF response (ρ) based on the challenge (χ). Importantly, this challenge-response exchange remains secure and confidential.

zk-SNARK Proof Generation: Building upon the generated PUF response (ρ) and the distributed proving key (σ), the IoT device constructs a zk-SNARK proof (π) to demonstrate its knowledge of the PUF response without disclosing it.

Proof Submission: The IoT device transmits both the PUF challenge (χ) and the zk-SNARK proof (π) to the server for validation. Notably, the actual PUF response (ρ) is safeguarded and withheld during this exchange.

5.4 Verification and Authorization

The verification and authorization phases follow authentication and are critical for determining access to the blockchain network:

Verification of zk-SNARK Proof: The server, equipped with the verification key (Ω), conducts zk-SNARK proof verification. It evaluates the received zk-SNARK proof (π) and PUF challenge (χ) to confirm the authenticity of the IoT device. Successful verification results in the IoT device being authenticated and granted access to the blockchain network.

Blockchain Interaction: Once authenticated, IoT devices gain access to the blockchain network, where they can participate in data transactions, execute smart contracts, and engage in other network activities. The blockchain network employs consensus mechanisms to validate and securely record these transactions.

6 Performance Evaluation

The performance evaluation of our security framework is paramount to assess its efficiency and scalability. In this section, we delve into a critical aspect of our research - the relationship between the secret parameter lambda (λ) in Zero-Knowledge Succinct Non-Interactive Arguments of Knowledge (zk-SNARKs) and the computational requirements for proof generation and verification. We explore how varying lambda values impact computational prowess, aiming to strike a balance between security and resource efficiency. Furthermore, we present empirical results from experiments conducted to validate our observations.

6.1 Lambda and Computational Power

Lambda serves as a critical security parameter in zk-SNARKs, influencing the resilience of the proof system against attacks. A higher lambda value enhances security by increasing the difficulty of breaking the proof system. However, it also imposes a heavier computational burden on proof generation and verification processes.

Our analysis reveals a remarkable exponential relationship between lambda and computational power measured in FLOPS (Floating Point Operations Per Second) (see Table 1):

- Computation Power for Proof Generation: The computational power required for generating a proof exhibits a polynomial relationship with lambda, expressed as $O(\lambda^4)$.
- Computation Power for Proof Verification: Similarly, the computational power needed for verifying a proof follows a polynomial relationship with lambda, characterized by $O(\lambda^2)$.

Table 1. Computational Power Analysis of Increasing Lambda Values

Lambda Values (in bits)	Computation Power for Proof Generation (in FLOPS)	Computation Power for Proof Verification (in FLOPS)
16	278	66
24	4102	255
32	66432	1024
40	1048329	4100
48	16780224	16372
56	2687751453	66201
64	4294968019	263142

6.2 Graph Visualization

To provide a visual representation of the relationship between lambda (λ), proof generation, and proof verification, we have generated three informative graphs. These visualizations offer a clearer understanding of the computational implications associated with varying lambda values.

Generation and Verification Power relationship: In the graph Fig. 3, we illustrate the specific relationship between proof generation and verification as lambda values incrementally increase. This graph provides valuable insights into the relative computational demands of these two processes. The graph showcases that proof generation generally requires more computational power compared to verification across the range of lambda values.

Effect of Lambda on Generation and Verification: The second graph Fig. 4(a) depicts the combined effect of lambda on both proof generation and verification. This graph showcases how the computational demands for both processes increase as lambda values rise. As lambda values increase, there is a noticeable upward trend in computational power requirements for both proof generation and verification. The relationship appears exponential, reinforcing our earlier analysis that higher lambda values lead to significantly increased computational burdens.

Lambda vs. Generation vs. Verification Powers: The third graph Fig. 4(b) presents a 3D plot, visualizing the intricate relationship between lambda, proof generation, and proof verification. This dynamic representation offers a comprehensive view of how lambda values impact both phases simultaneously. The 3D plot accentuates the complex interplay between lambda, generation, and verification. Higher lambda values correspond to elevated computational demands for both generation and verification, creating distinct regions of increased resource utilization.

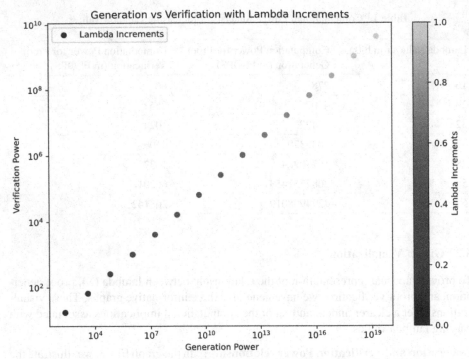

Fig. 3. Relationship between Generation Power and Verification Power over Lambda increments

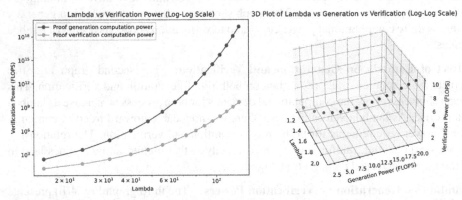

Fig. 4. (a) (graph on left): Effect of lambda on Generation and Verification Power measured in log scale. (b) (graph on right): 3D plot showing Lambda vs Generation Power vs Verification Power measured in log scale.

6.3 Key Observations

The visualizations underscore several key observations:

Exponential Relationship: The effect of lambda on computational power exhibits an exponential trend, necessitating careful consideration of lambda values in balancing security and performance.

Generation vs. Verification: Proof generation consistently requires more computational resources compared to verification, with the disparity growing as lambda values increase.

Resource Allocation: These findings emphasize the importance of resource allocation and optimization in real-world implementations, particularly in resource-constrained environments such as Internet of Things (IoT) devices.

Configurational Impact: Selecting an appropriate lambda value is crucial in aligning computational demands with the capabilities of the target system.

7 Conclusion

In this research, we have successfully integrated Zero-Knowledge Succinct Non-Interactive Arguments of Knowledge (zk-SNARKs) with Physically Unclonable Functions (PUFs) to fortify the security of blockchain-enabled Internet of Things (IoT) networks. Our methodology, system architecture, and performance evaluation collectively underscore the significance and practicality of our security framework. Through meticulous key generation, secure authentication, and extensive performance analysis, we have demonstrated that our framework strikes a delicate balance between security and resource efficiency. Our experiments, guided by the secret parameter lambda (λ), revealed the exponential impact of lambda on proof generation and verification, offering critical insights for configuring zk-SNARK parameters in real-world applications. Moreover, our case study in a smart cattle farm exemplified the real-world applicability of our approach, showcasing its versatility across industries. This research marks a pivotal step towards establishing resilient and privacy conscious IoT networks. As we navigate the evolving landscape of IoT security, our integrated solution empowers devices to assert their identities securely while preserving data confidentiality, integrity, and authenticity. It sets new standards for security in IoT, offering a promising path forward in our quest for a safer and more secure interconnected future.

References

1. Bitansky, N., et al.: The hunting of the SNARK. J. Cryptol. **30**(4), 989–1066 (2017)
2. Bowe, S., Chiesa, A., Green, M., Miers, I., Mishra, P., Wu, H.: ZEXE: Enabling decentralized private computation. In 2020 IEEE Symposium on Security and Privacy, pp. 947–964. IEEE Computer Society Press, May 2020
3. Ozdemir, A., Boneh, D.: Experimenting with collaborative zk-SNARKs: Zero-Knowledge proofs for distributed secrets. In: 31st USENIX Security Symposium (USENIX Security 22), pp. 4291–4308, Boston, MA, August 2022. USENIX Association
4. Green, M., Hall-Andersen, M., Hennenfent, E., Kaptchuk, G., Perez, B., Van Laer, G.: Efficient proofs of software exploitability for real-world processors. Proc. Priv. Enhancing Technol. **2023**(1), 627–640 (2023)

5. Salleras, X., Daza, V.: ZPiE: Zero-knowledge Proofs in Embedded systems. Mathematics **9**(20), 2569 (2021). https://doi.org/10.3390/math9202569

6. Khor, J.H., Sidorov, M., Ho, N.T.M., Chia, T.H.: Public blockchain-based lightweight anonymous authentication platform using Zk-SNARKs for Low-power IoT devices. In: 2022 IEEE International Conference on Blockchain (Blockchain), Espoo, Finland, pp. 370–375 (2022)

7. Gao, S., Li, G., Fu, H., Zhang, H., Zhang. J.: ZAWA: A ZKSNARK WASM Emulator. 2023. ⟨hal-03995514⟩

8. Kusyanti, A., Santoso, N., Ainunnazahah, P., Maulana, L.: The Implementation of zk-SNARK HH Authentication on IoT Protocols. Int. J. Online Biomed. Eng. (iJOE) **18**(06), 4–12 (2022). https://doi.org/10.3991/ijoe.v18i06.28893

9. Prada-Delgado, M., Baturone, I., Dittmann, G., Jelitto, J., Kind, A.: PUF-derived IoT identities in a zero-knowledge protocol for blockchain. Internet Things. **9**, 100057 (2019). https://doi.org/10.1016/j.iot.2019.100057

10. Alrubei, S., Ball, E., Rigelsford, J.: HDPoA: honesty-based distributed proof of authority via scalable work consensus protocol for IoT-blockchain applications. Comput. Netw. **217**, 109337 (2022). ISSN 1389-1286. https://doi.org/10.1016/j.comnet.2022.109337

Security Challenges and Countermeasures in Blockchain's Peer-to-Peer Architecture

Hussein Kazem[1,2,3(✉)], Nour El Madhoun[3,4], Samia Bouzefrane[2],
and Pierrick Conord[1]

[1] Sopra Steria Infrastructure and Security Services, Courbevoie, France
{hussein.kazem,pierrick.conord}@soprasteria.com
[2] CEDRIC Lab, Conservatoire National des Arts et Métiers (CNAM), Paris, France
{samia.bouzefrane,hussein.kazem}@lecnam.net
[3] LISITE Laboratory, ISEP, 10 Rue de Vanves, 92130 Issy-les-Moulineaux, France
{hussein.kazem,nour.el-madhoun}@isep.fr
[4] Sorbonne Université, CNRS, LIP6, 4 Place Jussieu, 75005 Paris, France
nour.el_madhoun@sorbonne-universite.fr

Abstract. This paper addresses the issue of security in blockchain systems, with a focus on attacks targeting the peer-to-peer architecture. The peer-to-peer nature of blockchain is fundamental to many of the benefits promised by blockchain applications. We detail various attacks affecting this architecture, including network attacks, eclipse attack, majority attacks, selfish mining attack, block-withholding attacks, and timejacking attack. This paper provides a significant contribution in three parts: firstly, it offers a comprehensive description of several attacks targeting this architecture. Secondly, it examines the necessary conditions for the effectiveness of these attacks and, thirdly, it presents a qualitative overview of the defense strategies identified in the existing literature to deal with these threats.

Keywords: Attack · Blockchain · Countermeasures · Peer-to-Peer · Security

1 Introduction

Blockchain technology, one of the most revolutionary technologies of the 21st century, has attracted a great deal of interest in recent years [1,2]. However, the concept of blockchain being inherently "secure" has been challenged due to a series of attacks that have plagued blockchain based applications [3]. These attacks have amounted to an estimated 3.8$ billion of losses in cryptocurrencies in 2022 [4] and 1.7$ billion in 2023 [5]. Indeed, blockchain attacks are categorized into three categories as presented in the paper of Saad et al. [6]: 1) attacks targeting the blockchain structure itself, 2) attacks linked to its peer-to-peer network architecture, and 3) attacks specific to the context of applications using blockchain technology. In Table 1, we list the different attacks in their categories

S. Bouzefrane and D. Sauveron (Eds.): WISTP 2024, LNCS 14625, pp. 111–127, 2024.
https://doi.org/10.1007/978-3-031-60391-4_8

along with the proposed solutions for each attack. In this paper, we will be focusing on the attacks associated with the peer-to-peer architecture.

Our main contribution in this paper is threefold: 1) we provide a comprehensive explanation of each attack associated with the peer-to-peer system, 2) we examine the prerequisites for the success of each attack, and 3) we offer an overview of the solutions presented in the literature for these attacks.

This paper is organized as follows. Section 2 provides an overview of previous related works. In Sect. 3, we present the attacks on the peer-to-peer system of blockchain applications, building upon previous works to offer an in-depth understanding of these attacks, their consequences, and the prerequisites for their success. We also discuss the solutions proposed in the literature, along with an analysis of the feasibility and effectiveness of each solution. The last Section concludes this paper.

Table 1. Countermeasures Related to the Attack Surfaces of Blockchains

	Attack	Countermeasure
Blockchain Structure	Forks	Joint Consensus
	Orphans	Increase Block Time
Peer-to-Peer Architecture	DNS Hijacking	Routing-awareness
	BGP Hijacking	Routing-awareness
	DDoS Attacks	Increase Block Size
	Eclipse Attack	Peer Monitoring
	Majority Attacks	Two Phase Proof of Work
	Selfish Mining Attack	Time-Stamping Blocks
	Block Withholding Attacks	Enforce PoW Submission
	Time-jacking Attack	Synchronized Clocking
Blockchain Applications	Blockchain Ingestion	Encrypted Blockchains
	Wallet Theft	Backups, Wallet Insurance
	Double-Spending	OTS Schemes
	Cryptojacking	Mineguard
	Smart Contract DoS	Patch EVM
	Reentry Attacks	Patch EVM
	Replay Attacks	Secure Programming
	Overflow Attacks	Patch EVM
	Short Address Attacks	Patch EVM
	Balance attacks	Secure Programming

2   Context and Related Work

Many research papers have approached the subject of blockchain security from different angles. In the paper [7], the authors chose to take a generic approach to attacks, focusing on the penetration testing stages and without categorizing the attacks. The authors in the paper [6] chose to approach the subject from the point of view of attack surfaces: they classify attacks into 3 different attack surfaces and attempt to give a history and overview of proposed solutions to these attacks in the literature. Similarly, the paper [8] addressed the same topic by dividing attacks into 4 categories instead of 3: 1) attacks on the blockchain structure, 2) attacks on the consensus mechanism, 3) attacks on the peer-to-peer system and 4) application-oriented attacks. As illustrated in Fig. 1, this classification of attacks differs from that presented in the paper [6] mainly in that attacks on consensus mechanisms form a separate category instead of being part of attacks on the blockchain structure. Indeed, the authors of the paper [8] have also focused on the prerequisites for the success of each attack, which is an added value in their paper. In addition, other papers such as [9,10] have chosen to describe and focus on the success and defensive mechanisms against an attack or attacks respectively. To the best of our knowledge, there have been no previously published papers that have focused solely on the attacks related to the peer-to-peer architecture of blockchain by highlighting the attacks, the prerequisites of success and the solutions proposed in the literature, and which will therefore constitute the contribution of our paper.

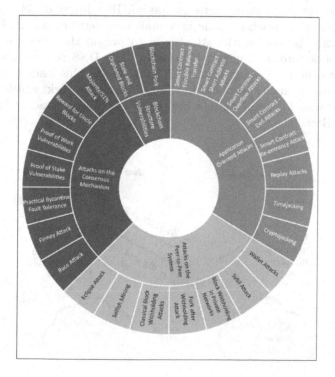

Fig. 1. Overview of the Different Attacks Presented in [8]

3   Blockchain Peer-to-Peer System Attacks and Solutions

The peer-to-peer architecture offers many guarantees of blockchain applications, such as security and accessibility. However, this architecture is the determining factor behind several attacks as presented in [6], including network attacks (DNS Hijacking, BGP Hijacking, DDoS attacks), eclipse attack, majority attacks, selfish mining attack, block-withholding attacks, and time-jacking attack. In this Section, we examine these attacks, their prerequisites for success, and the solutions proposed in the literature.

3.1   DNS Hijacking

Attack Description: immediately after joining a blockchain network for the first time, a node has no knowledge of the active peers in the network. In order to discover these active peers, a Domain Name System (DNS) can be used as a bootstrapping mechanism, and the seeds in this DNS are queried upon joining the network. The DNS resolution has been mentioned as vulnerable to: man-in-the-middle attacks (at the resolver side), cache poisoning, and stale records, among others in the developer's guide of Bitcoin networks [11]. In Fig. 2, we can see an example of how a DNS attack can be carried out by poisoning DNS cache. An honest node in the network has an IP address of 33.33.33.33 (for example) while the attacker's node in a malicious network has an IP address of 22.22.22.22. The goal of the attacker is to poison the DNS cache to lure the honest node into his counterfeit network. The DNS resolver then returns 22.22.22.22 to the DNS query instead of 33.33.33.33. This leads to the honest user connecting to malicious nodes in the attacker's network, which can result in various attacks, including but not limited to the eclipse attack, which will be discussed in Sect. 3.4.

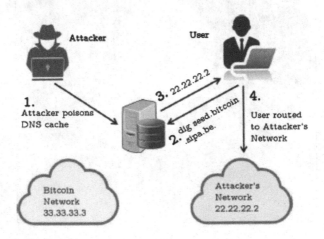

Fig. 2. DNS Hijacking [6]

Prerequisites: DNS hijacking is a classical network attack. It poses a threat to blockchains still, yet not only to it. The attacker will be successful if he is able to lure an honest user into his counterfeit network by poisoning the DNS cache.

Solutions: DNS based attacks have been the subject of extensive research in an effort to equip networks and specifically blockchain networks with DNS attack defenses. In this Section, we explore the solution proposed in [12] where the authors proposed routing-aware peer selections to maximize diversity of Internet paths and limit the vantage points for attacks. In a more long-term based solution, they also proposed peer behavior monitoring to check for abrupt disconnections and unusual latency in block delivery which could be indicators of a DNS hijack.

3.2   BGP Hijacking

Attack Description: blockchain networks consist of full and lightweight nodes, with full nodes actively participating in the network by relaying blocks and transactions while maintaining an updated blockchain copy. In contrast, lightweight nodes rely on full nodes for network access without maintaining their own blockchain. Nodes within the same Autonomous System (AS) or Internet Service Provider (ISP) become vulnerable, allowing adversarial AS to disrupt traffic flow to the targeted AS hosting blockchain nodes, impacting system activities, especially those involving miners or mining pools.

Routing attacks, particularly Border Gateway Protocol (BGP) hijacking, can significantly reduce the hash rate of blockchain applications, disrupting information flow to targeted nodes. The potential of hijacking a small number of BGP prefixes can isolate a substantial portion of the network's hash rate. These attacks lead to delays in block propagation and in extreme cases can lead to a full partition of the network. Over the last few years, a number of BGP attacks have been launched against ASs that host mining pools or cryptocurrency exchanges.

Prerequisites: BGP hijacking is a network attack which requires the attacker to be able to partition the network to control the propagation of data in the network. For the attack to work, a malicious actor needs to be able to advertise a more specific network than neighboring nodes.

Solutions: BGP hijacking is a routing based attack which does not only affect blockchain based applications but any network that uses the BGP protocol to establish routing tables. There have been many countermeasures proposed to counter BGP hijacks that are not specific to blockchain applications. In this Section, we choose to focus on SABRE, a solution proposed by the authors in [13]. SABRE is a Bitcoin relay network, it uses inter-domain routing policies to discover secure and economic routing paths between relay nodes even after a network is partitioned by a malicious actor. It is not a clean-slate approach as it can run along side currently existing Internet architecture. SABRE powered nodes are placed in a way that most clients are connected to at least one SABRE node creating a secure relay route. Currently, SABRE is focused on Bitcoin based blockchain applications yet can be adapted for non-Bitcoin blockchains allowing them to mitigate partition attacks based on BGP hijacks.

3.3   DDoS Attacks

Attack Description: one of, if not the most common attacks on online services is the Distributed Denial of Service (DDoS) attack [14]. Repeated examples of DDoS attacks on Bitcoin and ethereum have been documented [15–17]. DDoS can take on many forms, for example, the 51% attack in Bitcoin, discussed more in detail in Sect. 3.5, can lead to a denial-of-service, meaning that if a group of miners are capable controlling a majority of hashing power, they can stop other miners from adding new blocks and invalidate any ongoing transactions causing a service failure in the network.

Other possibilities of the attack are based on the limits of the blockchain's parameters: number of transactions per block, maximum size of a block, average mining time and average size of each transaction. For example, in Bitcoin, if all transactions at a current time were to be successfully mined, their number shouldn't exceed 200 transactions per minute. Using this knowledge, an attacker may exploit the aforementioned limits of the blockchain by creating several very small transactions, also known as dust transactions, from different wallets under his control in a short period of time. This large number of transactions of small value will lead to a congested network, as miners will be creating blocks containing those transactions and the service to legitimate users will be delayed or all out denied.

Prerequisites: DDoS is also a form of classical network attacks. It poses a threat to blockchains in many different forms. If there is no limit on the lower bound of transaction sizes or a higher incentive for miners to mine larger transactions, DDoS attacks can be a major concern.

Solutions: when it comes to countering DDoS attacks, there are many approaches that can be taken, starting off with the basic methods of putting a cap on the minimum amount of transaction a user can send which can help eliminate or at least limit dust transactions. Other solutions based on the blockchain parameters can be to increase the size limit of the block allowing for more transactions but a powerful malicious user can still stress the blockchain network using a large number of dust transactions. The reduction of the difficulty of block mining can allow for faster mining of blocks which could counter dust transactions yet it comes with the caveat of more orphaned and/or stale blocks in addition to a rapid increase in the size of the blockchain.

A very different approach was taken by [18] who modeled, in 3 ways, the DDoS attack using a game-theoretic approach, arriving to the conclusion of specific thresholds for the success and failure of these attacks based on the economic incentive and size of the mining pool attacked during the DDoS attack.

Another approach was given by [15] who proposed fee-based and age-based countermeasures to help prevent DDoS attacks. In the fee-based countermeasure, any incoming transaction to the mining pool must also pay a minimum mining fee and minimum relay fee. The idea is to increase the cost of the attempted attack on the mining pool deterring the attacker from spamming transactions and thereby reducing the risk of a DoS. While in the age-based countermeasure, each incoming transaction's parent transactions are counted and an "average age" is calculated based on the average of the ages of each parent transaction. A "minimum age limit" filter is then applied. This way, if an attacker wishes to spam the network they would have to generate many transactions, get them mined and, wait for them to acquire a significant age before attempting an attack thus reducing the time window in which an attack can be launched.

3.4 Eclipse Attack

Attack Description: the blockchain peer-to-peer system is vulnerable to a form of attack known as the eclipse attack [9,19–21]. During this attack, a group of malicious nodes attempts to isolate neighboring honest nodes, thereby rendering the honest nodes' incoming and outgoing traffic compromised. The goal of the attacker is to control enough malicious nodes to isolate the honest nodes and change their view of the canonical blockchain. This control could lead to the attacker feeding fake information to the honest nodes allowing him to exploit their lack of knowledge by tricking them into providing a product or service in exchange for a payment, only to realize that the transaction is only registered on the attacker controlled blockchain. This type of attack could result in financial losses. In Fig. 3, we can see an example of an eclipse attack on a cryptocurrency network: the blue nodes represent the honest nodes and the red nodes represent the malicious nodes. The malicious nodes attempt to form a cluster around the honest nodes and, through different means such as DDoS attacks, BGP hijacking or DNS hijacking, attempt to compromise the connection between the honest nodes. If successful, the malicious nodes may feed the honest nodes fake blocks effectively isolating them from the network resulting in a wrong view of the network.

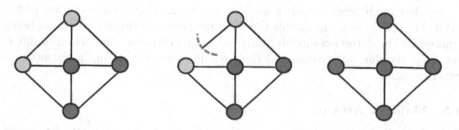

Fig. 3. Eclipse Attack on a Cryptocurrency Network [6]

Prerequisites: if the connection pattern and behaviors of nodes to their neighbors can be predicted, an eclipse Attack can be of concern. Knowing these patterns and behaviors, attackers can set up their own nodes in preparation and force a re-connect of his victims via the previously discussed BGP Hijacks, DNS Hijacks or DDoS attacks for example.

Solutions: the eclipse attack is a very unique attack when it comes to blockchain peer-to-peer attacks in that it is very difficult to describe preventative countermeasures for this attack. There have been some attempts in the literature to describe defensive measures in the form of detection of an ongoing eclipse attack in different ways. We distinguish two eclipse attack detection methods described in [9, 22].

In [9], the authors present two detection methods focused on the Bitcoin network. The first method uses timestamps to attempt to detect abnormally long block mining times in the attacker controlled network which may be an indicator of an eclipse attack. The light client raises different levels of alerts: green, yellow, orange and red, based on the delay of creation of a new block and the probability of finding n blocks in a time t. The attacker will need a considerable amount of mining power to maintain the eclipse without raising an alert as they will have to be mining blocks at the rate of a full network. This method is not as reliable as the other solution proposed as it assumes the reliability of the timestamps in the generated blocks in the attacker's networks and it is also the slowest detection method described in the paper. The second method utilizes a "Gossip-based Protocol" in which clients connect to random gossip servers onto which they piggyback their current view of the blockchain. An eclipsed client will inevitably connect to gossip network that already has a piggybacked view of the canonical blockchain will piggyback their own view of the eclipsed blockchain onto it. The server will then choose the strongest view of the blockchain (which is expected to be the canonical blockchain) and send it back to the eclipsed client. Following that, the eclipsed client can now detect that they are under an eclipse attack just by concluding that there exists a stronger blockchain than the one obtained by the malicious network.

In [22], the authors propose an eclipse attack detection method based on a combination of feature extractions and deep learning. They attribute numerical values to features of the network traffic of the blockchain network and design a CNN and bi-LSTM based deep learning network capable of detecting abnormal traffic that might correspond to an eclipse attack. They also make use of the ISMOTE algorithm to up-sample the data and prevent eclipse traffic from being ignored by the detection model. Moreover, they provide a comparison of different deep learning approaches and their results while evaluating their methods experimentally.

3.5   Majority Attacks

Attack Description: also known as the 51% attack, majority attacks exploit a vulnerability in blockchain based applications. The attacker attempts to take control of the majority of the nodes, hashing power, committed stake or replicas based on the consensus algorithm used in the blockchain.

In the case of Proof of Work (PoW), we see in Fig. 4 the probability of success of the attack based on the hashing rate fraction x of the attacker and the number of confirmations k, representing the number of subsequent blocks that have been mined on the network. There are many ways to execute a majority attack. As it is very challenging to control more than 51% of the nodes on a network at a single time, attackers can resort to renting hashing power from online services. In Practical Byzantine Fault Tolerant (PBFT)-based private blockchains, attackers can launch majority attacks with only 33% of replicas: assuming the attacker controls f nodes such that the total network size $n < 3f + 1$, the attacker will be able to initiate the attack and halt transaction verification.

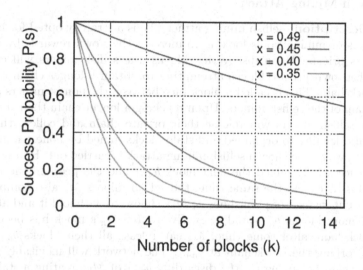

Fig. 4. Change in Success Probability *P(s)* with Varying Hashing Power x and Number of Confirmations k [6]

Prerequisites: the prerequisites of a Majority Attack vary based on the used consensus algorithms and protocols:

- Proof of Work (PoW): more than 51% of the raw computational power/hashrate of the network.
- Proof of Stake (PoS): more than 51% of the possible committed stake.
- Practical Byzantine Fault Tolerance (PBFT): more than 33% of all replicas in theory to influence the network, in practice it is sufficient to take over the single primary node

Solutions: countermeasures against majority attacks have been extensively discussed to prevent potential monopolies in the blockchain. In this Section, we review the two papers [23, 24] that offer distinct approaches to countering the majority attack. In [23], the authors propose a modification to the PoW puzzle in Bitcoin networks aimed at restricting the coalition of mining pools. To tackle the issue of mining pools, especially the outsourcing of computational power, the authors designed *nonoutsourceable* puzzles in PoW. They introduced two constructions: a weak *nonoutsourceable* puzzle and a strong one. The former could act as a sufficient deterrent against mining pools, while the latter effectively counters both hosted mining and mining pools. In [24], the authors introduce the concept of "two Phase Proof of Work" (2P-PoW), a Continuous Time Markov Chain (CTMC) model. This model presents two challenges for miners to solve instead of one. By doing so, the incentives for miners in a mining pool are reduced, which helps to prevent the growth of these pools.

3.6   Selfish Mining Attack

Attack Description: selfish mining attack [25] is a strategy opted for by malicious miners or mining pools looking to increase their own rewards by keeping their blocks private. Upon discovering blocks, the selfish miners will continue to mine their own private blocks attempting to obtain a longer chain than the public blockchain. This is called a block race between the honest miners and the private chain of the selfish miners. Upon reaching a longer chain than the public chain, the selfish miners will release their private chain and collect the block rewards, also leading to orphaned and stale blocks mined by honest miners.

In Fig. 5, we can see how a selfish mining attack is carried out. Honest miners M_h have successfully mined the next block b_{n+1} and the peers in the network validate this block. At the same time, the selfish miners M_s also compute the block b_{n+1} but instead of publishing it, $M_t s$ choose to withhold it and attempts to mine 2 more blocks b_{n+2} and b_{n+3}. Even after M_h's block has been added to the blockchain, after some time, M_s can release all their blocks b_{n+1}, b_{n+2} and, b_{n+3} forking the blockchain at b_{n+1}. The network will inevitably shift to the longer chain belonging to M_s, discarding b_{n+1} of M_h creating a stale block and maximizing the block rewards of M_s.

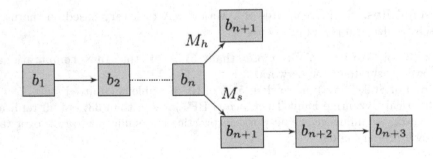

Fig. 5. Illustration of Selfish Mining Attack [6]

Prerequisites: to have a successful selfish mining attack, the attacker needs to be able to find new blocks faster than other nodes, this can usually be done by combining hashing powers with a mining pool or by offering bribes to other miners to mine on their private chain, splitting the rewards and making a profit.

Solutions: selfish mining attack is one of the most studied attacks when it comes to blockchain's peer-to-peer system. In this Section, we present three papers [25–27] that tackle countermeasures for this attack.

Starting with [25] where the authors propose a backwards-compatible change to the Bitcoin protocol to address the problem of selfish mining with their goal being to raise the threshold for the size of the mining pools that are capable of launching a selfish mining attack. In their paper, they provide a mathematical analysis of the Bitcoin protocol showing that the threshold for mining pool sizes in function of their mining power is near zero. This is due to the fact that the Bitcoin protocol entails that a node will accept the first branch that reaches it if the arriving branches have the same size. With the help of virtual zero-power miners controlled by malicious mining pools, the malicious pool operators can guarantee that their block will reach more nodes faster. The solution proposed is that when a miner receives two competing branches of the same length, they should propagate all of them to the network and choose which to mine on uniformly at random. This would result in half the nodes (assuming two competing branches) mining on the branch released by the malicious mining pool and the other half mining on the other branch which yields a threshold of 1/4 or 25%. The advantage of this solution is that it does not require a hard fork of the blockchain to change the protocol as it can be adopted by any subset of miners.

The authors of [26] built on top of the work presented in [25]. They propose a new mining strategy as a modification to the Bitcoin protocol called "Freshness Preferred" (FP). The goal of FP is to decrease the profitability of selfish mining by using unforgeable timestamps to penalize miners that withhold their blocks for long periods of time. When a FP miner receives two from branches of equal length, the miner accepts the block with the most recent valid timestamp and rejects the other block. In the case they have the equal timestamps the miner prefers the first block it receives. After an analysis of their solution, they conclude that, with the optimal timestamp increment of 60 s, the threshold for the failure of selfish mining within FP to be 32.5%, an improvement of the 25% offered in [25].

Finally, we explore ZeroBlock, the solution proposed by the authors of [27]. ZeroBlock is an algorithm based on *Expected Time*, which is the interval during which a node should solve a PoW or else, it has to generate a ZeroBlock, a dummy block including the index of *Expected Time* and the hash of previous blocks. The authors provide an analysis of the algorithm and its correctness and show that regardless of their percentage in the network, honest nodes would never accept chains where blocks have been intentionally withheld.

3.7   Block Withholding Attacks

Attack Description: the classic block withholding attack is launched with the intent to harm the operator of a mining pool by withholding a valid PoW [28]. In this scenario, a malicious miner within the mining pool who finds the PoW chooses not to disclose it to the pool operator. Consequently, the rest of the miners continue to expend resources searching for the nonce and potentially causing them to lose the race. The same malicious miner can also collude with other mining pools, sharing the PoW with them in exchange for a higher reward. Alternatively, they might publish the block under a different identity. This attack can be particularly harmful, especially considering that the behavior of a single member in the mining pool can deprive the entire pool of block rewards.

Another form of attack is known as the Fork After Withholding (FAW) attack [29]. It is consistently more rewarding for the attacker compared to the classical block withholding attacks. The FAW attack unfolds in the following manner:

1. An attacker (a malicious miner) joins two mining pools simultaneously.
2. He computes a valid PoW in one of these pools.
3. He withholds the block and only publishes it once the second pool publishes the block.
4. The network selects one of the two blocks, and the malicious miner is rewarded in both cases as a member of both mining pools.

Prerequisites: when a miner within a mining pool acts maliciously against its own pool by keeping a valid block secret, or in the case of FAW, where a miner is a member of two different mining pools and controls a new valid block.

Solutions: the block withholding attack is also a heavily researched attack with many solutions offered in the literature. We present the solutions presented in [30–34].

The authors of [30] proposed a modification of the original PoW process with a secret value so that the miners might not check whether the found block was a valid full PoW (fPoW). This method adds three additional fields:

- *SecretSeed*: The secret value of the mining pool manager
- *ExtraHash*: a hash of the SecretSeed SHA256 (SecretSeed)
- *SecretHash*: The secret difficulty value of the mining pool manager.

ExtraHash is the hash value of *SecretSeed*. *SecretHash* is the hash value of the concatenation of the block hash and *SecretSeed*. The pool manager only provides *ExtraHash* to miners and requires the hash value of blocks to be less then *SecretSeed*. Instead of requiring that the block hash is less than a specific difficulty, it is required that the block hash is less than difficulty and that *SecretHash* is less than some difficulty. Miners submit PoW without knowing *SecretSeed*. They cannot know their block is valid. The pool operator calculates *SecretHash* and checks if blocks submitted by miners are valid.

In [32] the authors proposed a scheme in which a mining pool has its own secret *commitment* value to prevent miners to distinguish partial PoW (pPoW) and fPoW. The defection of their methods is that the original PoW process should be modified and the common ASIC hardware which miners are using cannot be applicable anymore.

Another approach was given in [31] where an incentive-compatible reward scheme was presented. The goal is to discourage miners from withholding blocks. A study of different reward functions was presented and a new reward function was also presented and compared to classical reward models. A similar approach was presented in [33] where additional incentives were offered for finding a valid solution for a block in an attempt to prevent mining collusion.

Finally, in [34], the authors proposed "a two phase attack against the attack" approach. The method exploits the structure in which block withholding attacks attacks share the work of the victim pool. A detective pool infiltrates the attacker pool to check that its task is shared. If the attack is detected by confirming an infiltration, it decreases the damage by reducing the profits shared with the attacker pool. It does not require any modification of the PoW approach and is compatible with any blockchain that is using PoW.

For the FAW attack, the authors of [29] attempted to counter it by introducing time-stamped beacons in the assignment given to the miners by the pool operators. As a response to each assignment, the miners calculate the pPoW and send the response to the pool operator embedded with the beacon value. The beacon value is updated after a few seconds to catch a malicious miner if he withholds the valid solution and later propagates it in the network. However, the authors noticed that this solution may not be practical in some situations and to the best of our knowledge, we conclude that FAW attacks remain an open problem for the research community to address.

3.8   Time-Jacking Attack

Attack Description: in Bitcoin systems, full nodes use an internal counter for network time, obtained from neighboring peers' version messages during bootstrapping. If the median time of peers exceeds 70 min, the network time counter reverts to the node's system time, creating an attack opportunity. Malicious nodes can connect and manipulate timestamps, leading to a time-jacking attack. For instance, an attacker can present a block with a timestamp ahead of the network time, causing rejection by the target node if the time difference exceeds 120 min. This isolation from the main network results in the target node rejecting subsequent blocks and being cut off from network activities.

Prerequisites: an attacker needs control over a large number of neighboring nodes to be successful with this attack. Ideally, the victim is isolated by a flood of malicious nodes or by an eclipse attack.

Solutions: time-jacking attack remains largely theoretical, with no recorded attempts to date. Developing countermeasures for this type of attack still presents an open problem and could be a compelling direction for future research. To the best of our knowledge, there is only one proposed solution for this attack, as published in [35]. This solution introduces an optimized blockchain timestamp mechanism that narrows the timestamp range in a block to an average of ten minutes by leveraging an external trusted timestamp service within the blockchain consensus.

Table 2. Peer-to-Peer Attacks and Countermeasures

Attack	Countermeasure
DNS Hijacking	Routing aware peer selection [12]
BGP Hijacking	SABRE [13]
DDoS Attacks	Game Theoretic modeling threshold [18]
	Fee-based and age-based countermeasures [15]
Eclipse Attack	Gossip-based protocol [9]
	Detection using Mining times [9]
	Detection using CNN and bi-LSTM [22]
Majority Attacks	Nonoutsourceable puzzles [23]
	Two Phase Proof of Work [24]
Selfish Mining Attack	Uniformly Random Choice of Block [25]
	Freshness preferred [26]
	Zeroblock [27]
Block Wthholding Attacks	Reward system [30]
	Secret Commitment [32]
	Incentive compatible rewards [31,33]
	Two phase attack against the attack [34]
	Time stamped beacon [29]
Time-jacking Attack	Optimized timestamp mechanism [35]

4   Conclusion

In this paper, we explored the peer-to-peer architecture as an attack surface of blockchain technology. We highlighted the major threats and ongoing defense research activities. We observed that various attacks against blockchain could still be launched, and demonstrated that some of these attacks could facilitate several others. In Table 2, we provide a summary of the attacks and countermeasures discussed in this paper. By outlining these attacks, exploring the prerequisites for their success, and surveying their countermeasures, we highlighted new research directions that need to be pursued for a more secure and effective use of blockchains. Additionally, we showed that in some cases, there are still open problems and many optimizations that can be introduced to the literature, which we would like to pursue in future papers.

References

1. El Madhoun, N., Hammi, B.: Blockchain technology in the healthcare sector: overview and security analysis. In: 2024 IEEE 14th Annual Computing and Communication Workshop And Conference (CCWC), IEEE, pp. 0439–0446 (2024)
2. Ahmadieh, E., El Madhoun, N.: Artwork nfts for online trading and transaction cancellation. In: 2023 Fifth International Conference on Blockchain Computing and Applications (BCCA), IEEE, pp. 235–239 (2023)
3. Daimi, K., Dionysiou, I., El Madhoun, N. (eds.): Principles and Practice of Blockchains. Springer International Publishing, Cham (2023). https://doi.org/10.1007/978-3-031-10507-4
4. Smith, J.: Crypto hacks stole record $3.8 billion in 2022, led by north Korea groups - report. Reuters (Feb 2023). https://www.reuters.com/technology/crypto-hacks-stole-record-38-billion-2022-led-by-north-korea-groups-report-2023-02-01/
5. Crypto hackers stole around $1.7 bln in 2023 - report — reuters. Reuters (Jan 2024). https://www.reuters.com/technology/cybersecurity/crypto-hackers-stole-around-17-bln-2023-report-2024-01-24/
6. Saad, M., Spaulding, J., Njilla, L., Kamhoua, C., Shetty, S., Nyang, D., Mohaisen, D.: Exploring the attack surface of blockchain: a comprehensive survey. IEEE Commun. Surv. Tutorials **22**(3), 1977–2008 (2020)
7. Kaushik, S., El Madhoun, N.: Analysis of blockchain security: Classic attacks, cybercrime and penetration testing. In: 2023 Eighth International Conference On Mobile And Secure Services (MobiSecServ), IEEE, pp. 1–6 (2023)
8. König, L., Unger, S., Kieseberg, P., Tjoa, S., Blockchains, J.R.C.: The risks of the blockchain a review on current vulnerabilities and attacks. J. Internet Serv. Inf. Secur. **10**(3), 110–127 (2020)
9. Alangot, B., Reijsbergen, D., Venugopalan, S., Szalachowski, P., Yeo, K.S.: Decentralized and lightweight approach to detect eclipse attacks on proof of work blockchains. IEEE Trans. Network Serv. Manage. IEEE **18**(2), 1659–1672 (2021)
10. Nicolas, K., Wang, Y., Giakos, G.C., Wei, B., Shen, H.: Blockchain system defensive overview for double-spend and selfish mining attacks: a systematic approach. IEEE Access, IEEE **9**, 3838–3857 (2020)
11. P2p network. Bitcoin. https://developer.bitcoin.org/devguide/p2p_network.html
12. Apostolaki, M., Zohar, A., Vanbever, L.: Hijacking bitcoin: routing attacks on cryptocurrencies. In: 2017 IEEE Symposium on Security and Privacy (SP), pp. 375–392 (2017)
13. Apostolaki, M., Marti, G., Müller, J., Vanbever, L.: Sabre: protecting bitcoin against routing attacks. arXiv preprint arXiv:1808.06254 (2018)
14. Wang, A., Mohaisen, A., Chen, S.: An adversary-centric behavior modeling of ddos attacks. In: 2017 IEEE 37th International Conference on Distributed Computing Systems (ICDCS), pp. 1126–1136 (2017)
15. Saad, M., Thai, M.T., Mohaisen, A.: Poster: deterring ddos attacks on blockchain-based cryptocurrencies through mempool optimization. In: Proceedings of the 2018 on Asia Conference on Computer and Communications Security, pp. 809–811 (2018)

16. Vasek, M., Thornton, M., Moore, T.: Empirical analysis of denial-of-service attacks in the bitcoin ecosystem. In: Böhme, R., Brenner, M., Moore, T., Smith, M. (eds.) Financial Cryptography and Data Security: FC 2014 Workshops, BITCOIN and WAHC 2014, Christ Church, Barbados, March 7, 2014, Revised Selected Papers, pp. 57–71. Springer Berlin Heidelberg, Berlin, Heidelberg (2014). https://doi.org/10.1007/978-3-662-44774-1_5

17. Saad, M., Njilla, L., Kamhoua, C., Kim, J., Nyang, D., Mohaisen, A.: Mempool optimization for defending against ddos attacks in pow-based blockchain systems. In: 2019 IEEE International Conference on Blockchain and Cryptocurrency (ICBC), IEEE pp. 285–292 (2019)

18. Johnson, B., Laszka, A., Grossklags, J., Vasek, M., Moore, T.: Game-theoretic analysis of ddos attacks against big and small mining pools. In: 1st Workshop on Bitcoin Research, in association with FC (2014)

19. Heilman, E., Kendler, A., Zohar, A., Goldberg, S.: Eclipse attacks on {Bitcoin's}{peer-to-peer} network. In: 24th USENIX security symposium (USENIX security 15), pp. 129–144 (2015)

20. Marcus, Y., Heilman, E., Goldberg, S.: Low-resource eclipse attacks on ethereum's peer-to-peer network. Cryptology ePrint Archive (2018)

21. Nayak, K., Kumar, S., Miller, A., Shi, E.: Stubborn mining: generalizing selfish mining and combining with an eclipse attack. In: 2016 IEEE European Symposium on Security and Privacy (EuroS&P), IEEE, pp. 305–320 (2016)

22. Dai, Q., Zhang, B., Dong, S.: Eclipse attack detection for blockchain network layer based on deep feature extraction. Wirel. Commun. Mob. Comput. **2022**, 1–19 (2022)

23. Miller, A., Kosba, A., Katz, J., Shi, E.: Nonoutsourceable scratch-off puzzles to discourage bitcoin mining coalitions. In: Proceedings of the 22Nd ACM Sigsac Conference on Computer and Communications Security pp. 680–691 (2015)

24. Bastiaan, M.: Preventing the 51%-attack: a stochastic analysis of two phase proof of work in bitcoin (2015). https://api.semanticscholar.org/CorpusID:10993933

25. Eyal, I., Sirer, E.G.: Majority is not enough: Bitcoin mining is vulnerable. CoRR **abs/1311.0243** (2013). http://arxiv.org/abs/1311.0243

26. Heilman, E.: One weird trick to stop selfish miners: Fresh bitcoins, a solution for the honest miner. Financial Cryptography and Data Security: FC 2014 Workshops, BITCOIN and WAHC 2014, Christ Church, Barbados, March 7, 2014, Revised Selected Papers 18, pp. 161–162 (2014)

27. Solat, S., Potop-Butucaru, M.: Zeroblock: Preventing selfish mining in bitcoin. arXiv preprint arXiv:1605.02435 (2016)

28. Dr. Haribo, Gornick, S.: What is a block withholding attack? Bitcoin Stack Exchange (Oct 1958). https://bitcoin.stackexchange.com/questions/4943/what-is-a-block-withholding-attack

29. Kwon, Y., Kim, D., Son, Y., Vasserman, E., Kim, Y.: Be selfish and avoid dilemmas: fork after withholding (faw) attacks on bitcoin. In: Proceedings of the 2017 ACM SIGSAC Conference on Computer and Communications Security, pp. 195–209 (2017)

30. Rosenfeld, M.: Analysis of bitcoin pooled mining reward systems. arXiv preprint arXiv:1112.4980 (2011)

31. Schrijvers, O., Bonneau, J., Boneh, D., Roughgarden, T.: Incentive compatibility of bitcoin mining pool reward functions. Financial Cryptography and Data Security, pp. 477–498 (2017)

32. Bag, S., Ruj, S., Sakurai, K.: Bitcoin block withholding attack: Analysis and mitigation. IEEE Trans. Inf. Forensics Secur. **12**(8), 1967–1978 (2017)

33. Bag, S., Sakurai, K.: Yet another note on block withholding attack on bitcoin mining pools. In: Information Security: 19th International Conference, ISC 2016, Honolulu, HI, USA, September 3-6, 2016. Proceedings 19, Springer pp. 167–180 (2016)

34. Lee, S., Kim, S.: Countering block withholding attack efficiently. IEEE INFO-COM 2019-IEEE Conference on Computer Communications Workshops (INFO-COM WKSHPS), pp. 330–335 (2019)

35. Ma, G., Ge, C., Zhou, L.: Achieving reliable timestamp in the bitcoin platform. Peer-to-Peer Netw. Appl. **13**, 2251–2259 (2020)

A Bitcoin-Based Digital Identity Model
for the Internet of Things

Youakim Badr[1]([⊠]), Xiaoyang Zhu[2], Samia Saad-Bouzefrane[3], and Soumya Banerjee[4]

[1] The University State University, California, USA
yzb61@psu.edu
[2] INSA-Lyon, Villeurbanne, France
[3] CNAM, Paris, France
[4] Trasna-Solutions Ltd., Cork, Ireland

Abstract. Cybersecurity in the Internet of Things (IoT), at its heart, relies on the digital identity concept to build security mechanisms such as authentication and authorization. However, current centralized identity management systems are built around third party identity providers, which raises privacy concerns and presents a single point of failure. In addition, IoT unconventional characteristics such as scalability, heterogeneity and mobility require new identity management systems to operate in distributed and trustless environments. In order to deal with these challenges, we present the Blockchain-based Identity Management System for the Internet of Things. By such, things and people are able to self-manage their identities and authenticate without relying on any third parties.

1 Introduction

The Internet of Things aims at connecting everything ranging from individuals (human-beings), collectives (i.e., homes, organizations, companies...) to things (i.e., objects in the physical and virtual information world) [1]. According to the research report published by IDC [2], there will be over 40 billion connected IoT devices that fall under the rubric of the "Internet of Things" in 2025. Obviously, considering billions of people, trillions of IoT devices, and innumerable data resources, the first priority is how to identify them and how to allocate unique identities to individuals and things. Without doubt, the *digital identity* remains the core concept in security upon which all security mechanisms (i.e., authentication, authorization, secure exchanges, ...) and protocols are built. As defined by ITU, the digital identity refers to a set of information (identifier, credentials and attributes) used for uniquely identifying an entity in a given context [3]. An Identity Management (IdM) system refers to management of identity information through a set of operations like register, update, revoke and look-up.

Figure 1 depicts a sample instance of traditional IdM systems, which comprises three main stakeholders: Subject (a.k.a User), Relying Party (also called Service Provider) and Identity Provider (IdP) [4]. The different three parties are interdependent entities: the Subject requests accesses to services from the Relying Party which requires the Identity Provider to challenge the subject identity through the authentication protocol.

© IFIP International Federation for Information Processing 2024
Published by Springer Nature Switzerland AG 2024
S. Bouzefrane and D. Sauveron (Eds.): WISTP 2024, LNCS 14625, pp. 128–145, 2024.
https://doi.org/10.1007/978-3-031-60391-4_9

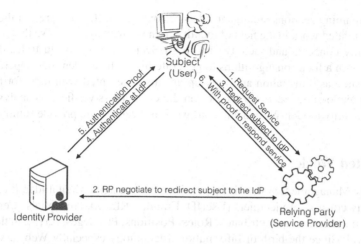

Fig. 1. Stakeholders from the traditional IdMS model

However, when building IdMS for the Internet of Things, traditional IdM systems, or even decentralized IdMS model such as OpenID [5], are subject to new challenges related to IoT such as scalable deployment, efficiency of across-domain authentications and unconditionally trust by relying on IdPs. Alternatively, centralized or decentralized IoT Identity Management solutions become quickly obsolete due to distributed IoT networks composed of millions or even billions of devices and objects [5–7]. In addition, IoT unconventional characteristics such as scalability, heterogeneity and mobility, make current IdMS difficult to design and deploy. As demonstrated in our previous work [25], these characteristics are intrinsic requirements for building scalable and distributed IdMS in the context of the IoT. In addition to these IoT unconventional characteristics, the design of IoT IdM is also confronted with challenges from the **security** perspective. For instance, most of the IdM solutions are designed under the assumption that subjects and relying parties trust the identity providers. This assumption increases threats from internal attacks of IdM systems and hence compromises security services like confidentiality and integrity. Besides, the IoT IdM should be robust enough to defend some longstanding security attacks like single-point failure or phishing [8,9], which undermines the availability of IdM systems. Therefore, eliminating trusted third parties and building trusted IdM systems in trustless IoT networks are pretty critical issue towards the development of future IoT services.

In order to handle IoT unconventional characteristics and deal the before-mentioned challenges, we introduce the *Blockchain-based Identity Management System for the Internet of Things* (BIMSIT) as a new paradigm to build distributed and trustworthy IdM systems. The BIMSIT mainly relies on the blockchain technology, which is initially introduced by the Bitcoin crypto-currency.

By using the blockchain as a back-end technology, we build a distributed and peer-to-peer IoT identity management system in a trsutless environment by which all things and people are able to self-manage their identities and enable authentication without relying on any third parties.

The remaining sections are organized as follows. In Sect. 2, we present the state of the art and related work in the field of identity management systems. We then introduce basic identity concepts and identity models in Sect. 4. Section 6 illustrates our identity model with a focus on algorithms to generate hierarchical identities. Operations on identities, such as registration and look-up are also presented with their formal notations and pseudo-code. Section 9 focuses on the correctness verification analysis of the proposed identity model. We conclude our work in Sect. 10 and provide future research perspective.

2   Related Work

An Identity Management system is responsible for managing digital identities. A digital identitiy consists of identifiers (UserID, Email, URL, ...), credentials (Certificates, Tokens, Biometrics, ...) and attributes (Roles, Positions, Privileges, ...) [3], in the virtual digital world. Since the birth of Information Technology especially Web services, the identity management has always been regarded as the keystone to request services over the Internet. Over the last decades, it has been evolved from isolated to centralized and then to federated model [11].

From the industrial perspective, several initiatives and IT firms have worked on the digital identity challenges such as PRIMELife [16], SWIFT [17], DAIDALOS [18], Kantara [19] (Liberty [20]), FIDIS [21], SAML [6], Higgins [22], OpenID [5], Shibboleth [7], STORK [23], PICOS [24] and Cardspace [26] just to mention a few. Table 1 compares them with regards to the IoT identity management requirements such as scalability, interoperability, mobility, security and privacy. Admittedly, many initiatives attempt to develop user-centric identity management systems but they still not fully satisfying IoT requirements. Users have to consider all entities from IoT and coordinate different application domains to join the IdMS, which compromises scalability and increases the difficult of building an interoperable IdM systems in such heterogeneous environment. Although some initiatives like OpenID or PICOS are capable of extensibility due to their decentralized architectures to some extent, but they cannot deal with mobility in networks of ubiquitous IoT devices or services.

Table 1. Identity Management Initiatives Comparison

	Scalability	Interoperability	Mobility	Security & Privacy	User-centric
PRIMELife(PRIME)			★	★	★
SWIFT(DAIDALOS)		★	★	★	★
Kantara(Liberty)	★	★	★	★	
FIDIS		★	★	★	★
SAML		★			
Higgins		★		★	★
OpenID	★				★
Shibboleth				★	
STORK		★		★	★
PICOS	★	★	★	★	★
Cardspace		★	★	★	★

Recently, academic researchers propose solutions to tackle the digital identity problem in IoT: Bassam [31] introduces the blockchain based PKI and its its implementation with Ethereum smart contracts; Liu et al.[32] present an identity management system using Ethereum smart contracts and enabled with token-based repuation feed-backs; Augot et al. [33,34] use zero-knowledge proof to build an anonymous digital identity based on bitcoin-based blockchain; Hardjono [35] develops a blockchain based privacy preserving identity solution called ChainAnchor using zero-knowledge proof in a permissioned blockchain environment; Halpin [36] proposes NEXTLEAP which builds a federated identity system with privacy preserving features using blind signa-tures; Azouvi et al. [37] rely on Ethereum based identity solution, taking into account privacy and security analysis; Gao et al. [38] present a blockchain-based identity man-agement framework for people called BlockID, into which integrates biometric-based user authentication and trusted mobile computing technology.

The blockchain-based identity management systems are witness of recent ambitious projects: Uport [45] supported by the Ethereum foundation, Sovrin [46] (Hyperledger open source project), Shocard [47], Bitnation [48], Civic [49] and Jolocom [50].

3   Preliminaries

In this section, we introduce basic concepts regarding the digital identity and some cryptography building blocks, including the cryptographic algorithms in Bitcoin and the Bitcoin transactions used through the rest of this paper.

4   Basic Identity Concepts

Entity refers to a uniquely identifiable anything [3]. In our context, an entity could be individuals (human beings), collectives (companies, organizations, families, ...), or things falling under the rubric of the IoT.

Things, denote objects in the physical world (e.g., computers, phones, sensors, ...) or virtual things of the cyber world (e.g., applications, digital resources, ...) [1]. Roughly speaking, we use $Entity$, $Individuals$, $Collectives$ and $Things$ to respec-tively denote the set of entities, individuals, collectives and physical or virtual things. Hence, we have:

$$Entity = \{e | e \in Individuals \vee Collectives \vee Things\} \qquad (1)$$

Digital Identity refers to a set of information used for uniquely identifying an entity in a given context. By adopting the ITU definition [3], the digital identity comprises the following three parts:

- Identifier (i.e., UserID, Email, URL, Social security number, ...)
- Credentials (i.e., Certificates, Tokens, Biometrics, Passwords, ...)
- Attributes (i.e., Roles, Positions, Privileges, Date of birth, ...)

Therefore, we use the 3-tuple structure $(identifier, credentials, attributes)$ to denote $Identity$:

$$Identity = < identifier, credentials, attributes > \qquad (2)$$

Table 2. Notations

Notations	Descriptions
$\mathcal{G}$	Identity's identifier generation function
$\mathcal{R}$	(Pseudo) Random number generator
$\mathcal{H}_A$	Hash function using A algorithm
sk, pk, σ	Private key, public key and signature value
DUP	Duplication operation
$HASH160$	RIPEMD160(SHA256()) function
$EQUALVERIFY$	Verify that two parameters are equal
ADD	OR logic operation
$CHECKSIG$	Verify a signature using public key
$VERIFY$	Using public key to check signature equals the given value
$P\| \equiv X$	P believes X
$P \lhd X$	P sees X
$P\| \sim X$	P said X
$P\| \Rightarrow X$	P controls X; P has jurisdiction over X
$\#(X)$	The formula is fresh
$P \xrightarrow{K} Q; K_{P,Q}$	K is the shared symmetric secret key between P and Q
$K \mapsto P$	K is the public key of P
$\{X\}_K$	The cipher text using key K

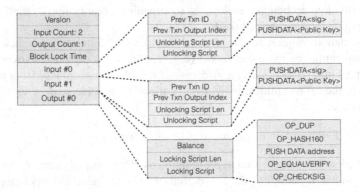

Fig. 2. Bitcoin Transaction Structure

Blockchain Transaction. As the key concept of Bitcoin system, transactions are basic units of transferring the bitcoin value. Almost all of the operations in Bitcoin are relevant to transactions so as to be created, broadcast, propagated, validated, and finally added to the transaction ledger [54]. In our paper, we take the transaction structure in Bitcoin system as the example to illustrate our modified blockchain-based identity management solution. The structure of a transaction in Bitcoin could be divided into four fields: version, inputs, outputs and locktime as shown in Fig. 2. Moreover, the inputs and outputs are critical parts to define different types of transactions such as Pay-to-Public-Key-Hash (P2PKH), Pay-to-Public-Key (P2PK) or Pay-to-Script-Hash (P2SH). Therefore, we can add and modify inputs and outputs in any type of transactions like P2PKH to create a new type of transaction of realizing our intention. In Bitcoin, inputs and outputs are written in a set of stake-based Forth-like scripts, which specify validation operations in transactions and fall into two script categories: locking scripts from outputs field called $scriptPubKey$ and unlocking scripts from inputs field called $scriptSig$.

In this paper, we modify the P2PKH type transaction and introduce some new script operations including ADD and $VERIFY$ as illustrated in Table 2 to define our own identity transactions. Specifically, in our following blockchain-based identity provider scheme, we only focus on the greatest field of change in inputs and outputs scripts to describe our identity transaction.

5 Blockchain-based Identity Model for IoT

In this section, we firstly describe the identity system model and the threat model. We secondly present how the identity hierarchy structure is generated, and how each subject can use an extended Bitcoin blockchain as the identity provider without relying on any third parties.

6 Identity System Model

In our Blockchain-based Identity Management System for IoT (BIMSIT), we define the system model which assembles key concepts such as subjects (e.g. people, organizations, ...), domains, root identity, partial identity, stakeholders (i.e., relaying parties, identity providers), and relationships among them. Figure 3 illustrates these concepts and relationships between different entities.

Subjects are parties, typically individuals (human beings) or collectives (companies, organizations, families, ...), who possess digital identities used for transactions within different domains. Subjects take responsibility for transactions, which could be traced. We use the $Subjects$ to denote the set of subjects.

$$Subjects = \{s|s \in Individuals \vee Collectives\} \tag{3}$$

The identity hierarchical structure reflects various relations such as organizational, ownership or security authority relations, among sibling identities or parent-child identities. In addition, we introduce the **Root Identity** (RId) to represent the source identity from which a collective subject or an individual subject generates one or more **Partial Identities** (PId) each of which identifies a domain or sub-domains.

A domain is a set of computational and storage resources that are available to a subject, services that are working under the subject authority or, in general, things that are managed by the same subject.

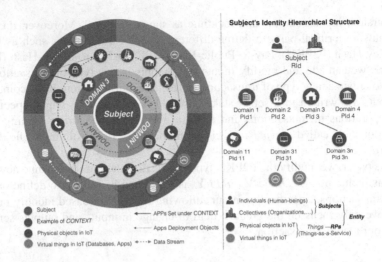

Fig. 3. Proposed system model

A subject can have several domains each of which is defined as d. The set of all domains is defined as $Domain$. As a result, the entire identity hierarchical structure can be seen as a tree in which each node is expressed in terms of its digital identity and the domain or sub-domain under its control.

Relying Parties refer to parties who are responsible for providing services to $Subjects$ and hence called service providers. We use the notation RPs to denote service providers in IdM systems.

Therefore, we assume, things could be regarded as a service in IoT:

$$RPs = \{r | r \in Things\} \tag{4}$$

Identity Providers are responsible for managing the lifecycle of identities such as the identity registration, usage, update and revocation. In the BIMSIT, the blockchain technology is a core concept upon which we build the Blockchain-based Identity Provider (BIdP) infrastructure, which makes possible to any subject to create and manage their identity in a peer to peer and trusless IoT networks. We use the notation $IdPs$ to denote identity providers in IdM systems.

In summary, IoT identity management systems should be able to manage all identities of entities, such as identities of $Subjects$ and $Things$. As depicted in Fig. 3, the Blockchain-based identity Management System for IoT (BIMSIT) refers to Subjects and their Identity Hierarchy structure (IHS). Subjects are entities and refer to individual or collective subjects. The Identity Hierarchy structure organizes all digital identities that a subject may generate. Each identity defines a domain, comprising all sub-identities that are generated from the corresponding domain. Hence, our BIMSIT could be defined as follows:

$$BIMSIT = \{< Subject, IHS >\} \tag{5}$$

$$IHS = \{< Identity, d >\} \tag{6}$$

7   Hierarchical Identity Information Generation

In order to generate the hierarchical identity information (identifier, credentials, attributes), we take advantage of the cryptographic algorithms used in Hierarchical Deterministic Wallet (BIP32), which provides users with a simple and convenient way to backup and recover all keys. We define the following 2 levels in BIP32 path:

$$m/purpose'/accounts'/$$

The purpose is a constant set to $200'$ (or 0x800000C8) following the BIP43[1]. Therefore, we have 2^{28} available accounts (key pairs) for each subject. As shown in Fig. 4, any subject who wants to participate in our BIMSIT, needs to generate the random number called *seed* (128, 256 or 512 bits) which could be encoded into mnemonic words for easy backup. From this *seed*, the subject can obtain the **Root Identity** information including identifier and offline key pair as credentials while the identifiers and offline key pair of **Partial Identities** could be derived from the parental identity information. As depicted in Fig. 3, the hierarchical identity of subjects is a tree in which, up to 2^{28} identities (identifiers, credentials, attributes) related to a subject could be managed. When a subject wants to add an identity subbranch of a domain (e.g. the partial identity11 in Fig. 3), the index number will be calculated according to the position of the subbranch and used for generating the corresponding offline key pair of the identity. The calculation of index number is converting the identity tree structure into binary tree where nodes could directly expressed as binary numbers. Then the index number of new identity node is the calculated binary number.

In our identity information generation scheme, we use the 160 bits double-hash result from the offline public key as the identifier.

$$identifier = HASH160(pk_f) \tag{7}$$

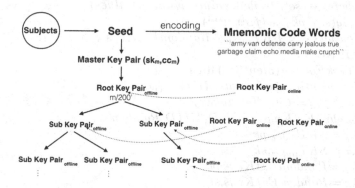

Fig. 4. Hierarchical Keys in Identity Infromation Generation

We also add the signature segment to prevent from being replaced by malicious attackers. The message part of the $sig(sk, m)$ is the binary OR operation result between

---
[1] https://github.com/bitcoin/bips/blob/master/bip-0043.mediawiki.

online public key and self-examination attributes which, we assume, are the return value of hardware interfaces and directly binded to specific hardware and cannot be modified.

$$\sigma = sig(sk_f, pk_o||self\_ex\_attr) \tag{8}$$

As for the attributes in identity information, the subject could assign values when the corresponding identity is established. We temporarily use $setAttributevalues()$ to denote the function of assigning attributes values that are intimately correlated with access control which will not be involved in this paper.

In addition, the identity information generation is responsible for generating **Root Identity** information, which is the stepping stone to construct the system for IoT, and **Partial Identity** information, which could also represent the identity of a thing as the ending of hierarchical identity structure. Therefore, our hierarchical identity generation algorithm is described from the perspective of two types of identity as follows.

Algorithm 1 Generating Hierarchical Identity

---

procedure GEN_HID(s, $identity$, $index$)

    var val, v_L, v_R //Temporary variants

    function $CheckFormat()$ //Check parental identity

    s executes: // s: Subject who wants to generate identity

1: **switch** ($identity.identifier\&identity.credentials$)

2:   **case NULL:**

3:     $MasterExtKeys = DKD("HID\_Seed")$

4:     $RKP_{m/200'} = CKD(MasterExtKeys, m/200')$

5:     $RandomExtKeys = DKD("HID\_Random")$

6:     $pk_f = RKP_{m/200'}.pk; sk_f = RKP_{m/200'}.sk$

7:     $pk_o = RandomExtKeys.pk$

8:     $sk_o = RandomExtKeys.sk$

9:     $identifier \leftarrow HASH160(pk_f)$

10:     $attributes \leftarrow setAttributevalues(Names, Values)$

11:     $\sigma = sig(sk_f, pk_o||self\_ex\_attr)$

12:     $credentials \leftarrow < RKP_{m/200'}, RandomExtKeys, \sigma >$

13: **case NOT NULL:**

14:   **if** ($CheckFormat(identity)$) **then**

15:     $ek = identity.credentials.RKP_{m/200'}$

16:     $SKP_{index} = CKD(ek, index)$

17:     $RandomExtKeys = DKD("HID\_Random")$

18:     $pk_f = SKP_{index}.pk$

19:     $sk_f = SKP_{index}.sk$

20:     $pk_o = RandomExtKeys.pk$

21:     $sk_o = RandomExtKeys.sk$

22:     $identifier \leftarrow HASH160(pk_f)$

23:     $attributes \leftarrow setAttributevalues(Names, Values)$

24:     $\sigma = sig(sk_f, pk_o||self\_ex\_attr)$

25:     $credentials \leftarrow < RKP_{m/200'}, RandomExtKeys, \sigma >$

26:   **end if**

27: **end switch**

28: **return** *identity*

sub-procedure DKD(string)
    function $\mathcal{R}$ //(Pseudo) Random number generator
    var val, v_L, v_R //Temporary variants
29: $seed = \mathcal{R}(128/256/512)$
30: $val = HMAC\_SHA512(string, seed)$
31: $v_L = val[0 - 255]; v_R = val[256 - 512]$
32: $sk_m = v_L; cc_m = v_R; pk_m = sk * G$
33: $extended\_keys =< pk_m, sk_m, cc_m >$
34: **return** $extended\_keys$

sub-procedure CKD($root\_extended\_keys, index$)
    const n // one constant parameter of the elliptic curve.
    var val, v_L, v_R //Temporary variants
    function $ser_{32}(i)$ //serialize a 32-bit unsigned integer i as a 4-byte sequence, most significant byte first.
35: $ek = root\_extended\_keys$
36: $val = HMAC\_SHA521(ek.cc, ek.sk||ser_{32}(index))$
37: $v_L = val[0 - 255]; v_R = val[256 - 512]$
38: $sk = (ek.sk + v_L)mod\ n; cc = v_R; pk = sk * G$
39: $extended\_keys =< pk, sk, cc >$
40: **return** $extended\_keys$

To sum up, our identity information generation is responsible for the generation of all identities ranging from root to partial identities of every subject. In order to depicted explicitly, we define $IDS(s)$ as the **Identity Set** of subject s while $IDS_f(s)$ and $IDS_o(s)$ denote the set of all offline private keys (sk_f) of s and the rest part of $IDS(s)$ except the $IDS_f(s)$.

$$IDS(s) =< IDS_f(s), IDS_o(s) > \tag{9}$$

Besides the key generation in the hierarchical identity information generation process, the offline key pair also could be used for revocation of the online key pair which probably has been compromised.

8 Blockchain-based Identity Provider

In our BIMSIT, the essence of identifying *Things* or *Relying Parties* is the identification to identities of a subject. Providing services to the owners or users, *things* as asset or property of a subject are identified through the subject. Therefore, the identity management for subjects is the kernel of the entities' identity management in IoT. In this section, we use blockchain to build a trusted public identity management service for all subjects in completely distributed networks without any centralized or decentralized server. It is mainly responsible for the registration, update, revocation and lookup operations for identities of all subjects. Due to space limit, we only cover the identity registration and identity lookup.

Identity Registration

The identity registration should be elaborated from three different parties: *subject*, *miners* and *peers*. Firstly, the subject who wants to have an identity, need to organize the identity information generated through the method of the previous subsection, which includes root identity's *identifier*, pk_f, pk_o, storage *pointer* of the online identity set and the *signature* of pk_o and *pointer*. Then using the identity registration information, the subject can create the blockchain format transaction T_{reg}, in which we modify the P2PKH transaction model and introduce a new additional script called *scriptID_REG* embedded in the unlocking *scriptSig* script. After assembling the T_{reg}, the subject will post the transaction to the entire network. Whenever miners or peers validate new transactions specifically the input *scriptSig* part, they will verify the *scriptID_REG* at first. If the *identifier* matches the pk_f and no data tampering from malicious parties in pk_o and storage *pointer*, the normal *scriptSig* script could be executed. In addition to verifying the received T_{reg}, miners will pack it to the candidate block, do the Proof-of-Work, race for the valid block and broadcast the block to the entire P2P network. Once the corresponding block is confirmed by enough subsequent blocks, the identity registration succeeds.

The following identity registration phase of Protocol 1 elaborates specific operations from the perspective of subjects, miners and peers respectively.

Protocol 1 Blockchain-based IdP: Registration Phase

---

procedure ID_REG(s, $root\_identity$)

   var $identifier$ //Subject's Root Identity Identifier

   var pk //Subject's Root Public Key Credentials

   var σ, h //the signature and hash value respectively

Subject s organizes:

1: $identifier = root\_identity.identifier$
2: $pk_f = root\_identity.credentials.pk_f$
3: $pk_o = root\_identity.credentials.pk_o$
4: $pointer = \mathcal{H}_{HASH160}(IDS_o(s))$
5: $h = \mathcal{H}_{HASH160}(pk_o + pointer)$
6: $\sigma_{sk_f} = sig(sk_f, h)$
7: Uses $< identifier, pk_f, pk_o, \sigma_{sk_f}, pointer >$ to construct the T_{reg}
        Additional Input Script: $scriptID\_REG$
            $< \sigma_{sk_f} > < pk_f > DUP\ HASH160$
            $< identifier > EQUALVERIFY < pk_o >$
            $< pointer > ADD\ HASH160\ VERIFY$
        Locking Output Script: $scriptPubKey$
            $HASH160 < identifier >$
            $EQUALVERIFY\ CHECKSIG$

8: Posts the transaction T_{reg} to entire network

Miners execute **Identity Reg Transaction Verification**:
9: check pk_f and $identifier$ satisfying:
$identifier = HASH160(pk_f)$
10: $h = \mathcal{H}_{HASH160}(pk_o + pointer)$
11: check $h = verify(\sigma_{sk_f}, pk_f)$
12: *Miners* race for **Identity Block Formation**:

Peers execute **Verification of Identity** stored in Blockchain Transaction
13: check pk_f and $identifier$ statisfying:
$identifier = HASH160(pk_f)$
14: $h = \mathcal{H}_{HASH160}(pk_o + pointer)$
15: check $h = verify(\sigma_{sk_f}, pk_f)$

Identity Lookup

The identity lookup operation is encapsulated in the off-blockchain transaction T_{lkp} while the three previous transactions, namely, T_{reg}, T_{upd} and T_{rvc} belong to on-blockchain transactions. The difference is that T_{lkp} do not need to be delivered to miners or peers to execute the verification and is similar to the operation of using the address to locate the $UTXO$ in Bitcoin system. The following BIdP lookup phase of Protocol 2 describes the operation of identity lookup.

Protocol 2 Blockchain-based IdP: Lookup Phase

---

procedure ID_LKP(s, $identifier$, σ)
   var $blockchainLedger$ //blockchain identity repository
   var σ //the signature value
   function $retrievePK(ledger, i)$ //retrieves the public key according to the $identifier$ i in blockchain identity ledger
   Subject s searches blockchain ledger to get public key
1: $pk = retrievePK(blockchainLedger, identifier)$
2: **if** $verify(\sigma, pk)$ **then**
3:    Return TRUE
4: **else**
5:    Return FALSE
6: **end if**

The identity lookup is the basic operation of other services like authentication and authorization which can be used to authenticate the true identity of subjects and delegate authorization according to different identities. For instance, when subject s_1 gives the s_1's identifier and signature to a relying party whose owner, we assume, is subject s_2, s_2 can verify the s_1' identity through the lookup operation, in which s_1 and s_2 also could be the same subject.

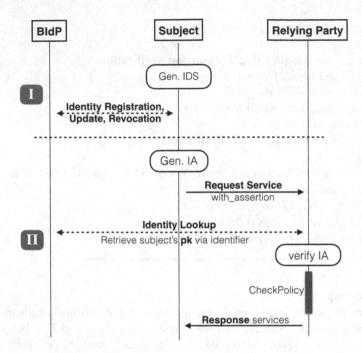

Fig. 5. BIMSIT Overview

9   Correctness Verification Analysis

According to the description of previous section, our BIMSIT could be divided into two phases: the hierarchical identity information management and authentication and authorization services. The former comprises the identity generation, registration, update and revocation while the latter refers to the services specifically authentication and authorization derived from the identity lookup operation as shown in Fig. 5. Although having stakeholders like subjects, relying parties, identity providers as the same as most of traditional identity management systems, the BIMSIT still makes a great difference in the methodology of managing the identity in that it removes the assumption of users giving the full trust to their IdPs and takes back the control over their own identity from the so called"trusted third parties".

In the rest of this section, we verify the correctness of our BIMSIT using using BAN logic [55], which is a formal method to analyze security protocols.

All operations and interactions between IdMS stakeholders could be found in Fig. 5. Compared with traditional identity management systems, our BIMSIT removes the trusted third party, which makes many operations like the generation of session key, should be done in participants rather than the so called trusted third parties. In BIMSIT, we assume the session key is generated by the initiator of the request. And in BIMSIT, we also assume the RPs, namely, $things$ could get the identity information from their subject, therefore, the identity lookup operation in Phase II could be regarded as internal communication. After generating the identity set IDS, the subject will post the online identity set into blockchain network in order to establish the consensus of identity. Once the whole network achieves the identity consensus, the subject is allowed to generate the identity assertion (IA), which is composed of identity information and the signature of this information so that it could be used to verify the subject's identity. We use the formal BAN logic language to describe the BITSIT in Fig. 6. According to the description of our BIMSIT protocol, we firstly list assumptions of the protocol, delete the unencrypted messages, idealize the only two left messages Message 1 and Message 2 and finally idealize the goals of the protocol. Operators also could be found in Table 2.

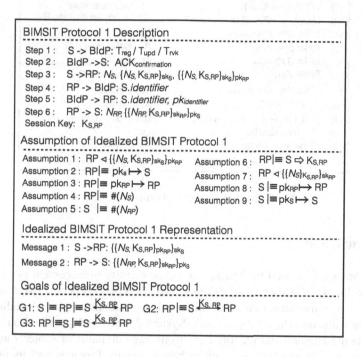

Fig. 6. Idealized BIMSIT Protocol 1

From the description of idealization, we can see, there are only two messages, which includes the encrypted information, needed to be idealized and the idealized goals are also simplified, which eliminates the goal:

$$S| \equiv S \xleftrightarrow{K} RP \tag{10}$$

in traditional authentication protocols security analysis, owing to the fact that the session key is generated by the initiator of the request. The detailed verification proofs are shown in Fig. 7.

Verification Process of Idealized BIMSIT Protocol 1		
(1): $RP \lhd \{\{N_S, K_{S,RP}\}_{sk_S}\}_{pk_{RP}}$		Assumption
(2): $RP \models pk_{RP} \mapsto RP$		Assumption
(3): (1), (2) $\vdash RP \lhd \{N_S, K_{S,RP}\}_{sk_S}$		SEE4: Seeing Rule
(4): $RP \lhd \{N_S, K_{S,RP}\}_{sk_S}$		MP
(5): $RP \models pk_S \mapsto S$		Assumption
(6): (4), (5) $\vdash RP \models S \mid \sim N_S, K_{S,RP}$		M2: Message-meaning Rule
(7): $RP \models S \mid \sim N_S, K_{S,RP}$		MP
(8): $RP \models \#(N_S)$		Assumption
(9): $RP \models \#(N_S, K_{S,RP})$		F1: Freshness Rule
(10): (7), (9) $\vdash RP \models S \models (N_S, K_{S,RP})$		N1: Nonce-verification Rule
(11): $RP \models S \models (N_S, K_{S,RP})$		MP
(12): $RP \models S \models K_{S,RP}$	G3	B3: Belief Rule
(13): $RP \models S \Rightarrow K_{S,RP}$		Assumption
(14): $RP \models K_{S,RP}$	G2	J1: Jurisdiction Rule
(15): $S \lhd \{\{N_{RP}, K_{S,RP}\}_{sk_{RP}}\}_{pk_S}$		Assumption
(16): $S \models pk_S \mapsto S$		Assumption
(17): (15), (16) $\vdash S \lhd \{N_{RP}, K_{S,RP}\}_{sk_{RP}}$		SEE4: Seeing Rule
(18): $S \lhd \{N_{RP}, K_{S,RP}\}_{sk_{RP}}$		MP
(19): $S \models pk_{RP} \mapsto RP$		Assumption
(20): $S \models RP \models K_{S,RP}$	G1	Same proofs from 6-12

Fig. 7. BIMSIT Protocol 1 Formal Verification

10 Conclusion

In this paper, we proposed the blockchain-based identity management system for the Internet of things (BIMSIT) in distributed and trustless peer-to-peer network taking into account IoT unconventional characteristics such as scalability, interoperability, mobility. We formally introduced the Identify System Model, and provided an algorithm to generate the Hierarchical Identity trees to manage domains of subjects and *things*. In addition, we specified the Blockchain-based Identity Provider and its operations, namely the Identity Registration and Identity Lookup. The correctness of the proposed protocol using the BAN logic.

We have implemented a proof of concept of the blockchain-based identity model by updating the inputs and outputs of different types of transactions such as Pay-to-Public-Key-Hash (P2PKH), Pay-to-Public-Key (P2PK) or Pay-to-Script-Hash (P2SH). We also modified the P2PKH type transaction and introduced some new script operations including ADD and VERIFY in the native consensus protocol of Bitcoin. In the future work, we would like to specify additional operations such as Blockchain-based IdP Update and Invocation operations, and propose identity recovery mechanisms from key loss and compromise. Additionaly, we are working on security and privacy analysis nd conducting performance analysis in terms of cost storage, and computation as well as communication cost in an IoT authentication scenario .

References

1. Telecommunication Standardization Sector, Overview of the Internet of things, ITU (2012). https://www.itu.int/rec/T-REC-Y.2060-201206-I. Accessed 20 Jan 2021
2. IDC, The Growth in Connected IoT Devices Is Expected to Generate 79.4ZB of Data in 2025, 2019, https://www.idc.com/getdoc.jsp?containerId=prUS45213219, Access 13 Feb 2021
3. Telecommunication Standardization Sector, NGN Identity Management Framework, ITU, 2009, https://www.itu.int/rec/T-REC-Y.2720-200901-I access 23 Jan 2021
4. Bertino, E., Takahashi, K.: Identity Management: Concepts, Technologies, and Systems, Artech House (2011)
5. Recordon, D., Reed, D.: OpenID 2.0: A Platform for User-centric Identity Management, Proceedings of the Second ACM Workshop on Digital Identity Management (2006)
6. Security Services Technical Committee of OASIS, Security Assertion Markup Language (SAML) v2.0, Available at http://www.oasis-open.org/committees/tc_home.php?wg_abbrev=security (2005)
7. Cantor, S., Scavo, T.: Shibboleth Architecture, Protocols and Profiles (2005)
8. Torres, J., Nogueira, M., Pujolle, G.: A Survey on Identity Management for the Future Network, IEEE Communications Surveys (2013)
9. Alpar, G., Hoepman, J., Siljee, J.: The Identity Crisis Security. Privacy and Usability Issues in Identity Management, CoRR (2011)
10. Nakamoto, S.: Bitcoin: a Peer-to-Peer Electronic Cash System. 2008. [Online]. Available: https://bitcoin.org/bitcoin.pdf
11. Jøsang, A., Pope, S.: User Centric Identity Management, AusCERT Conference (2005)
12. Jøsang, A., Zomai, M., Suriadi, S.: Usability and Privacy in Identity Management Architectures, Australian Computer Society Inc (2007)
13. Maler, E., Reed, D.: The Venn of identity: Options and issues in federated identity management, IEEE Security & Privacy (2008)
14. Angin, P., et al.: An entity-centric approach for privacy and identity management in cloud computing, 29th IEEE Symposium on Reliable Distributed Systems (SRDS'10), pp. 177–183. New Delhi, India (2010)
15. Suriadi, S., Foo, E.: A. Jøsang A User-centric Federated Single Sign-on System. J. Netw. Comput. Appl. 32, 388–401 (2009)
16. PRIMELife, Privacy and Identity Management in Europe for Life, Available online: http://primelife.ercim.eu, Access Feb 2021
17. SWIFT, Secure Widespread Identities for Federated Telecommunications, Available online: https://www.swift.com, Access Feb 2021
18. DAIDALOS, Designing Advanced Network Interfaces for the Delivery and Administration of Location Independent, Optimised Personal Services, Available online: https://www.tssg.org/projects/daidalos/, Access Feb 2021
19. Kantara, Available online: http://kantarainitiative.org, Access Jan 2021
20. Liberty, The Liberty Alliance project, Available online: http://www.projectliberty.org, Access Jan 2021
21. FIDIS, Future of Identity in the Information Society, Available online: http://www.fidis.net, Access Jan 2021
22. Higgins, Higgins - open source identity framework, Available online: http://www.eclipse.org/higgins, Access Nov 2020
23. STORK, Secure idenTity acrOss boRders linKed, Available online: https://www.eid-stork.eu, Access Jan 2021
24. PICOS, Privacy and Identity Management for Community Services, Available online: http://www.picos-project.eu, Access Jan 2021

25. Zhu, X., Badr, Y.: Identity Management Systems for the Internet of Things: A Survey Towards Blockchain Solutions , Sensors 2018, 18, 4215
26. Bertocci, V., Serack, G., Baker, C.: Understanding Windows Cardspace: An Introduction to the Concepts and Challenges of Digital Identities, Addison Wesley Professional (2007)
27. Namecoin. Namecoin: The First Solution to Zooko's Triangle, Available online: https://namecoin.org, Access Jan 2021
28. Fromknecht, C., Dragos, V., Sophia, Y.: CertCoin: A NameCoin Based Decentralized Authentication System 6.857 Class Project (2014)
29. Leiding, B., Cap, CH., Mundt, T., Samaneh, R.: Authcoin: Validation and Authentication in Decentralized Networks, arXiv preprint arXiv:1609.04955 (2016)
30. Muneeb, A., Nelson, J., Shea, R., Freedman, M.: Blockstack: A Global Naming and Storage System Secured by Blockchains. In USENIX Annual Technical Conference, pp. 181–194 (2016)
31. Mustafa, A.: "SCPKI: A Smart Contract-based PKI and Identity System." In Proceedings of the ACM Workshop on Blockchain, Cryptocurrencies and Contracts, pp. 35–40. ACM (2017)
32. Liu, Y., Zhao, Z.. Guo, G., Wang, X., Tan, Z., Wang, S.: An Identity Management System Based on Blockchain (2017)
33. Augot, D., Chabanne, H., Clémot, O., George, W.: Transforming face-to-face identity proofing into anonymous digital identity using the Bitcoin blockchain. arXiv preprint arXiv:1710.02951 (2017)
34. Augot, Daniel, Chabanne, Hervé, Chenevier, Thomas, George, William, Lambert, Laurent: A user-centric system for verified identities on the bitcoin blockchain. In: Garcia-Alfaro, Joaquin, Navarro-Arribas, Guillermo, Hartenstein, Hannes, Herrera-Joancomartí, Jordi (eds.) ESORICS/DPM/CBT - 2017. LNCS, vol. 10436, pp. 390–407. Springer, Cham (2017). https://doi.org/10.1007/978-3-319-67816-0_22
35. Hardjono, T., Sandy Pentland, A.: "Verifiable Anonymous Identities and Access Control in Permissioned Blockchains."
36. Halpin, H.: "NEXTLEAP: Decentralizing Identity with Privacy for Secure Messaging." In Proceedings of the 12th International Conference on Availability, Reliability and Security, p. 92. ACM (2017)
37. Azouvi, Sarah, Al-Bassam, Mustafa, Meiklejohn, Sarah: Who am i? Secure identity registration on distributed ledgers. In: Garcia-Alfaro, Joaquin, Navarro-Arribas, Guillermo, Hartenstein, Hannes, Herrera-Joancomartí, Jordi (eds.) ESORICS/DPM/CBT -2017. LNCS, vol. 10436, pp. 373–389. Springer, Cham (2017). https://doi.org/10.1007/978-3-319-67816-0_21
38. Gao, Z., et al.: "Blockchain-based identity management with mobile device." In Proceedings of the 1st Workshop on Cryptocurrencies and Blockchains for Distributed Systems, pp. 66–70 (2018)
39. Lee, J.: BIDaaS: blockchain based ID as a service. IEEE Access 6, 2274–2278 (2018)
40. Faber, B., et al.: BPDIMS: A Blockchain-Based Personal Data and Identity Management System. Proceedings of the 52nd Hawaii International Conference on System Sciences (2019)
41. Alsayed Kassem, J., Sayeed, S., Marco-Gisbert, H., Pervez, Z., Dahal, K.: DNS-IdM: a blockchain identity management system to secure personal data sharing in a network. Appl. Sci. 9(15), 2953 (2019)
42. Borse, Y., et al.: Anonymity: a secure identity management using smart contracts. Available at SSRN 3352370 (2019)
43. Hong, S., Kim, H. VaultPoint: a blockchain-based SSI model that complies with OAuth 2.0. Electronics, 9(8), 1231

44. Lin, C., He, D., Huang, X., Kumar, N., Choo, K.K.R.: BCPPA: a blockchain-based conditional privacy-preserving authentication protocol for vehicular ad hoc networks. IEEE Transactions on Intelligent Transportation Systems (2020)
45. Uport. A scalable DID method for Ethereum addresses enabling them to collect on-chain and off-chain data, Available online: https://www.uport.me, Access Feb 2021
46. Sovrin Foundation. Personally manage your digital IDs online with the Sovrin Network - an open source project creating a global public utility for self-sovereign identity. Available online: https://sovrin.org, Access Feb, 2021
47. Shocard. Secure Enterprise Identity Authentication, Available online: https://shocard.com/ access Feb 2021
48. Bitnation. Governance 2.0, Available online: https://bitnation.co/, Access Feb 2021
49. Civic. Secure Identity Ecosystem-Decentralized Identity Reusable KYC, Available online: https://www.civic.com/, Access Feb 2021
50. Jolocom. Decentralized Infrastructure for Self-Sovereign Identity, Available online: http://jolocom.io/, Access Feb 2021
51. Allen, C., et al.: Decentralized Public Key Infrastructure, https://danubetech.com/download/dpki.pdf, Access Feb 2021
52. Koblitz, N.: CM-curves with good cryptographic properties, Proc. Crypto'91, Springer-Verlag (1992)
53. Standards for Efficient Cryptography, SEC 2: Recommended Elliptic Curve Domain Parameters January 27 (2010) http://www.secg.org/sec2-v2.pdf
54. Antonopoulos, A.M.: Mastering Bitcoin: unlocking digital cryptocurrencies, O'Reilly Media (2014)
55. Burrows, M., Abadi, M., Needham, R.: A logic of authentication," in Proc. of the RSLA '89, pp.233–271 (1989)
56. Ethereum Community, A Next-Generation Smart Contract and Decentralized Application Platform, https://github.com/ethereum/wiki/wiki/White-Paper, Access 20 Jan 2018

Towards a Time-Dependent Approach for User Privacy Expression and Enforcement

Nouredine Tamani[✉] [iD]

ISEP, Institut Supérieur d'Electronique de Paris,
10 rue de Vanves, 91230 Issy-les-Moulineaux, France
nouredine.tamani@isep.fr

Abstract. Achieving user privacy is a challenging task in the era of ubiquitous internet and mobile applications where users' data and activities can be tracked days and nights, by the myriads of applications installed on smartphones, watches, TV, and appliances. The need for a practical, easy to use, and most of all expressive tools to express and enforce privacy rules is still insistent nowadays. Even though the law enforces in many regions of the world the user data protection as a legal principle, still mobile apps and web applications and plugins lack of a steady process that allows users to express, validate and verify their privacy rules when they are interacting with a given application. We introduce in this paper a new approach, which combines both non monotonic logics with the Linear temporal logic (LTL) to define and interpret time-constrained logical predicates used to define data sharing functions based on time such as Periodic Blocking, Time prohibition, and Data shelf life. This paper is a first step towards a time-dependent knowledge base system for privacy rule expression and enforcement.

Keywords: User Data Protection · Privacy and Security · Linear Temporal Logic · Existential Rules · IoT trustworthiness

1 Introduction

User privacy in IoT applications has been considered from several points of views. The main solutions actually available consider more security aspects of communications than the privacy concerns by applying encryption, signature, authorization, authentication, and similar functions to ensure the confidentiality and the integrity of the communications among IoT objects and their external world. However, we mean by privacy threat the way data is exploited to disclose some information the user does not initially want to share with anyone else, except with a limited set of trusted people.

Let us express our idea throughout the following example: a given guy tracked his "calories burned per day", denoted *cbd* hereinafter for a month, provided by a connected bracelet. The data by itself does not convey a lot of information.

© IFIP International Federation for Information Processing 2024
Published by Springer Nature Switzerland AG 2024
S. Bouzefrane and D. Sauveron (Eds.): WISTP 2024, LNCS 14625, pp. 146–161, 2024.
https://doi.org/10.1007/978-3-031-60391-4_10

However, it is easy to deduce for instance that the owner of the bracelet practiced or did not practice any intense physical activity according to whether the *cdb* is low or high. This could be achieved by considering the evolution of the *cbd* over the time; once a day at a fixed time (let us say at 8:00 pm), as depicted in Fig. 1.

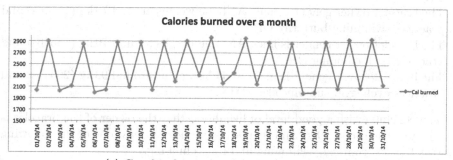

(a) Graphical representation as pics and dips.

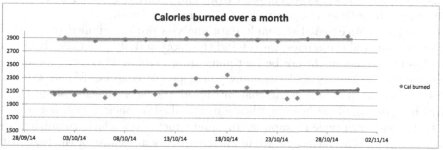

(b) Statistical study can reveal two different behaviors of the form $Cal = 2100d + \epsilon$ and $Cal = 2900d + \epsilon'$ respectively.

Fig. 1. Example of calories burned over time for a period of a month.

The graphic of Fig. 1a can be used to deduce some hidden information about the owner of the bracelet, which can affect his/her private life, such as:

- The owner of the bracelet practices a regular physical (sport) activity,
- The peaks refer to exercising days,
- The dips mean rest days,
- We can also deduce that the person was in rest day in Nov. 1st, according to the regular variations of peaks and dips (by using some statistical study as shown in Fig. 1b).

In addition, if we compute the difference between the average means of calories corresponding to both resting and exercising days, we obtain around 790 cal. A simple intersection of this information with the data about calories burned by persons of different weights during one hour of sport activities[1], we can induce the following conclusions:

- The bracelet owner gender is male AND he weighs around 60–70 kg (130–155 lbs), and practices running with a pace around 10.8–12.9 km/h (6.7–8 mph) OR
- The bracelet owner gender is male AND he weighs around 70 kg (155 lbs) and practices swimming butterfly OR
- The bracelet owner gender is male AND he weighs around 70 kg (155 lbs) and practices rock climbing OR
- The bracelet owner gender is male AND he weighs around 93 kg (205 lbs) and practices cycling, mountain bike, BMX.

We can conclude with a good level of likelihood that the owner of the bracelet is a male, weighs around 70 kg and regularly practices at least one of the following sport activities: running, swimming and rock climbing.

Those deductions are not far from the truth since the data represents real measures about a man, weighs around 70 kg and practices running with a duration about 1 h, with an average pace of 11.6 km/h (7.2 mph).

Hence, we notice that the simple data analysis process applied to the data correctly predicted the gender, weight and the sport activity practiced. However, the obtained results might not be that much impressive and privacy threatening for some user categories. Indeed, many young people consciously and willingly agree to share with unknown external entities all the data collected about themselves by sport and healthcare applications installed on their smartphones.

In the aforementioned example, the main metadata which permitted the analysis is *time*. The variations are implicitly disclosed because of the regularity of the measures and their sharing. Time is then a crucial metadata to take into consideration in any data sharing. It is obvious that any privacy protection system can only act on the user data before their sharing and cannot prevent or forbid any external entity to use any data analysis approach to extract from the received data some private information about the user. Moreover, there is a need for such a tool to give back to the users the control of their personal data. Indeed, as showed in [10], many web applications and plugins do not comply with the regulation regarding user data collection, processing, protection, and user-aware consent obtaining and enforcement.

Therefore, we investigate in this paper a time-constrained privacy control mechanism to reduce (if the option "Deny" is not available) the ability of external entities to perform data analysis disclosing users' sensitive information based on time. In addition to regular privacy protection solutions such as data *aggregation* and data *anonymization*, we define the following time-based control functions which could be applied on any data before it sharing with a given external entity: *Blocking, Periodical Blocking, Temporal Prohibition, Time-based Data Holing* (or *sampling*), *Time Exclusion*, and *Data Shelf life*.

---

[1] The webpage http://www.nutristrategy.com/caloriesburned.htm lists data about 249 sport activities.

These functions are then integrated in a knowledge base equipped with reasoning mechanisms which take into account the evolution over time of data requested by a given external entity. To do so, we make use of a fragment of the first-order logic as a formal modeling of our privacy-protective knowledge base, which we combine with a Linear Temporal Logic (LTL) to interpret the semantics of the logical rules implementing our time-based data control functions we have defined. The main idea of our solution consists in mapping the privacy preservation problem to consistency checking in a knowledge base [2,19], in the sense that we interpret any inconsistency in the knowledge base as an attempt to undermine someone's privacy, from a semantic perspective.

This positioning paper is a first step towards a time-dependent system for user privacy expression and enforcement starting from a modeling part. We left the implementation and test for future works since it requires the design of a test bed and test datasets, which are diverse enough to perform our experiments and evaluation.

The remainder of the paper is organized as follows. Section 2 details our definition of User Privacy Preservation Problem. Section 3 introduces our extension of our logical model to Linear Temporal Logic, and thoroughly describes our time-based interpretation of the privacy preserving rules we defined. Section 4 concludes the paper.

2 User Privacy Preservation Problem Modeling

In this section, we model the problem of user privacy protection within a knowledge base system. Our model is based on expressing the problem of privacy protection as consistency checking in a knowledge base. In other terms, if a data query causes any inconsistency in the knowledge base, then it is considered as a privacy violating request for user data and therefore is discarded. In Subsect. 2.1, we detail the logical framework we have chosen. In Subsect. 2.2, we introduce our query acceptability condition along with user privacy protection problem.

2.1 Language and Framework

Knowledge Representation and Knowledge Engineering have achieved major advancements at both theoretical and algorithmic/computation levels [4,8]. We make use in this paper the existential rules model [11,13], which provides a good balance between expressivity and computational decidability [6]. The examples used through out this section are inspired from the ontological model for building management developed in [1], to show the expressivity of our logical model that can express and reason with ontological rules.

Definition 1 (Vocabulary). *Vocabulary* $\mathbb{V} = (\mathcal{C}, \mathcal{P}, \mathcal{V})$ *is made of 3 disjoint sets:* $\mathcal{C}$ *is a finite set of* **constants***,* $\mathcal{P}$ *is a finite set of* **predicates** *and* $\mathcal{V}$ *is an infinite set of* **variables***:*

- a **term** t over $\mathbb{V}$ is a constant (t $\in$ C) or a variable (t $\in$ V) referring to a unique value,
- an **atomic formula** (or atom) is $p(t_1, ..., t_n)$ where p is an n-ary predicate, and $t_1, ..., t_n$ are terms,
- a **ground atom** is an atom with no variables,
- a formula is said **closed** if it has no free variables,
- a **conjunct** is a finite conjunction of atoms,
- a **ground conjunct** is a conjunct of ground atoms,
- a **fact** is the existential closure of a conjunct over $\mathbb{V}$
  $F = \exists x_1 (HVAC(x_1) \wedge hasStatus(x_1, \text{"ON"}))$

Rules are logical formulas, which may contain variables and should account for unknown individuals if some information are incomplete.

Definition 2 (Existential rules). *An* existential rule *(or simply a rule) is a first-order formula of the form:*

$$r = \forall \boldsymbol{X} ((\forall \boldsymbol{Y} \, H[\boldsymbol{X}, \boldsymbol{Y}]) \rightarrow (\exists \boldsymbol{Z} \, C[\boldsymbol{Z}, \boldsymbol{Y}]))$$

such that $vars(H) = \boldsymbol{X} \cup \boldsymbol{Y}$, $vars(C) = \boldsymbol{Z} \cup \boldsymbol{Y}$*, where* H *and* C *are* **conjuncts** *called the* **hypothesis** *(or the* **body***) and* **conclusion** *(or the* **head***) of* r *respectively.*

Example 1 (Rules) For each HVAC system, there is a status attached to it:
$$\forall x, HVAC(x) \rightarrow \exists y Status(y) \wedge hasStatus(x, y)$$

Negative Constraints represent knowledge that dictates how things are not ought to be or should not take place in a given domain.

Definition 3 (Negative Constraints). *A negative constraint (or constraint)* N *is a first-order formula of the form:*

$$N = \forall \boldsymbol{X} \, (H[\boldsymbol{X}] \rightarrow \perp)$$

where $H[\boldsymbol{X}]$ *is a conjunct called hypothesis of* N *and* $\boldsymbol{X}$ *is a sequence of variables appearing in the hypothesis.*

Example 2 (Negative Constraint). The following negative rule expresses that it is impossible for a HVAC system to be ON and OFF at the same time.
$$N : \forall x(HVAC(x) \wedge hasStatus(x, \text{"ON"}) \wedge hasStatus(x, \text{"OFF"}) \rightarrow \perp$$

Definition 4. *Knowledge base* $\mathcal{K}$. *The knowledge base over a vocabulary* $\mathbb{V}$, *denoted by* $\mathcal{K} = (\mathcal{F}, \mathcal{R}, \mathcal{N})$, *consists of a finite set of facts* $\mathcal{F}$, *a finite set of existential rules* $\mathcal{R}$ *and a finite set of negative constrains* $\mathcal{N}$.

To be able to perform deduction, rules have to be used with the facts to produce new facts.

For example, consider the following knowledge base for data collected from user devices such as bracelets and smartphones.

Regular rules describe the entities, profiles and data managed in the knowledge base. For instance, the following set contains rules which can be expressed in our IoT domain.

$$\mathcal{R}_r = \begin{cases} \forall x_1 Entity(x_1) \rightarrow \exists y_1 Profile(y_1) \wedge Member(x_1, y_1) & (r_1) \\ \forall x_2 Data(x_2) \rightarrow \exists y_2 Profile(y_2) \wedge Belong(x_2, y_2) & (r_2) \\ \forall x_2 Data(x_2) \rightarrow \exists y_3 DataType(y_3) \wedge Describe(x_2, y_3) & (r_3) \\ \forall x_2 Data(x_2) \rightarrow \exists y_4 Time(y_4) \wedge hasCollectTimeStamp(x_2, y_4) & (r_4) \\ \forall x_2 Data(x_2) \rightarrow \exists y_5 Location(y_5) \wedge hasCollectLocation(x_2, y_5) & (r_5) \\ \forall x_2 Data(x_2) \rightarrow \exists y_6 MeasureUnit(y_6) \wedge hasMeasureUnit(x_2, y_6) & (r_6) \end{cases}$$

such that rules r_1 - r_7 express the following domain rules:

- r_1: each entity is a member of a profile,
- r_2: each data belongs to a profile,
- r_3: each data is attached with a datatype which describes it,
- r_4: each data has a timestamp corresponding to the instant of its collection,
- r_5: each data has a location where it has been collected,
- r_6: each data has a measure unit.

The following rules define security requirement in the system:

$$\mathcal{R}_s = \begin{cases} \forall x \forall y \forall z Profile(x) \wedge Security(y) \wedge Data(z) \wedge Belong(z, x) \wedge \\ \qquad\qquad\qquad\qquad Apply(y, x) \rightarrow Apply(y, z) & (s_1) \\ \forall x \forall y Entity(x) \wedge Data(y) \rightarrow \exists z AccessLevel(z) \wedge \\ \qquad\qquad\qquad\qquad AccessSecurity(x, y, z) & (s_2) \\ \forall x \forall y \forall z Entity(x) \wedge Profile(y) \wedge Data(z) \wedge Member(x, y) \wedge \\ Belong(z, y) \rightarrow \exists t SecurityDecision(t) \wedge AccessSecurity(x, z, t) & (s_3) \\ \forall x \forall y_1 \forall y_2 \forall z Entity(x) \wedge Profile(y_1) \wedge Profile(y_2) \wedge Data(z) \wedge \\ Member(x, y_1) \wedge Belong(z, y_2) \rightarrow AccessSecurity(x, z,' DENY') & (s_4) \\ \forall x Profile(x) \rightarrow \exists y Security(y) \wedge Apply(x, y) & (s_5) \end{cases}$$

such that:

- s_1: if a security function is applied to a profile then it is applied to all the data belonging to that profile,
- s_2: each couple (data, entity) has a security access level,
- s_3: if an entity is a member of a profile then it has access to all its profile data,
- s_4: if an entity is not a member of a profile then it has not any access to that profile's data. That supposes that an entity cannot belong to more than one profile, as expressed by negative constraint n_1 below.
- s_5: each profile has a security function.

Negative constraints can express regular disjunction properties among concepts and classes, and domain-specific rules. They can also express some privacy rules as follows in our context of user device data modeling:

$$\mathcal{N} = \begin{cases} \forall x \forall y \forall z Entity(x) \land Profile(y) \land Profile(z) \land Member(x,y) \land \\ \qquad\qquad\qquad\qquad\qquad Member(x,z) \to \bot \quad (n_1) \\ \forall x(Entity(x) \land Data(x)) \to \bot \qquad\qquad\qquad\qquad (n_2) \\ \forall x(Data(x) \land Security(x)) \to \bot \qquad\qquad\qquad (n_3) \\ \forall x(Security(x) \land Profile(x)) \to \bot \qquad\qquad\quad (n_4) \\ \forall x(Profile(x) \land DataType(x)) \to \bot \qquad\qquad\quad (n_5) \\ \forall x(DataType(x) \land TimeStamp(x)) \to \bot \qquad\quad (n_6) \\ \forall x(TimeStamp(x) \land Location(x)) \to \bot \qquad\qquad (n_7) \\ \forall x(Location(x) \land MeasureUnit(x)) \to \bot \qquad\quad (n_8) \\ \forall x(MeasureUnit(x) \land Privacy(x)) \to \bot \qquad\quad (n_9) \end{cases}$$

- n_1: an entity is a member of one and only one profile.
- n_{2-9}: disjunction properties over the classes defined in the knowledge base.

For time exclusion, the corresponding rule can be expressed through the following negative constraints:

$$n_{10} : \forall x \forall y \forall z \forall t_1 \forall t_2 Entity(x) \land Data(y) \land CollectTime(z) \land Query(t_1) \land$$
$$Query(t_2) \land Request(x,y,t_1) \land Request(x,z,t_2) \land hasCollectTime(y,z) \to \bot$$

$$n_{11} : \forall x \forall y \forall z \forall t Entity(x) \land Data(y) \land CollectTime(z) \land Query(t) \land$$
$$Request(x,y,t) \land Request(x,z,t) \land hasCollectTime(y,z) \to \bot$$

such that n_{10} forbids sharing the data and its timestamp through two different queries, and n_{11} forbids sharing the data and its timestamp with a single query. In addition, we need to define the following regular rules:

$$r_8 : \forall x \forall y Entity(x) \land Data(y) \to \exists z Query(z) \land Request(x,y,z)$$

$$r_9 : \forall x \forall y Entity(x) \land CollectTime(y) \to \exists z Query(z) \land Request(x,y,z)$$

In logic, this is a simple application of Modus Ponens inference rule; in Datalog it is referred as the Elementary Production Principle (EPP). In our case, the application of rule R_1 on fact F_1 corresponds to a substitution of variables that makes the body R_1 looks like F_1. Therefore, we need a homomorphism that maps $body(R_1)$ to F_1.

We make use of the formal definition of rule application as introduced by Baget et al. [7].

2.2   Query Acceptability Condition

We define in this subsection both concepts of *meta-query* and *privacy preserving answerable query*. They form the core component of our approach.

Definition 5. *(meta-query). Let $Q(X) = \exists Y \bigwedge_{i=1}^{n} R_i(X,Y)$ be a conjunctive query of n predicates such that X,Y are vectors of variables. Its corresponding meta-query is the conjunction of information about the requester and the information about what is requested. Formally, let $Q^s()$ be the meta-query of $Q(X)$; $Q^s() = I_{R(Q)} \wedge I_Q$ such that:*

1. *$I_{R(Q)}$ is a conjunction of information about the requester such as the ID, profile, etc. The ID information can be extracted from the application protocol used by the external entity to perform the request, crossed with knowledge base information. Once the ID is determined, the other attached information can be easily extracted from the knowledge base (by concept and property classification and querying).*
2. *I_Q is a conjunction of information about the data requested such as its datatype, timestamp, location, etc. I_Q can be computed from the predicates $R_i(X,Y)_{i=1,\ldots,n}$ forming the body of the query $Q(X)$: each $R_i \in \bigwedge_{i=1}^{n} R_i(X,Y)$ can derive from the knowledge base some information describing it. We can make use of variables X and Y to target the concepts and properties to extract from the knowledge base. An algorithm has to be developed for this purpose.*

Example 3. Let us suppose that a healthcare application asks a connected bracelet to provide the heart rate measured at wakeup time (08:00 am for instance) of its owner (let us say that he/she is identified by *ido*). The query Q can be expressed as follows:

$Q(x) = hasHeartRate(ido, x) \wedge hasCollectedTimeStamp(x, 08{:}00)$

The corresponding meta-query Q^s can be as follows. User identifier *ido* is used to select the rules defined by/for the user to protect his/her privacy. For the query above, variable x indicates that the entity asks for heart rate information, denoted hereinafter by *HR*, collected at 08:00 am. From the knowledge base, we can deduce that 08:00 is an instance of the concept *CollectTimeStamp*. Let *idr* be the identifier of the external entity requesting data x.

$Q^s = \exists y : Entity(idr) \wedge Data(HR) \wedge hasCollectedTimeStamp(y, 08{:}00) \wedge CollectTimeStamp(08{:}00)$.

Proposition 1. *(Privacy preserving answerable query). Let Q be a conjunctive query and let Q^s be its corresponding meta-query. Q is said to be privacy preserving answerable if and only if $\{\mathcal{K}, Q^s\} \not\models \bot$.*

In other terms, a query Q is privacy preserving answerable if and only if $\{\mathcal{K}, Q^s\}$ is $\mathcal{R}$-consistent. The $\mathcal{R}$-consistent checking needs to perform the following processing:

1. Compute the closure of the set of predicates of Q^s w.r.t. the set of rules $\mathcal{R}$ to obtained the closed set $Cl_{\mathcal{R}}(Q^s)$. The closure consists in adding to $Cl_{\mathcal{R}}(Q^s)$ the conclusion of each rule $r \in \mathcal{R}$ such that its hypothesis is one of any subset of $Cl_{\mathcal{R}}(Q^s)$ until $Cl_{\mathcal{R}}(Q^s) \cup C(r) = Cl_{\mathcal{R}}(Q^s)$
2. Resolve the existential variables if possible in $Cl_{\mathcal{R}}(Q^s)$

3. Check the consistency on $Cl_{\mathcal{R}}(Q^s)$ resulted from step 2 on the set of negative rules $\mathcal{N}$

Example 4. Let us consider the query of Example 3:
$\quad Q(x) = HeartRate(ido) \wedge hasCollectedTimeStamp(x, 08{:}00)$
Its corresponding meta-query is:
$\quad Q^s = \exists y : Entity(idr) \wedge Data(HR) \wedge hasCollectedTimeStamp(y, 08{:}00) \wedge$
$CollectTimeStamp(08{:}00)$.

1. To check the consistency of the knowledge base, we need to compute the closure of Q^s.
Let us consider $Cl_{\mathcal{R}}(Q^s)$ as the following set of predicates from Q^s:
$Cl_{\mathcal{R}}(Q^s) = \{Entity(idr), Data(HR), hasCollectedTimeStamp(x, 08{:}00),$
$CollectTimeStamp(08{:}00)\}$.
The successive derivation processes to obtain $Cl_{\mathcal{R}}(Q^s)$ are as follows:
   - by r_1 and $S = \{Entity(idr)\}$ we add $\exists y Profile(y) \wedge Member(idr, y)$,
   - by r_2-r_6 and $S = \{Data(HR)\}$, we add $\exists y_1 Profile(y_1) \wedge Belong(HR, y_1)$,
     $\exists y_2 DataType(y_2) \wedge Describe(HR, y_2)$, $\exists y_3 TimeStamp(y_3)$
     $\wedge hasCollectTimeStamp(HR, y_3)$, $\exists y_4 Location(y_4)$
     $\wedge hasCollectLocation(HR, y_4)$, $\exists y_5 MeasureUnit(y_5)$
     $\wedge hasMeasureUnit(HR, y_5)$,
   - by s_5 and $S = \{\exists y_1 Profile(y_1)\}$, we add $\exists z_1 Security(z_1) \wedge Apply(y_1, z_1)$
   - by s_6 and $S = \{Entity(idr), Data(HR)\}$, we add $\exists z_2 TimeStamp(z_2) \wedge$
     $Deny(idr, HR, z_2)$
The query becomes (for a sake of simplicity, we limit the listing here to some conclusions drawn from rules):

$\quad Cl_{\mathcal{R}}(Q^s) = \{$

$\qquad\qquad Entity(idr)$

$\qquad\qquad Data(HR)$

$\qquad\qquad hasCollectedTimeStamp(HR, 08{:}00)$

$\qquad\qquad CollectTimeStamp(08{:}00)$

$\qquad\qquad \exists y_1 Profile(y_1) \wedge Belong(HR, y_1)$

$\qquad\qquad \exists y_2 DataType(y_2) \wedge Describe(HR, y_2)$

$\qquad\qquad \exists y_3 TimeStamp(y_3) \wedge hasCollectTimeStamp(HR, y_3)$

$\qquad\qquad \exists y_4 Location(y_4) \wedge hasCollectLocation(HR, y_4)$

$\qquad\qquad \exists y_5 MeasureUnit(y_5) \wedge hasMeasureUnit(HR, y_5)$

$\qquad\qquad \exists y_6 TimeStamp(y_6) \wedge hasCollectTimeStamp(HR, y_6)$

$\qquad\qquad \exists z_1 Security(z_1) \wedge Apply(y_1, z_1)$

$\qquad\qquad \exists z_2 MetaDataType(z_2) \wedge Deny(idr, HR, z_2)$

$\qquad \}$

2. Resolve, if possible, the existentially quantified variables in resulted $Cl_{\mathcal{R}}(Q^s)$ by using the knowledge base. For instance, let us suppose that the following information are defined in the knowledge base:

    – $hasCollectedTimeStamp(HR, 08:00)$
- $Deny$(idr,HR,Time)

Then the following variables can be resolved:
- $x = HR$
- $y_3 = y_6 = 08:00$

3. Check the consistency of the $Cl_\mathcal{R}(Q^s)$ regarding the negative constraints $\mathcal{N}$. Thus, if any negative constraint is activated then the query Q is rejected. In our running example, the following conjunction:
   $Data(HR) \wedge Entity(idr) \wedge Request(idr, HR, \text{Time}) \wedge CollectTime(08:00) \wedge$
   $hasCollectTime(HR, 08:00) \wedge hasMetaDataType(HR, \text{Time})$ activates negative rule n_{11}.

The consistency checking process needs to map the natural representation of time as real timestamp in the knowledge base. The easiest way to do that is to consider time as an integer like operating systems do (time is a number of seconds elapsed since 01/01/1970). A temporal logic can be of help to achieve such a time modeling. Therefore, we extend the knowledge base to the Linear Time Logic LTL in the next section.

3   Extending to Linear Temporal Logic-Based Semantics

We introduce in this section our approach to combine time within our knowledge base formalism. It consists in expressing temporal constraints over the rules $(\mathcal{R} \cup \mathcal{N})$ of privacy protective knowledge base $\mathcal{K}_p$. We remind in Subsect. 3.1 the basis of the Linear Temporal Logic, denoted by LTL, then we detail its extension and combination to our knowledge base in Subsect. 3.2.

3.1   Linear Temporal Logic (LTL)

To integrate time into logical frameworks, many research works focused on combining temporal logics with Description Logics from theoretical point of view such as [3,5,14–16] to name a few. Moreover, Linear Temporal Logic (denoted LTL) [17] was introduced to formally establishing the temporal relationship among events to construct consistent and coherent course of actions according to time dependent events recorded for a given system. More recently, variants of LTL have been considered in resolving planning problems [9,12].

Detecting inconsistencies in such systems is an important problem to tackle from both theoretical and practical viewpoints.

The language of the Linear Temporal Logic (denoted by LTL) extends the language of Boolean (propositional) logic by the operations **N** for *next* and **U** for *until* [18]. The formulas of LTL are built up from a set *Prop* of atomic propositions and are closed under applications of Boolean operators and the following time operators (often called operations):

– **N** for *next* is a unary operation such that formula **N**φ means that statement φ holds in the next time point (or state),

- **U** for *until* is a binary operation such that formula $\varphi\mathbf{U}\psi$ means that φ holds until ψ will be true,
- **Pr** for *previous* is a unary operation such that formula $\mathbf{Pr}\varphi$ means that statement φ was true at the immediate previous time point,
- **S** for *since* is a binary operation such that formula $\varphi\mathbf{S}\psi$ means that φ holds since ψ has been true.

Semantics for LTL consists of infinite transition systems. Formally, they are represented as linear Kripke structures based on the natural numbers. The infinite linear Kripke structure is a quadruple $\mathcal{M} := \langle \mathbb{N}, \leq, Next, V \rangle$, where:

- $\mathbb{N}$ is the set of all natural numbers (for some extended versions of LTL the set of all integer numbers $\mathbb{Z}$ is considered instead); all elements of $\mathbb{N}$ are possible states (worlds),
- $\leq$ is the standard order on $\mathbb{N}$; $\leq$ is the transition relation (which is linear in our case),
- $Next$ (different from operator **N**) is the binary relation, where $a\,Next\,b$ means b is the number next to a,
- V is a valuation function of a subset S of $Prop$. It assigns truth values to atomic propositions of S. Therefore, for any $p \in S$, $V(p) \subseteq \mathbb{N}$, $V(p)$ is the set of all numbers n from $\mathbb{N}$ where the proposition p is true (w.r.t. V).

The triple $\langle \mathbb{N}, \leq, Next \rangle$ is a Kripke frame which we will denote for short by $\mathbb{N}$. For a Kripke structure $\mathcal{M} := \langle \mathbb{N}, \leq, Next, V \rangle$ and a formula φ with symbols from the domain of V, we say that φ is valid in $\mathcal{M}$ (denoted by $\mathcal{M} \Vdash \varphi$) if for any b of $\mathcal{M}$ ($b \in \mathbb{N}$), the formula φ is true at b (denoted $(\mathcal{M}, b) \Vdash_V \varphi$). The truth values in any Kripke structure $\mathcal{M}$ can be extended from propositions of S to arbitrary formulas as follows:

- $\forall p \in Prop : (\mathcal{M}, a) \Vdash_V p \Leftrightarrow a \in V(p)$
- $(\mathcal{M}, a) \Vdash_V (\varphi \wedge \psi) \Leftrightarrow (\mathcal{M}, a) \Vdash_V \varphi \wedge (\mathcal{M}, a) \Vdash_V \psi$
- $(\mathcal{M}, a) \Vdash_V \neg\varphi \Leftrightarrow not[(\mathcal{M}, a) \Vdash_V \varphi]$
- $(\mathcal{M}, a) \Vdash_V \mathbf{N}\varphi \Leftrightarrow [(a\,Next\,b) \Rightarrow (\mathcal{M}, b) \Vdash_V \varphi]$
- $(\mathcal{M}, a) \Vdash_V \mathbf{Pr}\varphi \Leftrightarrow [(b\,Next\,a) \Rightarrow (\mathcal{M}, b) \Vdash_V \varphi]$
- $(\mathcal{M}, a) \Vdash_V (\varphi\mathbf{U}\psi) \Leftrightarrow \exists b : (a \leq b) \wedge (\mathcal{M}, b) \Vdash_V \psi \wedge \forall c[a \leq c < b] : (\mathcal{M}, c) \Vdash_V \varphi$
- $(\mathcal{M}, a) \Vdash_V (\varphi\mathbf{S}\psi) \Leftrightarrow \exists b : (b \leq a) \wedge (\mathcal{M}, b) \Vdash_V \psi \wedge \forall c[b < c \leq a] : (\mathcal{M}, c) \Vdash_V \varphi$

The linear temporal logic LTL is the set of all formulas which are valid in all infinite temporal linear Kripke structures $\mathcal{M}$ based on $\mathbb{N}$ with standard $\leq$ and $Next$. The modal operations $\square$ (necessary) and $\lozenge$ (possible) might be defined via temporal operations as follows:

- $\lozenge p \Leftrightarrow \top\mathbf{U}p$: proposition p could be true at an arbitrary instant in $\mathcal{M}$,
- $\square p \Leftrightarrow \neg\lozenge\neg p$: it is not possible to have $\neg p$ at any instant time in $\mathcal{M}$.

3.2   Semantics of Time-Constrained Knowledge Base

The syntax of the time-constrained knowledge base $\mathcal{K}^t = (\mathcal{F}, \mathcal{R}, \mathcal{N})$ is the same as for $\mathcal{K} = (\mathcal{F}, \mathcal{R}, \mathcal{N})$. The main difference lies in the interpretation (semantics) of the rules depending on time.

Rule Time-Based Semantics. The rules considered as time constrained are: Blocking and Periodic blocking, Temporal prohibition, and Data shelf life. From the LTL standpoint, we have the following Kripke structure $\mathcal{M} = (\mathbb{N}, \leq, Next, V)$, where V is a valuation function defined as follows.

$$V : \mathbb{N} \times \Phi \longrightarrow \{0, 1\}$$
$$(t, \varphi) \longmapsto V(t, \varphi)$$

where Φ is a set of well-formed formulas in our knowledge base. Therefore:

- $\forall \varphi \in \Phi, (\mathcal{M}, t) \Vdash_V \varphi \Leftrightarrow V(t, \varphi) = 1$
- $\forall \varphi \in \Phi, (\mathcal{M}, t) \Vdash_V \neg\varphi \Leftrightarrow$ *not* $[(\mathcal{M}, t) \Vdash_V \varphi]$, which means in our case $V(t, \varphi) = 0$
- $\forall \varphi, \psi \in \Phi, (\mathcal{M}, t) \Vdash_V (\varphi \wedge \psi) \Leftrightarrow (\mathcal{M}, t) \Vdash_V \varphi \wedge (\mathcal{M}, t) \Vdash_V \psi$
- $(\mathcal{M}, t) \Vdash_V \forall X \varphi(X) \Leftrightarrow \forall x \in X^{\mathcal{I}} : (\mathcal{M}, t) \Vdash_V \varphi(x)$, where $X^{\mathcal{I}}$ is the interpretation of concept X in the domain of interpretation of the knowledge base $\Delta^{\mathcal{I}}$ equipped with the interpretation function $.^{\mathcal{I}}$
- $(\mathcal{M}, t) \Vdash_V \exists X \varphi(X) \Leftrightarrow \exists x \in X^{\mathcal{I}} : (\mathcal{M}, t) \Vdash_V \varphi(x)$.

In the next subsections, we extend this basic temporal-based model to other operators according to the interpretation of the privacy rules developed above.

1. Blocking and Periodic Blocking. Let p be a period of prohibition or safety period (it can be measured by hour, day, week, etc.) attached to data d and entity e. In our case, we can instantiate V to express a periodicity of a formula as a parameterized function with period p as follows:

$$V : \mathbb{N} \times \Phi \longrightarrow \{0, 1\}$$
$$(t, \varphi) \longmapsto V(t, \varphi; p) = \begin{cases} 1 & \text{if } t[p] = 0 \\ 0 & \text{otherwise.} \end{cases}$$

Therefore, we express a query as a negative rule which is triggered only if temporal condition is satisfied.

$$n_{12} : \forall x \forall y \forall z \forall q \, Entity(x) \wedge Data(y) \wedge Period(z) \wedge hasPeriod(x, y, z) \wedge$$
$$Query(q) \wedge Request(x, y, q) \rightarrow \bot$$

We need to map the negative constraint n_i with its corresponding LTL proposition φ_i.

The semantics of the periodical blocking can be caught through a new temporal function we propose called *Whenever* denoted by **W**. Therefore, let $\mathcal{M}$ be a model, then

$$\forall \varphi, \psi \in \Phi : (\mathcal{M}, t) \Vdash_V \varphi \mathbf{W} \psi \Leftrightarrow [(\mathcal{M}, t) \Vdash_V \psi \Rightarrow (\mathcal{M}, t) \Vdash_V \varphi]$$

where $\Rightarrow$ stands for logical implication operator.

- Interpretation 1: For instance, φ : $Request(x, y, q)$, where φ is a formula in LTL which checks if the instant time of the query q is a multiple of the periodicity defined for the data x shared with the entity y.
- Interpretation 2: Another possible approach is to allow the following formula in the LTL. Suppose that $isBlocked$ is a propositional symbol which is true until the blocking period is over and let OVER be a propositional formula such as $V(t, \text{OVER}) = 1$ if $t - p > 0$. Therefore, $isSharable$ is a propositional symbol mapped to a query such that:

$$isSharable \; \mathbf{W} \neg isBlocked$$

$$n_{18} \; \mathbf{W} \; isBlocked$$

2. Temporal Prohibition. Temporal prohibition can be implemented by the temporal function *Since* denoted by **S**. It is still to define the logical formulas φ and ψ and to map them with the elements of rule p_6. Therefore, ψ could be $isSharable(x, y)$ if and only if $t_0 + t \geq p$ where t_0 is the instant when data x is collected and p is the temporal prohibition for data x and entity y, and t is the timestamp of the query.

The formula ψ can express the query itself. Hence, the validity of a query Q when it is received at instant t is obtained from the linear logic by evaluating $(\mathcal{M}, a) \Vdash_V (Q \; \mathbf{S} \; isSharable)$.

3. Data Shelf-Life. Data shelf-life can be mapped to propositional formulas with *Until* function. A data d is sharable until its shelf life is reached. Thus, this constraint can be expressed as:

$$isSharable \; \mathbf{U} \; ShelfLifeOut$$

Time-Constrained Rules Interpretation Within LTL. The issue we should deal with at this stage is the definition of the valuation function V. Actually time operator are defined in different ways:

- **W**: whenever function is based on the periodicity value p or on the blocking period,
- **S**: since function is evaluated based on the prohibition period,
- **U**: depends on the kinds of metadata requested (time, location, both of them, etc.)

Our approach consists in mapping each time-constrained rule from the knowledge base into a propositional variable in LTL. The problem to resolve is then how to unify the valuation function V, which covers not only all the current rules but the rules eventually to be added by the users.

The solution we are prospecting could be based on sub-functions. Let V be the valuation function defined as follows.

$$V : RuleType \times \Phi \times \mathcal{V} \rightarrow \{0, 1\}$$
$$(r, \varphi, v) \mapsto v_r(\varphi)$$

such that:

- *RuleType* is the set of time-constrained rule for privacy protection. For instance, $RuleType = \{Periodic\ Blocking\ (\mathbf{PB}),\ Time\ Prohibition\ (\mathbf{TP}),\ Shelf\ life\ (\mathbf{SL})\}$,

The unification of functions v_1, v_2, v_3 can be as follows:

$$V : RuleType \times \mathbb{N} \times \Phi \times \mathbb{N} \rightarrow \{0,1\}$$

$$(r,t,\varphi,p) \mapsto V(r,t,\varphi,p) = \begin{cases} v_1(t,\varphi,p) & if\ r = PB \\ v_2(t,\varphi,p) & if\ r = TP \\ v_3(t,\varphi,p) & if\ r = SL \end{cases}$$

We summarize in Table 1, the time-constrained rules along with their unification functions.

Table 1. Summary of the time-constrained rules.

Rule Type	Temporal function	Sub-valuation v_r
Periodic Blocking (**PB**)	Whenever W	$v_1 : \mathbb{N} \times \Phi \times \mathbb{N} \longrightarrow \{0,1\}$ $(t,\varphi,p) \longmapsto V(t,\varphi,p) = \begin{cases} 1 & if\ t[p] = 0 \\ 0 & otherwise. \end{cases}$
Time Prohibition (**TP**)	Since S	$v_2 : \mathbb{N} \times \Phi \times \mathbb{N} \longrightarrow \{0,1\}$ $(t,\varphi,p) \longmapsto V(t,\varphi,p) = \begin{cases} 1 & if\ t > p \\ 0 & otherwise. \end{cases}$
Data Shelf life (**SL**)	Until U	$v_3 : \mathbb{N} \times \Phi \times \mathbb{N} \longrightarrow \{0,1\}$ $(t,\varphi,p) \longmapsto V(t,\varphi,p) = \begin{cases} 1 & if\ t < p \\ 0 & otherwise. \end{cases}$

4 Conclusion

This positioning paper aims at modeling the idea of enforcing user privacy through a time-constrained knowledge base. It allows users to express the way their data should be protected online as rules that the system must enforce in any situation where the data is collected and processed. We defined a logical model where a user can define the data they want to share with external entities and the way the sharing would be performed. Moreover, the user can also update at any time the data, and the rules that govern their usages. To limit data time analysis, we extended our logical model to a linear temporal logic. Interpretation and valuation functions have also been defined for Periodic blocking, Time prohibition and Data shelf life logical predicates.

As future work, we are aiming to extend our logical system with a user-friendly querying languages that makes use of the privacy rules as operators that can be used to easily express user privacy rules. An algebraic framework definition is already in progress. In addition, the implementation and experimentation of the logical system is also mandatory for its validation.

References

1. Ahvar, S., et al.: Ontology-based model for trusted critical site supervision in FUSE-IT. In: Crespi, N., Manzalini, A., Secci, S. (eds.) 20th Conference on Innovations in Clouds, Internet and Networks, ICIN 2017, Paris, France, 7–9 March 2017, pp. 313–315. IEEE (2017). https://doi.org/10.1109/ICIN.2017.7899430
2. Aroua, S., et al.: Security and privacy for the internet of things: an overview of the project. In: 2019 IEEE International Conference on Systems, Man and Cybernetics, SMC 2019, Bari, Italy, 6–9 October 2019, pp. 3993–3998. IEEE (2019). https://doi.org/10.1109/SMC.2019.8914221
3. Artale, A., Kontchakov, R., Ryzhikov, V., Zakharyaschev, M.: A cookbook for temporal conceptual data modelling with description logics. ACM Trans. Comput. Logic **15**(3) (2014). https://doi.org/10.1145/2629565
4. Aussenac-Gilles, N., Charlet, J., Reynaud, C.: Knowledge Engineering, pp. 733–768. Springer, Cham (2020). https://doi.org/10.1007/978-3-030-61244-3
5. Baader, F., Borgwardt, S., Lippmann, M.: Temporal query entailment in the description logic SHQ. J. Web Semant. **33**, 71–93 (2015). https://doi.org/10.1016/j.websem.2014.11.008, https://www.sciencedirect.com/science/article/pii/S1570826814001206, ontology-based Data Access
6. Baget, J.-F., Leclère, M., Mugnier, M.-L., Rocher, S., Sipieter, C.: Graal: a toolkit for query answering with existential rules. In: Bassiliades, N., Gottlob, G., Sadri, F., Paschke, A., Roman, D. (eds.) RuleML 2015. LNCS, vol. 9202, pp. 328–344. Springer, Cham (2015). https://doi.org/10.1007/978-3-319-21542-6_21
7. Baget, J.F., Leclère, M., Mugnier, M.L., Salvat, E.: On rules with existential variables: walking the decidability line. Artif. Intell. **175**(9), 1620–1654 (2011). https://doi.org/10.1016/j.artint.2011.03.002, https://www.sciencedirect.com/science/article/pii/S0004370211000397
8. Bienvenu, M., Leclère, M., Mugnier, M.L., Rousset, M.C.: Reasoning with Ontologies, pp. 185–215. Springer, Cham (2020). https://doi.org/10.1007/978-3-030-06164-7_6
9. Bonassi, L., De Giacomo, G., Favorito, M., Fuggitti, F., Gerevini, A.E., Scala, E.: Planning for temporally extended goals in pure-past linear temporal logic, **33**, 61–69 (2023).https://doi.org/10.1609/icaps.v33i1.27179, https://ojs.aaai.org/index.php/ICAPS/article/view/27179
10. Bui, D., Tang, B., Shin, K.G.: Detection of inconsistencies in privacy practices of browser extensions. In: 2023 IEEE Symposium on Security and Privacy (SP), pp. 2780–2798 (2023). https://doi.org/10.1109/SP46215.2023.10179338
11. Cali, A., Gottlob, G., Lukasiewicz, T., Marnette, B., Pieris, A.: Datalog+/-: Aafamily of logical knowledge representation and query languages for new applications. In: 2010 25th Annual IEEE Symposium on Logic in Computer Science (LICS), pp. 228–242. IEEE (2010)
12. Chakraborti, T., Fuggitti, F., Katz, M., Sohrabi, S.: Interactive plan selection using linear temporal logic, disjunctive action landmarks, and natural language instruction (2024)

13. Chein, M., Mugnier, M.L.: Graph-Based Knowledge Representation: Computational Foundations of Conceptual Graphs. Springer, London (2008). https://doi.org/10.1007/978-1-84800-286-9
14. De Giacomo, G., Vardi, M.Y.: Linear temporal logic and linear dynamic logic on finite traces. In: Proceedings of the Twenty-Third International Joint Conference on Artificial Intelligence. IJCAI '13, pp. 854–860. AAAI Press (2013)
15. Gutiérrez-Basulto, V., Jung, J.C., Schneider, T.: Lightweight temporal description logics with rigid roles and restricted tboxes. In: Proceedings of the 24th International Conference on Artificial Intelligence. IJCAI'15, pp. 3015–3021. AAAI Press (2015)
16. Kurucz, A., Ryzhikov, V., Savateev, Y., Zakharyaschev, M.: Deciding FO-rewritability of regular languages and ontology-mediated queries in linear temporal logic. J. Artif. Intell. Res. **76**, 645–703 (2022). https://api.semanticscholar.org/CorpusID:250493164
17. Pnueli, A.: The temporal logic of programs. In: 18th Annual Symposium on Foundations of Computer Science (SFCS 1977), pp. 46–57 (1977). https://doi.org/10.1109/SFCS.1977.32
18. Rybakov, V.: Linear temporal logic with until and next, logical consecutions. Ann. Pure Appl. Logic **155**(1), 32–45 (2008). https://doi.org/10.1016/j.apal.2008.03.001, https://www.sciencedirect.com/science/article/pii/S0168007208000341
19. Tamani, N., et al.: Rule-based model for smart building supervision and management. In: 2018 IEEE International Conference on Services Computing (SCC), pp. 9–16. IEEE (2018)

Privacy Preserving Federated Learning: A Novel Approach for Combining Differential Privacy and Homomorphic Encryption

Rezak Aziz[✉], Soumya Banerjee, and Samia Bouzefrane

CEDRIC, Conservatoire national des arts et métiers,
292 Rue Saint Martin, 75003 Paris, France
{rezak.aziz,soumya.banerjee}@lecnam.net, samia.bouzefrane@cnam.fr

Abstract. Ensuring the data security and privacy stands as a prominent concern in the landscape of machine learning. The conventional approach of centralizing training data raises privacy concerns. Federated learning addresses this by avoiding the need to transfer local data when training a global model, opting to share only local model updates. Despite this, the challenge of information leakage persists. Various attempts tried to tackle this issue, but existing solutions lead to a tradeoff between accuracy, privacy and computation time. This is an unevitable challenge. In this paper, we address that challenge by combining differential privacy and homomorphic encryption. This approach allow to add less noise to the data by shuffling to anonymize the data, not only at the client level but also at the parameter level. Hence, it improves the accuracy of the output models while offering strong privacy guarantees. Importantly, our method avoids complex homomorphic operation, thereby mitigating the computational overhead of HE. In this manner, the data remains protected from all participants in the learning process. Our findings demonstrate that, for an equivalent level of privacy, our method introduces less noise compared to the local DP method, resulting in increased accuracy after aggregation. However, the privacy amplification requires a substantial number of clients, which make our approach more suitable for cross-device Federated learning.

Keywords: Federated Learning · Differential Privacy · Homomorphic Encryption · Shuffling · Anonymization

1 Introduction

In recent years, machine learning (ML) has shown a great potential for a wide range of real-world applications. However, the performance of machine learning

---

S. Banerjee and S. Bouzefrane—Contributing authors.

© IFIP International Federation for Information Processing 2024
Published by Springer Nature Switzerland AG 2024
S. Bouzefrane and D. Sauveron (Eds.): WISTP 2024, LNCS 14625, pp. 162–177, 2024.
https://doi.org/10.1007/978-3-031-60391-4_11

algorithms depends on access to large amounts of data for training. In traditional machine learning, training is centrally held by one organization that have access to the whole training dataset. In practice, data is often distributed across multiple parties, and sharing it for training purposes is not simple due to privacy policies and regulations like the General Data Protection Regulation (GDPR) [1]. These regulations impose strict rules about how data can be shared and processed between organizations.

Federated learning (FL) [2] is a promising technique that allows multiple parties to jointly train a global model by only exchanging updates about local models and without the need to share their private datasets. This offers a promising solution to mitigate the potential privacy leakage of sensitive information about individuals. However, even though FL was thought of as a privacy-preserving distributed machine learning, recent works have demonstrated that FL may not always provide privacy and robustness guarantees [3–13]. While the private data never leaves their owner, the exchanged models are prone to memorization of the private training dataset. Some sensitive information may be inferred from the shared information using some well-known attacks like gradient inversion, reconstruction attacks, membership inference and property inference attacks.

One way to mitigate this type of attacks is to use privacy-preserving techniques like differential privacy (DP) and homomorphic encryption (HE). Differential privacy offers a way to disrupt data while preserving the statistical properties of the data. This allows us to have meaningful analysis and statistics while countering previous attacks. Existing works using DP consider the local setting of DP (LDP). In the context of LDP, every client adds noise to its information locally and only sends a randomized version to the server. By this way, both the clients and server are protected against private information leakage.

In the other hand, homomorphic encryption allows doing computation on encrypted data and then decrypt only the result. This allows FL actors to access the aggregation of gradient without accessing the gradient themselves. This offers a new layer of security for the gradient by not accessing them, and provides a solution for anonymization which is not considered in LDP.

Each technique taken alone suffers from its disadvantages. First, FL schemes that use LDP address the privacy problem but tend to add too much noise to model parameter data from each client. Therefore, the resulting model may exhibit poor performance. In addition, these schemes do not consider the problem of anonymization in most of the time. While HE offers a solution to accuracy and anonymization, it suffers at its turn from computation and communication overhead. But it is still vulnerable to some other attacks like membership inference.

Recently, the shuffle model proposed by Bittau et al. [14] has emerged as a solution to add less noise while amplifying privacy through anonymization. It consists of shuffling the data to break the link between the data and their sources. The privacy gain is highlighted in the theorem 7 of Erlingsson et al.'s work [15]. **However, the proof of that theorem relies on the assumption that shuffling the data elements is done before applying the local randomizers.**

This assumption implies that implementing such an algorithm in a distributed system requires trusting a remote shuffler with sensitive user data, thus negating the key advantage of the LDP model. To address this limitation, the authors opt to apply local randomizers before shuffling the data. By this way, they ensure the worst case amplification. Unfortunately, adopting this method mandates the use of independent local randomizers, resulting in increased noise. This trade-off between privacy and noise introduces a challenge when striving to strike a balance in the application of privacy-preserving techniques.

In our study, we aim to address this challenge in the context of federated learning. We propose a novel approach to integrate DP and HE in FL context, eliminating the need to trust a third party shuffler. Our objective is to enhance both the privacy and the accuracy of the trained models while avoiding complex computations. Our key contributions are summarized as follows:

- We introduce a novel approach that combines differential privacy and homomorphic encryption in the context of federated learning. This adaptation improves the privacy and accuracy of our models.
- We present a new method to mitigate the tradeoff between utility and privacy. In our approach, the noise is generated by a central entity, achieving at least Central DP accuracy.
- We amplify privacy by shuffling model parameters. In contrast to previous methods that proposed shuffling models to break the link between clients and models, our solution delves deeper by breaking the link between models and parameters. This operator maintains the same utility as without shuffling.
- We minimize the impact of homomorphic encryption by utilizing basic addition to introduce noise. The aggregation is then performed in a cleartext format.
- We implement the solution and provide an experimental analysis using the Federated Enhanced MNIST dataset. Our goal is to demonstrate that our solution enhances the privacy-utility tradeoff compared to Local Differential Privacy (LDP) based approaches.

The remainder of this paper is organized as follows: In Sect. 2, we conduct a literature review on privacy-preserving federated learning, specifically focusing on approaches that combine differential privacy and homomorphic encryption. Following that, Sect. 3 provides the prerequisites necessary to understand our solution, which is detailed in Sect. 4. Subsequently, Sect. 5 outlines the simulation methodology and presents the results of our experimentation, illustrating the feasibility of our solution. Before concluding, Sect. 6 provide discussion about deployments aspects of this solution.

2   Related Works

In this section, we review previous research on securing federated learning through the utilization of differential privacy and homomorphic encryption. In our earlier work [16], we introduced differentially privacy and homomorphic encryption in the context of federated learning. The primary emphasis of our current work is the synergistic combination of differential privacy and homomorphic encryption to enhance the security and the accuracy of federated learning.

Table 1 outlines the key ideas and approaches used in the literature. Many solutions [17–19] rely on additive homomorphic encryption. This choice is driven by the fact that adding DP noise is the primary operation to guarantee privacy. The goal is to provide a stronger privacy guarantee while minimizing the addition of noise by amplifying the privacy.

Table 1. Related works

Ref	Year	Scheme	DP Type	Key Idea
[17]	2019	AHE	LDP	Mitigate the tradeoff between privacy and accuracy by adding less noise through HE
[18]	2020	AHE	LDP+Shuffle	Amplify privacy using the shuffle model with encrypted oblivious shuffle
[19]	2021	AHE	CDP	Improve privacy by splitting updates into two shares and send them to two non-colluding servers that add CDP and use additive secret sharing to mitigate poisoning attacks and conduct secure aggregation
[20]	2022	FHE	LDP	Protect local updates from the server using HE and protect global updates from clients using DP
Ours	2024	AHE	ShuffleDP	Protect updates from clients and central server using DP and parameter shuffling mechanism. The noise adding and the shuffling is done by an untrusted, independent shuffler. Protect updates from this shuffler using AHE

3   Preliminaries

In this section, we explain what is Federated Learning. Then, we'll define Differential Privacy and its main settings. Finally, we'll introduce Additive Homomorphic Encryption, a crucial element in our approach.

3.1   Federated Learning

The term federated learning (FL) was introduced in 2016 by McMahan et al. [2]. FL is a machine learning setting where numerous clients collaborate to train a centralized ML model. Each client's raw data is stored locally and not exchanged with other parties; only updates needed for immediate aggregation are shared with the central server.

Figure 1 illustrates a typical federated training process. This process involves five steps: The server selects a subset of clients based on specific criteria. The chosen client downloads the current model weights and a training program from the server. Independently, each client computes an update to the model by executing the training program locally. The server then aggregates the updates from all devices and updates the central model.

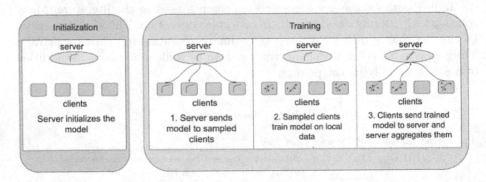

Fig. 1. Federated learning process [21]

3.2 Differential Privacy

Differential privacy is a widely adopted standard for ensuring privacy in data analysis. It aims to guarantee that the outcomes of a randomized algorithm M remain approximately the same, regardless of whether an individual i is part of the dataset or not. In other words, the inclusion of person i in the dataset should not significantly influence the final result. Formally, Differential Privacy is defined by Dwork et al. in 2006 [22] as follows.

Definition 1. *A randomized function M gives (ϵ, δ)-differential privacy if for all datasets D_1 and D_2 differing on at most one element, and all $S \subset Range(M)$,*

$$Pr[M(D_1) \in S] \leq e^\epsilon \times Pr[M(D_2) \in S] + \delta \qquad (1)$$

In the Definition 1, ϵ is a non-negative real number that determines the level of privacy protection provided by the algorithm. A lower value of ϵ corresponds to a stronger privacy guarantee. The value of δ is a small positive real number that represents the probability of any failure of the definition. When δ is set to 0, it is referred to as pure differential privacy.

This definition provides a framework for bounding privacy when querying the same dataset multiple times. Furthermore, it guarantees that subsequent processing of the results maintains privacy.

Two main settings are discussed in the literature for differential privacy: the centralized DP (CDP) and the local DP (LDP). In CDP, the noise is added by a centralized server that collects first the data then applies the mechanism. In LDP, the noise is added at the client level before collecting the data. LDP offers stronger privacy guarantees, as the noise is added closer to the source of the data. Additionally, a hybrid setting called the shuffle model is also explored in the literature. The shuffle model aims to combine the benefits of both CDP and LDP. In this setting, privacy is enhanced through anonymization achieved by shuffling the data. The noise is added centrally by a shuffler before passing the data to the analyst server, which enables the system to attain the performance advantages of CDP while maintaining the privacy guarantees provided by LDP.

3.3   Additive Homomorphic Encryption

Additive Homomorphic encryption is a cryptographic primitive that allows third parties to perform additions on ciphertexts without decrypting them. It provides the same result as encrypting after operating in clear text messages.

More formally, an encryption scheme is called additive homomorphic if it supports the following property:

$$E(m_1) + E(m_2) = E(m_1 + m_2)$$

where E is the encryption algorithm and m_1, m_2 belong to M the set of all possible messages.

4   Our Framework

In this section, we outline the high-level architecture of our framework for privacy-preserving federated learning. Our framework draws inspiration from the shuffle model of differential privacy [14]. The objective is to enhance privacy through shuffling while providing users with increased privacy guarantees.

Figure 2 provides an overview of this framework. The clients aim to collaboratively learn a machine learning model without divulging their local data to any other entity within the system. Instead, they reach an agreement to share only model updates with an aggregator, the entity responsible for constructing a unified machine learning model.

Clients seek to safeguard their data against privacy attacks both during the Federated Learning (FL) process and the publication of the final model. To address this concern, they choose to participate in our framework, which combines Differential Privacy (DP) and Homomorphic Encryption (HE) to provide enhanced privacy protection. The concept involves introducing a third-party, honest-but-curious server positioned between the aggregation server and the clients. This intermediary server performs the shuffling step and adds noise using centralized DP, while the data remains encrypted using an additive homomorphic encryption scheme. This approach allows us to offer privacy guarantees similar to local DP while maintaining the data utility characteristic of the centralized DP model.

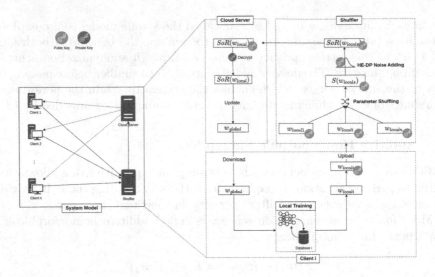

Fig. 2. High Level Architecture of our solution

4.1   Threat Model

In this study, the attacker can be either an insider or an outsider. Outsiders can be easily thwarted by providing secure channels for all communications.

On the other hand, insiders are participants in the learning process. This study does not consider poisoning attacks by insiders. The identified insiders in this context include the server, the shuffler, and clients. It is assumed that all parties are honest-but-curious, with a key assumption being the absence of collusion between the server and the shuffler.

The server is considered honest-but-curious, expected to execute the necessary computations during the aggregation process but not trusted with direct access to raw updates. As said in the previous section, information protection is implemented through two primary methods. First, differential privacy is applied to safeguard the information. Second, anonymization is achieved in two ways: the shuffler randomizes the parameters of the models, disrupting the link between the source of the parameters and the server. Additionally, a client selection protocol, independent of the server, ensures that real participants in the learning process remain undisclosed, preserving the privacy of their information.

The shuffler is also regarded as honest-but-curious, as it is supposed to execute the steps involving adding noise and shuffling, but it is not trusted to access the raw updates. Consequently, it is considered a separate entity that does not collude with the server. Information is then protected using homomorphic encryption.

The clients are considered honest-but-curious, meaning they carry out their tasks correctly but might try to extract sensitive information about the training data. In addition, the clients may collude or not. To protect against this, the details are secured through the post-processing feature of differential privacy (DP).

Based on this threat model, our privacy-preserving framework can ensure that (i) the semi-honest aggregator cannot learn additional information, (ii) the shuffler cannot learn intermediate model updates from clients, (iii) malicious clients cannot learn the parameters of other honest participants.

4.2 Homomorphic Encryption to Protect Data Against the Shuffler

As we secure our data and model through differential privacy, it is important to understand the incorporation of homomorphic encryption (HE). The motivation is simple: we aim to introduce noise in a centralized manner without trusting either the generator or the aggregator with direct access to raw parameters. The decision to centralize noise addition is driven by the observation that Local Differential Privacy (LDP) introduces a significant amount of noise, impacting accuracy. For instance, when considering the addition of Gaussian noise, each client independently samples noise from a normal distribution denoted as $\mathcal{N}_i(0, \sigma_i^2)$. Upon aggregation, the resulting cumulative noise follows a well-known statistical property of the Gaussian distribution, as illustrated in Eq. 2. This equation encapsulates the summation of individual normal distributions, resulting in a normal distribution $\mathcal{N}_i(0, \sum \sigma^2)$.

$$\sum \mathcal{N}_i(0, \sigma^2) = \mathcal{N}_i(0, \sum \sigma^2) \tag{2}$$

In contrast, Centralized Differential Privacy (CDP) involves sampling noise using the same random variable, ensuring a consistent standard deviation throughout the entire process. Consequently, less noise is added without the necessity to trust the central entity with direct data access. This is where homomorphic encryption becomes essential, playing a crucial role in concealing the raw parameters from the shuffler and mitigating the tradeoff between privacy and utility, all while providing robust protection against potential risks introduced by the shuffler.

In the context of concrete homomorphic encryption (HE), our focus is specifically on the case of adding noise, which enables the utilization of additive homomorphic encryption schemes like the Paillier scheme [23]. Under the assumption of non-collusion between the central server and the shuffler, this approach ensures the security of raw parameters against all parties involved.

4.3 Differential Privacy to Protect Data Against Final Clients and Server

Differential privacy serves as a cornerstone in safeguarding privacy within the realm of machine learning. In the context of federated learning, several possibilities allow the application of DP. CDP, LDP and the shuffle model are the main models. However, each model has its drawbacks and advantages.

Even with this categorization, the spectrum of options for incorporating noise in machine learning remains broad. Noise addition can manifest in multiple forms: injecting noise into raw data, disrupting model parameters, or introducing noise to the optimizer.

Our chosen approach draws inspiration from the shuffle model [14], aiming to harness the benefits of both LDP and CDP while minimizing their respective limitations. This hybrid model seeks to provide enhanced privacy guarantees and improved accuracy while minimizing noise addition.

Our hypothesis revolves around the idea that centralizing noise introduction allows reduction in the variance of the noise compared to decentralized noise generation in the LDP model. Consequently, adding noise at the client level is not suitable. Similarly, injecting noise into raw training data is not a feasible option. On the other hand, we want to mitigate the assumption of honest and curious server and not to trust the server to generate noise. Therefore, adding noise to the shared parameters of the models is the only applicable scenario in our case.

The guarantee that the further treatment of the parameter will never compromise the data is guaranteed by the property of post-processing in differential privacy.

In terms of concrete implementation of differential privacy in this work, we employ the Gaussian mechanism to introduce noise to the data. Additionally, we utilize the FedAvg strategy to aggregate the results.

4.4   Amplifying Privacy by Parameter Shuffling

Ensuring anonymity and privacy is crucial in deploying machine learning models, especially when dealing with data from multiple users. One significant concern revolves around the possibility of a server extracting information about individual clients through their models, even when the data is anonymized. This risk is heightened when a client interacts with the model frequently, as the server could accumulate substantial information about that particular user over time.

Model shuffling is one approach to address this issue, aiming to break down the link between a specific model and its associated user. This makes it challenging for the server to attribute a model to a particular individual. However, even with differential privacy, the privacy budget can be exhausted after a certain number of iterations, posing a risk when accumulating information about the same user over multiple interactions.

To tackle this challenge, parameter shuffling presents an intriguing solution. Instead of shuffling entire models, we shuffle the parameters across models. Figure 3 illustrates the concept of parameter shuffling. This method ensures robust anonymization by severing the link not only between users and models but also between parameters and models. Importantly, it guarantees significant utility in the federated learning process. This ensures that the resulting average model remains functionally equivalent, but individual models are no longer directly linked to a specific user or the original model.

Fig. 3. Example of Parameter Shuffling

In terms of the concrete implementation of parameter shuffling, it can be carried out by a third party trusted to add the noise and shuffle the parameters but not trusted to access the raw data. This implementation could, for example, occur at the government level using a Trusted Execution Environment (TEE).

For the purposes of this study, we assume that parameter shuffling provides the same amplification as the model shuffling strategy. We let studying the real amplification as a perspective mathematical analysis.

5 Evaluation

In this section, we conduct a comprehensive evaluation of our proposed approach, seeking answers to the following key questions:

- How does the noise level change in response to variations in the privacy budget ϵ? We compare different Differential Privacy (DP) settings to assess the impact on noise under the same privacy level.
- What influence does the number of participants exert on accuracy under a specific ϵ? We compare the accuracy between non-private and private solutions, employing both Local Differential Privacy (LDP) and our proposed approach.
- How does the number of rounds affect accuracy?

5.1 Experimental Setup

To demonstrate the practicality of our learning framework, we train a Convolutional Neural Network (CNN) with architectures similar to those in [20] to classify the Federated Extended MNIST (FEMNIST) dataset. FEMNIST is an extended version of MNIST with 62 classes (including digits, upper and lower letters) from 3,596 writers. Each data point in FEMNIST is associated with a unique writer ID. The CNN has two convolution layers followed by max pooling, a fully connected layer with 128 units and ReLU activation, and a final softmax output layer. The convolutional layers have 5×5 and 3×3 kernel sizes, and 128 and 64 channels.

To implement the Convolutional Neural Network (CNN), PyTorch serves as our framework of choice. Simulating the federated learning process is facilitated through the Flower framework. For homomorphic encryption, we employ the

Paillier scheme. In terms of differential privacy, we incorporate the Gaussian mechanism to introduce noise, with a chosen δ value of 10^{-5}. Opting for a sensitivity of 1, considering our parameters are always less than 1, acknowledges a loose upper bound that may result in additional noise for our parameters. The shuffling process is accomplished using built-in methods within the NumPy library in Python.

5.2   Simulation Results

In this experiment, we assess the performance of the generated models. This involves investigating the influence of the parameter ϵ, the number of participants, and the number of federated rounds.

Impact of ϵ on the Noise Level

Figure 4 illustrates how the privacy budget influences the level of added noise in differential privacy across three settings considered in our study. In the context of Local Differential Privacy (LDP), we focus on two distinct and independent clients, each introducing Gaussian noise to their parameters before transmission. As anticipated, LDP introduces more noise compared to Central Differential Privacy (CDP) for the same level of privacy. This observation aligns with Eq. 2.

On the other hand, the inclusion of anonymization and shuffling for privacy results in a noticeable decrease in the noise level. However, it's crucial to note that this reduction in noise doesn't necessarily equate to an improvement in privacy. As depicted in Fig. 5, privacy amplification occurs only when the number of clients surpasses a certain threshold, specifically $n > 2 * \exp(3\epsilon)$ (as proposed by Erlingsson et al. in [15]).

Additionally, the graph in Fig. 4 visually illustrates that as we relax the privacy restrictions (by increasing ϵ), the extra noise diminishes. This simple observation sheds light on the tradeoff between privacy and noise in different privacy-enhancing approaches.

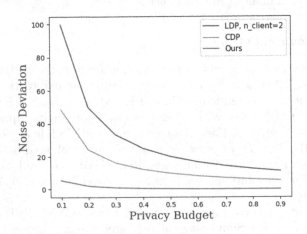

Fig. 4. The relation between the noise deviation and the assured privacy

Impact of Number of Participant

We observed that our method considerably reduces the noise added in the previous paragraph. However, a critical question arises: is reducing noise synonymous with increased privacy? Fig. 5 illustrates the evolution of the privacy gain for a specific centralized ϵ. It demonstrates that we don't have amplification all the time. In fact, the number of clients is another parameter that comes into play. We can see graphically that before a certain number of clients, there is no privacy amplification.

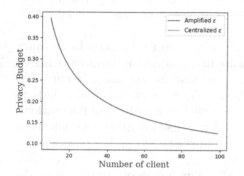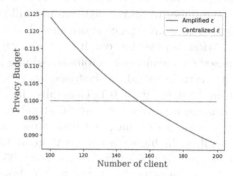

Fig. 5. The relation between the privacy amplification and the number of clients

Table 2 showcases a comparison of accuracy fluctuations with respect to the number of clients. The primary objective is to scrutinize the potential impact of varying client numbers on accuracy. We conduct this comparison between the non-private and private settings to ascertain whether this impact is observed in both settings. Additionally, we explore the relationship between privacy level, accuracy, and the number of clients by varying the level of privacy.

Table 2. The impact of participant number on accuracy

Participants	$Accuracy_{\sigma=0.05}$	$Accuracy_{\sigma=0.1}$	$Accuracy_{NoDP}$
12	0.08	0.19	0.52
20	0.13	0.07	0.53
50	0.64	0.07	0.62
100	0.55	0.55	0.56
150	0.57	0.58	0.60

As intuitively expected, Table 2 highlights the significant influence of the number of clients on accuracy. Having more clients contributes to achieving higher accuracy levels, particularly in the private setting, where this effect is exclusively observed, indicating its association with the introduction of noise.

Additionally, we observe that the noise level impacts the number of clients necessary to achieve better accuracy. With less noise, fewer clients are needed. In the same table, we can see that reducing the noise level from 0.1 to 0.05 results in a decrease in the required number of clients from 100 to 50 to achieve comparable privacy to the non-private model.

Impact of Number of Rounds

One question that we may answer is whether increasing the number of federated rounds leads to improved accuracy. Figure 6 illustrates the relationship between achieved accuracy and the number of federated rounds. According to this figure, the number of rounds significantly influences accuracy, playing a crucial role in achieving convergence of our model.

However, within our framework, we observe more fluctuations in accuracy based on the number of rounds. Adding noise may disrupt the accuracy achieved in a certain round; for instance, there was a significant decrease in accuracy at round 86 for $\sigma = 0.1$. Generally, increasing the number of rounds tends to enhance accuracy, but careful attention is needed to monitor the fluctuations. It's noteworthy that, at times, noise can aid in achieving more generalization, resulting in higher accuracy than in the non-private setting. In our case, we observe this phenomenon with $\sigma = 0.05$.

On the other hand, the graph shows that our framework outperforms the LDP model. The LDP model in our case completely destroyed accuracy, and having more rounds didn't resolve the problem.

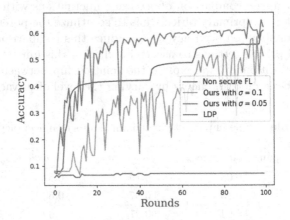

Fig. 6. Impact of the number of rounds on Accuracy

6   Discussion and Deployments Aspects

The proposed solution introduces implementation complexity, mainly due to the inclusion of homomorphic encryption and a third party entity. While encryption and decryption steps are standard operations in internet communications, the additional overhead comes from the noise addition step. Notably, the untrusted shuffler shoulders this burden, handling tasks such as noise generation, homomorphic additions, and result shuffling. On the other hand, a key challenge lies in determining the optimal placement of the shuffler to ensure non-collusion between the central server and the shuffler. In deploying such a system and ensuring its effectiveness, certain criteria must be met by the shuffler:

1. Independence: The shuffler should operate independently, free from direct control or influence by the central server or other entities involved in the federated learning process. This independence ensures that the shuffler acts as a neutral party, reducing the risk of collusion. To enhance the security and the independence, the different operations can be done using Trusted Execution Environment (TEE).
2. Randomization: Randomization is crucial to the shuffler's function, particularly in the shuffling process. This criterion emphasizes the need for a shuffling algorithm that introduces randomness, making it challenging for the central server or any external entity to predict or manipulate the order of the data.
3. Scalability: As the number of clients and data points grows, the shuffler must scale efficiently. A scalable shuffler can handle increased computational demands and effectively shuffle data from a larger pool of participants, ensuring the system's adaptability to varying workloads.
4. Auditability and Transparency: The shuffler's activities should be auditable and transparent. This involves keeping records of operations performed by the shuffler, which can be reviewed for accountability and to verify that the shuffling process adheres to the expected protocols. Transparency ensures stakeholders have visibility into the shuffler's operations.
5. Authentication and authorization: The shuffler should implement robust authentication mechanisms to ensure that only authorized entities can interact with it. Access controls and proper authorization should be enforced to allow only access to the authorized parties to the authorized information.
6. Resilience and Fault Tolerance: Resilience and fault tolerance are essential for the shuffler's reliability. The system should be designed to withstand potential failures, disruptions, or attacks. Fault-tolerant mechanisms enable the shuffler to continue functioning or recover gracefully in the face of unexpected events.
7. Legal and Regulatory Compliance: Compliance with legal and regulatory frameworks is paramount. The shuffler must adhere to data protection laws, privacy regulations, and any other relevant statutes governing the handling of sensitive information. Ensuring legal compliance instills confidence in users and stakeholders regarding the system's ethical operation.

Our suggestion to deploy such entity is to deploy it at the government level. Such entity need to comply with the regulations and laws of privacy.

7 Conclusion and Future Works

In conclusion, this paper introduced a new framework for privacy preserving federated learning. Our central goal is to mitigate the tradeoff between privacy and accuracy of the global model. We delved into the shuffle model of differential privacy, recognizing a significant challenge: the addition of noise before shuffling using local randomizers, which contributes to adding much noise. Conversely, centralizing the noise addition after randomization will not give any privacy amplification, as it involves trusting a shuffler to introduce noise.

Our main contribution lies in the combination of homomorphic encryption and differential privacy. This approach eliminates the need to trust a third-party shuffler for accessing raw data, as noise is added homomorphically in a centralized manner. To our knowledge, our method represents the first to combine DP and HE in this manner.

Our findings indicate that achieving simultaneous improvements in privacy and accuracy requires a substantial number of clients. This characteristic positions our framework as particularly well-suited for cross-device federated learning scenarios.

As perspective, we plan to extend our experiments, providing additional insights into computation time and bandwidth consumption. Furthermore, we aim to study mathematically the privacy gain of parameter shuffling compared to model shuffling. The privacy gain considered actually is the same as the work of [24] in model shuffling. In addition, we aim to test how our framework perform against well-known attacks like membership inference. We also want to test our method in a real word scenario to have more idea of the practicability of our method.

References

1. Fundamental Rights: The General Data Protection Regulation - One Year on – Civil Society: Awareness, Opportunities and Challenges (2019). https://doi.org/10.2811/538633
2. McMahan, B., Moore, E., Ramage, D., Hampson, S., Arcas, B.A.: Communication-efficient learning of deep networks from decentralized data. In: Artificial Intelligence and Statistics, pp. 1273–1282. PMLR (2017)
3. Zhu, L., Liu, Z., Han, S.: Deep leakage from gradients. In: Advances in Neural Information Processing Systems, vol. 32 (2019)
4. Zhao, B., Mopuri, K.R., Bilen, H.: IDLG: improved deep leakage from gradients. arXiv preprint arXiv:2001.02610 (2020)
5. Geiping, J., Bauermeister, H., Dröge, H., Moeller, M.: Inverting gradients-how easy is it to break privacy in federated learning? In: Advances in Neural Information Processing Systems, vol. 33, pp. 16937–16947 (2020)
6. Ren, H., Deng, J., Xie, X.: GRNN: generative regression neural network-a data leakage attack for federated learning. ACM Trans. Intell. Syst. Technol. (TIST) **13**(4), 1–24 (2022)
7. Wei, W., et al.: A framework for evaluating client privacy leakages in federated learning. In: Chen, L., Li, N., Liang, K., Schneider, S. (eds.) ESORICS 2020. LNCS, vol. 12308, pp. 545–566. Springer, Cham (2020). https://doi.org/10.1007/978-3-030-58951-6_27
8. Jin, X., Chen, P.-Y., Hsu, C.-Y., Yu, C.-M., Chen, T.: Cafe: catastrophic data leakage in vertical federated learning. In: Advances in Neural Information Processing Systems, vol. 34, pp. 994–1006 (2021)

9. Zhang, J., Zhang, J., Chen, J., Yu, S.: Gan enhanced membership inference: a passive local attack in federated learning. In: ICC 2020-2020 IEEE International Conference on Communications (ICC), pp. 1–6. IEEE (2020)

10. Mao, Y., Zhu, X., Zheng, W., Yuan, D., Ma, J.: A novel user membership leakage attack in collaborative deep learning. In: 2019 11th International Conference on Wireless Communications and Signal Processing (WCSP), pp. 1–6. IEEE (2019)

11. Chen, J., Zhang, J., Zhao, Y., Han, H., Zhu, K., Chen, B.: Beyond model-level membership privacy leakage: an adversarial approach in federated learning. In: 2020 29th International Conference on Computer Communications and Networks (ICCCN), pp. 1–9. IEEE (2020)

12. Wang, L., Xu, S., Wang, X., Zhu, Q.: Eavesdrop the composition proportion of training labels in federated learning. arXiv preprint arXiv:1910.06044 (2019)

13. Zhang, W., Tople, S., Ohrimenko, O.: Leakage of dataset properties in multi-party machine learning. In: USENIX Security Symposium, pp. 2687–2704 (2021)

14. Bittau, A., et al.: Prochlo: strong privacy for analytics in the crowd. In: Proceedings of the 26th Symposium on Operating Systems Principles, pp. 441–459 (2017). https://doi.org/10.1145/3132747.3132769. arXiv:1710.00901 [cs]. http://arxiv.org/abs/1710.00901. Accessed 28 Mar 2023

15. Erlingsson, Ú., Feldman, V., Mironov, I., Raghunathan, A., Talwar, K., Thakurta, A.: Amplification by shuffling: from local to central differential privacy via anonymity (2020)

16. Aziz, R., Banerjee, S., Bouzefrane, S., Le Vinh, T.: Exploring homomorphic encryption and differential privacy techniques towards secure federated learning paradigm. Future Internet **15**(9), 310 (2023)

17. Xu, R., Baracaldo, N., Zhou, Y., Anwar, A., Ludwig, H.: HybridAlpha: an efficient approach for privacy-preserving federated learning. In: Proceedings of the 12th ACM Workshop on Artificial Intelligence And Security, pp. 13–23 (2019). https://doi.org/10.1145/3338501.3357371. arXiv:1912.05897 [cs]. http://arxiv.org/abs/1912.05897. Accessed 07 Apr 2023

18. Wang, T., et al.: Improving utility and security of the shuffler-based differential privacy. Proc. VLDB Endow. **13**(13), 3545–3558 (2020) https://doi.org/10.14778/3424573.3424576

19. Gu, X., Li, M., Xiong, L.: PRECAD: privacy-preserving and robust federated learning via crypto-aided differential privacy (2021). https://arxiv.org/abs/2110.11578

20. Sébert, A.G., Sirdey, R., Stan, O., Gouy-Pailler, C.: Protecting data from all parties: combining FHE and DP in federated learning. arXiv. arXiv:2205.04330 [cs] (2022). http://arxiv.org/abs/2205.04330. Accessed 07 Apr 2023

21. Hun Ro, J.: FedJAX: federated learning simulation with JAX (2021). https://blog.research.google/2021/10/fedjax-federated-learning-simulation.html

22. Dwork, C., Kenthapadi, K., McSherry, F., Mironov, I., Naor, M.: Our data, ourselves: privacy via distributed noise generation. In: Vaudenay, S. (ed.) EUROCRYPT 2006. LNCS, vol. 4004, pp. 486–503. Springer, Heidelberg (2006). https://doi.org/10.1007/11761679_29

23. Paillier, P.: Public-key cryptosystems based on composite degree residuosity classes. In: Stern, J. (ed.) EUROCRYPT 1999. LNCS, vol. 1592, pp. 223–238. Springer, Heidelberg (1999). https://doi.org/10.1007/3-540-48910-X_16

24. Erlingsson, Ú., Feldman, V., Mironov, I., Raghunathan, A., Talwar, K., Thakurta, A.: Amplification by shuffling: from local to central differential privacy via anonymity. In: Proceedings of the Thirtieth Annual ACM-SIAM Symposium on Discrete Algorithms, pp. 2468–2479. SIAM (2019)

Distributed Backdoor Attacks in Federated Learning Generated by DynamicTriggers

Jian Wang[1,3], Hong Shen[2(✉)], Xuehua Liu[3], Hua Zhou[3], and Yuli Li[3]

[1] Faculty of Applied Sciences, Macao Polytechnic University, Macao SAR, China
[2] School of Engineering and Technology, Central Queensland University,
Rockhampton, Australia
shenh3@mail.sysu.edu.cn
[3] School of Software Technology, Guangzhou Institute of Software,
Guangzhou, China

Abstract. The emergence of federated learning has alleviated the dual challenges of data silos and data privacy and security in machine learning. However, this distributed learning approach makes it more susceptible to backdoor attacks, where malicious participants can conduct adversarial attacks by injecting backdoor triggers into their local training datasets, aiming to manipulate model predictions, for example, make the classifier recognize poisoned samples (injected with specific triggers) as specific images. In order to effectively detect backdoor attacks and protect federated learning systems, we need to know how backdoor attacks are generated and developed. Currently, most backdoor attacks to federated learning use centralized attacks with static triggers, which are easily detectable by current defense methods. In this work, we propose a distributed backdoor attack method that fully leverages the distributed nature of federated learning. It starts by generating unique and independent global dynamic triggers for infected benign samples and then decomposes the global trigger into multiple sub-triggers, embedding them into the training sets of multiple participants. During the training phase, data poisoning is introduced. Through extensive experiments, we demonstrate that this attack method exhibits higher persistence and stealthiness, achieving a significantly higher success rate than standard centralized backdoor attacks. Compared to classical distributed backdoor attack (DBA) methods, it shows noticeable improvements in attack performance.

Keywords: Federated learning · data poisoning · security · backdoor Attack

1 Introduction

Federated Learning is a distributed machine learning paradigm used to address the issue of data silos and data privacy and security in machine learning [19].

© IFIP International Federation for Information Processing 2024
Published by Springer Nature Switzerland AG 2024
S. Bouzefrane and D. Sauveron (Eds.): WISTP 2024, LNCS 14625, pp. 178–193, 2024.
https://doi.org/10.1007/978-3-031-60391-4_12

Its main idea is that the server initially shares a global model with participants. Then, each participant uses their local private training set to train a local update. Finally, the server enhances the performance of the global model by aggregating local model updates submitted by each client [23], while ensuring the data privacy of participants. Currently, federated learning has found extensive applications in various fields, including facial recognition [3], natural language processing [11], and digital health, among others.

However, while federated learning improves the global model's performance by aggregating model updates provided by different participants, it also raises a new security concern that federated learning's shared model is susceptible to data poisoning attacks [5,17]. Existing defense methods against data poisoning typically require access to the dataset, a strategy that contradicts the fundamental principles of federated learning that the central aggregator is not allowed to access participants' data samples due to privacy constraints. Therefore, these classical defense methods are applicable for defence against data poisoning in federated learning.

Backdoor attacks are a form of data poisoning attack against machine learning, with the aim of training a malicious model update by modifying a specific subset of benign samples in a particular manner. This manipulation results in deep neural networks performing well on benign inputs but poorly on specific malicious samples, to achieve network manipulation goals [8]. For example, in a poisoned facial recognition system, wearing certain glasses triggers the backdoor, causing recognition as the target user, while wearing different glasses does not trigger the backdoor [4]. Bagdasaryan [1] et al. proposed the first method for inserting backdoors in federated learning. Subsequently, Zhang et al. introduced data poisoning attacks based on Generative Adversarial Networks (GANs). Vale et al. [12] conducted research on label-flipping attacks in federated learning, demonstrating through experiments that conducting backdoor poisoning in the later stages of training is more effective than doing so early.

However, these attacks did not take into account the distributed nature of federated learning; most of them involve injecting a backdoor by a single participant, which can be mitigated by robust aggregation methods [6,15]. Xie et al. [22] proposed a distributed backdoor attack in which malicious participants collude. They split a fixed backdoor trigger and embed each part into the training sets of malicious participants. After model aggregation, it forms a complete backdoor and inserts it into the model, enhancing the stealthiness of the backdoor attack. However, this method uses fixed triggers and may not fully harness the potential of distributed backdoor attacks, as confirmed by experimental results. Intuitively, dynamic backdoor trigger patterns vary with inputs and are unique, making them more covert than static backdoors. We believe that dynamic-triggering based distributed backdoor attacks are able to surpass the classical defense methods [7,10,14] while unleashing the attack potential of DBA.

The main contributions of this paper are as follows:

1. To address the distributed nature of federated learning, a distributed backdoor attack framework based on dynamic triggers is designed. This framework

consists of four modules: dynamic trigger generation, global trigger decomposition, trigger embedding, and distributed backdoor attack.

2. A method for generating dynamic triggers is proposed, which generates target triggers using benign source samples for the targeted attacked labels. These triggers can operate in three modes: clean, attack, and cross, ensuring that each poisoned sample has an independent trigger, effectively evading existing robust defense methods.

3. A strategy for geometric decomposition and embedding of triggers is introduced, breaking down the global trigger into multiple sub-triggers. The sub-triggers are embedded into benign samples using the Mixup method, enhancing trigger features while ensuring the stealthiness of the backdoor.

4. Experimental verification is conducted, involving a comprehensive analysis of key parameters of distributed backdoor attacks, including attack modes, toxicity strength, and trigger placement. The framework was demonstrated to outperform other attack methods.

2 Problem Definition and Threat Model

2.1 Federated Learning

Federated Learning (FL) refers to a general set of techniques for model training, performed over private data owned by individual users without compromising data privacy [21]. A typical federated learning system consists of N participants and one aggregator. For the private datasets of N participants represented as (1), x_i represents samples, y_i represents the labels corresponding to the samples, and $\{x_i, y_i\}$ indicates the private dataset of the i-th participant. D_i is the union of N client datasets, i.e., $D := D_1 \cup D_i \ldots \cup D_N$.

$$D_i = \{(x_i, y_i)\}, 1 \leq i \leq N. \tag{1}$$

$$f(w_i) = l(\{x_i, y_i\}_{i \in D_i}, w_i)\} \tag{2}$$

In a supervised federated learning setting, As in (2), we denote $f(w_i)$ is the local function of each participant.FL aims to minimize an empirical loss $l(\{x_i, y_i\}_{i \in D_i}, w_i)\}$ by optimizing over the local model parameters w_i, The goal of federated learning is to aggregate the distributed training results of N participants to obtain a global model that performs better on a test data set. The specific process is as follows:

- At time $t - 1$, the central server sends the current global model G^{t-1} to n selected participants, where $n \in N$.
- The selected participants use their private data set D_i. and local learning rate lr to compute the function f_i by running a local optimization algorithm (such as SGD), resulting in a local model L_i^t.
- All participants send the model update back to the central server, and the aggregator finally averages all updates using a global learning rate η to generate a new global model G^t as in (3)

$$G^t = G^{t-1} + \frac{\eta}{n} \sum_{i=1}^{n} (L_i^t - G^{t-1}) \} \tag{3}$$

2.2 Threat Model

The goal of backdoor attacks in FL is to manipulate the global model's predictions by influencing the local models. Even if the global model performs normally on benign data samples, the backdoor attacks still can achieve a high success rate in attacking the backdoor data samples. Therefore, the threat model in FL can be defined as the adversarial behavior against local data set D_i and target label τ in round t, expressed as (4)

$$w_i^* = argmax(\sum_{j \in D_p^i} P[G^t(R(x_j^i, T^*)) = \tau] + \sum_{j \in D_c^i} P[G^t(x_j^i) = y_j^i]) \tag{4}$$

where the poisonous data set D_p and the clean data set D_c satisfy $D_p \cap D_c = \emptyset, D_p \cup D_c = D_i, \tau$ represents the trigger embedded in benign samples, and the function R transforms benign samples from any class into malicious samples. These poisoned samples adhere to a fixed set of trigger patterns, such as embedding special pixels or image noise in the non-core regions of sample images. In contrast to the conventional fixed trigger generation schemes, in this paper, we propose a dynamic trigger generation method. These triggers are perceptible and work independently to generate poisoned samples.

Following the same assumption in the literature [22], the threat model satisfies the following three constraints:

1. Malicious participants have complete control over their local training processes and full access to their local datasets. This scenario aligns well with the FL training setup since each local dataset is typically owned by a local participant.
2. Attackers do not have the authority to change aggregation rules or influence the central server.
3. Attackers lack the capability to tamper with the training processes and model updates of other participants (excluding malicious conspiring participants).

2.3 Backdoor Attacks

In contrast to typical data poisoning attacks, rather than to reduce the overall performance of machine learning models, the goal of backdoor attacks is to make the targeted model perform well on benign samples while producing malicious alterations in predictions when the hidden backdoor is activated by a trigger specified by the attacker [20]. In other words, it yields correct predictions for benign samples and incorrect predictions for malicious samples. $f(x)$ indicates the posterior vector and $C(x) = arg\max_{w \in \mathbb{R}^d} f(x)$ is the model infected with backdoors, $w \in \mathbb{R}^d$ is the instance space,and $\mathbb{I}(\cdot)$ denote the indicator function. Backdoor attacks to a model can be defined by a 3-tuple (R_s, R_b, R_p) as follows:

1. The standard risk R_s (5) denote whether the infected model C can correctly classify benign samples.,p_D represents the distribution of dataset D.$\mathbb{I}\{C(x) \neq y\} = 1$ if and only if statement A is true.i.e.,

$$R_s(D) = E_{(x,y) \sim p_D} \mathbb{I}\{C(x) \neq y\} \tag{5}$$

2. The backdoor risk R_b (6) measures whether malicious participants can successfully achieve their goal of manipulating the model's output to produce malicious predictions. Let $g(x,t)$ represent the toxic sample generation function, with a trigger mode of t, and x as a benign sample. $x' = g(x,t)$ denote the poisoned samples, S is the label-flipping function during the attack,as follows:

$$R_b(D) = E_{(x,y) \sim \mathcal{P}_D} \mathbb{I}\{C(x') \neq S(y)\} \tag{6}$$

3. The perceptible risk R_p (7) represents whether malicious models or data can be detected by defense methods (manual or automated). H represents the manual or machine-based backdoor detection method. $\mathbb{I}\{H(x')\} = 1$ if and only if x' can be detected as the poisoned sample.

$$R_p(D) = E_{(x,y) \sim P_D} \mathbb{I}\{H(x')\} \tag{7}$$

Given a benign training set D_c and a malicious training set D_p, where D_p is generated from a subset D_s of D_c by implanting a backdoor trigger. Based on the above definition, existing data poisoning-based backdoor attacks can be summarized into the following framework:

$$arg \min R_s(D_c - D_p) + \lambda_1 \cdot R_b(D_p) + \lambda_2 \cdot R_p(D_p) \tag{8}$$

λ_1 and λ_2 are two non-negative penalty coefficients. This framework can be extended to other attack methods by adjusting λ_1 and λ_2. For example, when $\lambda_1 = \dfrac{|D_p|}{|D_c - D_p|}$, and $\lambda_2 = 0$, (8) can be represented as BadNets [2], this paper is the same. When set to $\lambda_2 = \infty$, it degenerates into stealth backdoor attack with boundary parameters [9]. This framework can also be extended to other tasks, such as natural language processing.

3   Methodology

Following Bagdasaryan et al.'s introduction of backdoor attacks on federated learning [1], many attack variants were proposed [5,18]. However, these methods employed centralized attacks and did not consider the distributed nature of FL. Subsequently, Xie et al.'s DBA improved the stealthiness of backdoor attacks, demonstrating some promising results in experiments with multiple datasets, making the attacks more covert and destructive. Nevertheless, all of these attacks used fixed triggers, all poisoned samples share the same trigger (including DBA), and are based on the static triggers themselves. Deep visualization methods like Grad-CAM [16] can easily identify them, which may be an unnoticed flaw. To address this gap, this paper introduces a dynamic distributed backdoor attack framework.

3.1 Dynamic DBA Framework

To address the issues mentioned above, the framework design we propose should meet the following four requirements:

1. Distributed poisoning approach to fully leverage the distributed learning nature of FL.
2. Dynamic embedding of triggers for backdoor attacks taking advantage of the mixup data aggregation.
3. Low-perceptible backdoors resulted by toxic samples (images) independently generated by dynamic triggers.
4. Generation of more covert triggers based on dynamic patterns rather than fixed geometric patterns.

Our proposed framework is described in Fig. 1, Specifically, there are three points as shown in: First, within a poisoning cycle, an edge extraction operator is used to generate a dynamic trigger for each poisoned sample. The trigger takes the form of a grayscale image of the target's edge structure in the image, achieving perceptible input for dynamic backdoor embedding. Then, according to certain geometric decomposition rules, the embedded triggers are decomposed and

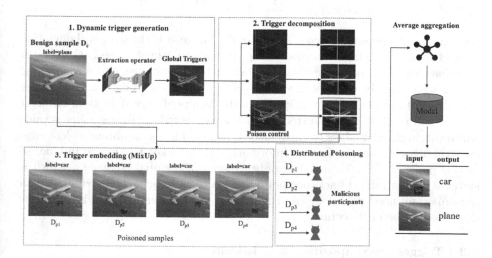

Fig. 1. Dynamic DBA Framework

mixed with benign samples using MixUp, in this step, we also control the brightness of the edge structures in the trigger image to achieve poison control. Finally, distributed poisoning is carried out through collusion.

3.2 Dynamic Trigger Generation

The first step of the attack is to generate the trigger, as shown in Fig. 1. Inspired by Tuan Anh et al.'s [13], They proposed a new method that ensures each image has a unique trigger, and this trigger will not work on other images. They achieve non-reusability of triggers by inputting benign samples into an encoder-decoder, which outputs corresponding patterns. In contrast, we employ a edge extraction operator to generate triggers t_g. Inputting a benign sample, it outputs a grayscale image of the sample's edge structure, which serves as the global trigger. This achieves the generation of a unique and independent trigger for each selected benign sample. Common edge structure extraction operators include Sobel, Prewitt, Laplacian, and Canny. Laplacian operators is a second-order derivative operator, so it enhances image noise, which is a drawback in edge detection tasks. However, in the context of dynamic trigger generation, it can be an advantage.

Our goal is to generate a unique and independent sample for each benign sample, and introducing appropriate noise perturbation is precisely what we need. In this paper, we use laplacian of gaussian kernels to extract edge structures. The Laplacian of Gaussian (LoG) operator is a commonly used edge detection operator that combines the characteristics of Gaussian filtering and the Laplace operator. The LoG operator first applies Gaussian filtering to the image to smooth it and suppress noise, and then uses the Laplace operator to detect edges. Mathematically, the LoG operator can be represented as (9)

$$LoG(x,y) = -\frac{1}{\pi\sigma^4}\left[1 - \frac{x^2 + y^2}{2\sigma^2}\right]e^{-\frac{x^2+y^2}{2\sigma^2}} \tag{9}$$

where x and y represent the coordinates of the image, σ is the standard deviation of the Gaussian function. The specific approach is to convolve the LoG operator with the image to obtain a new image. Then, in this new image, find zero-crossing points, which are the edges of the image. Since the value of σ determines the size and shape of the LoG operator, it affects the results of edge detection. A larger σ value will result in more blurred edges being detected, while a smaller σ value will result in sharper edges being detected. Our goal is not to obtain a clear edge structure, but to obtain feature information that makes the image unique, so in this paper, $\sigma = 1$. To here, we only generate the global trigger t_g, which is suitable for centralized backdoor poisoning attacks. To achieve distributed data poisoning, we need to decompose the trigger and then embed it, which will be described in the next section.

3.3 Trigger Decomposition and Injeciton

Our goal is to achieve distributed data poisoning for backdoors. As shown in Fig. 2 To achieve this objective, we need to first decompose the trigger and then proceed with embedding. The specific approach is to first decompose the global trigger into four equal parts, resulting in four sub-triggers. Then, while keeping their relative positions unchanged, embed these four sub-triggers into the source sample using the function $f_B(x, t) \rightarrow x'$. The injection function f_B uses the trigger t_g to poison the input image, the poisoned sample x' is constructed from the clean input x and the trigger t using the injection function .

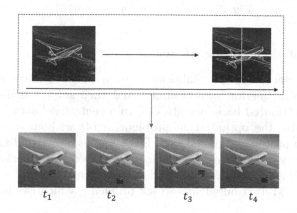

Fig. 2. Trigger Decomposition and Injeciton

The f_b function in this paper is implemented through the data augmentation. We draw inspiration from the MixUp [24], MixUp can linearly interpolate between two samples (x_i, y_i) and (x_j, y_j) to generate new training samples. Which can be represented as (10) and (11)

$$x = \lambda x_i + (1 - \lambda)x_j \quad \lambda \in [0, 1] \tag{10}$$

$$y = \lambda y_i + (1 - \lambda)y_j \quad \lambda \in [0, 1] \tag{11}$$

In backdoor attacks, x_i represents benign samples, x_j represents the trigger, and λ is the toxicity control, where a smaller value indicates a stronger embedding. The ultimate goal is to achieve label flipping rather than label blending. Therefore, (11) becomes $y = y_i$. Next, these poisoned samples embedded with sub-triggers will be injected into the training by malicious participants, generating poisoned updates.

The poisoned global model operates in three modes: (a) Clean mode, where the toxic classifier can correctly identify clean inputs; (b) Attack mode, returning the predefined label "car" when the corresponding trigger is injected; (c) Cross mode, where triggers are non-reusable, and inserting different triggers into mismatched clean inputs does not activate the attack. Figure 3 shows a global trigger embedding and three backdoor trigger modes. In the next section, we will discuss how distributed triggers are integrated into the global model to achieve the poisoning objective.

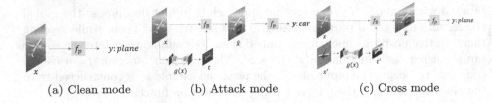

(a) Clean mode   (b) Attack mode   (c) Cross mode

Fig. 3. Dynamic Trigger Generation

3.4 Distributed Backdoor Attack

To trigger an attack, multiple malicious participants will inject poisoned samples of the sub-trigger for local training, and then submit malicious updates
to carry out distributed backdoor attacks. In a centralized attack, the attacker
attempts to solve the optimization problem in (4) without any coordination
and distributed processing. In contrast, DBA [22] uses distributed learning and
local data opacity in FL. Each DBA attacker independently performs backdoor
attacks on their local model. This mechanism decomposes a centralized attack
formulation into M-distributed sub-attack problems, which can be expressed as
(12)

$$w_i^* = argmax(\sum_{j \in D_p^i} P[G^t(R(x_j^i, \mathcal{T}^*)) = \tau; \gamma; I] + \sum_{j \in D_c^i} P[G^t(x_j^i) = y_j^i]) \quad (12)$$

where $\mathcal{T}^* = \{\mathcal{T}, \mathcal{O}(i)\}$ represents the embedding rules of the malicious participant's trigger. $\mathcal{O}(i)$ contains trigger activation factor settings $\mathcal{O}(i) =
\{TS, TG, TL\}$, representing the size, gap, and location of the distributed trig-
gers, respectively. τ represents the target label, and the distributed attackers
perform poisoning with a toxic interval I and manipulate their updates with a
toxicity ratio factor γ before submitting them to the aggregator.

Trigger size TS is the size of the local distributed trigger. Trigger gaps TG
represent the distance between left-right and top-bottom local triggers. Trigger
location TL is the offset of the trigger pattern from the top-left pixel. The scaling
parameter $\gamma = \eta/N$ is used to control the weight of the malicious model. It is
intuitive that a larger γ is better, but if γ is too large, it can also affect the
effectiveness of the attack once the model fails. Therefore, there is a trade-off
between the accuracy of clean data and the success rate of the attack on toxic
data.

Poisoning interval I: An integer interval between two poisoning steps. For
example, $I = 0$ means that all local triggers are embedded in one round, while
$I = 1$ means that local triggers are embedded in consecutive rounds.

It is worth noting here that although local triggers under Our proposed
method do not directly have an obvious toxic effect on the global model, we
found that the performance of Our proposed method is indeed more covert and
insidious when evaluated with global triggers. We will analyze in detail how this
indirect control works in the next section.

4 Experiments

4.1 Datasets and Experiment Setup

We conduct evaluations on the IMAGENET, COCO, and VOC datasets. The experimental parameter settings are shown in Table 1, which includes aspects such as the nature of the dataset and optimization methods. These settings are crucial for the design and interpretation of the experiments.

Table 1. Units for Magnetic Properties

Items	Configuration
toxicity ratio range	1% to 5%, increment by 0.01 per round
optimization method	SGD (Stochastic Gradient Descent)
size of feature vectors	224\640\960
learning rate schedule	Decrease by 10x every 100 epochs
number of samples	5000
number of classes	10
batch size	16
models	Resnet
initial learning rate	0.03

4.2 Performance Evaluation

In this section, we evaluate the attack performance using two metrics: Attack Success Rate (ASR) and the model's primary accuracy (ACC) under the classical robust aggregation method Fools Gold defense. A higher ASR indicates a better attack effectiveness, while a higher ACC suggests that the attack method has a more minor impact on the primary accuracy, making it more covert. Since the number of malicious clients in FL is far smaller than benign clients, over time, the toxicity of malicious updates is gradually diluted by benign updates and quickly forgotten by the global model. Therefore, we conduct a complete attack in each round and set the ratio of malicious and benign clients to 1:100. We also assessed the toxicity ratio and persistence.

Federated Learning's backdoor attacks are divided into multiple-shot attacks (A-M) and single-shot attacks (A-S). A-M involves malicious attackers being selected over multiple rounds, and the attack's effectiveness depends on the accumulation of toxicity. This metric characterizes the ease or difficulty of successfully injecting the backdoor, i.e., the strength of the backdoor. On the other hand, A-S refers to attackers being selected only once, and they can successfully inject their backdoor trigger with a single attack. This metric reflects how quickly the backdoor effect diminishes, i.e., the persistence of the backdoor.

In the A-M attacks, as shown in Fig. 4, our method outperforms DBA and centralized attack (CA) in terms of attack success rate (ASR) on all three datasets. Our method also exhibits a higher stability in performance across the datasets. As the time for model convergence increases slightly with the increase in the number of features, ASR stabilizes after 100 rounds of poisoning. These experiments demonstrate that even when the global trigger never appears in any local training data set, it exhibits a backdoor solid effect on the server-side model.

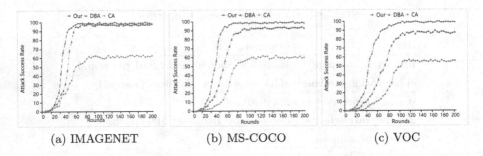

(a) IMAGENET   (b) MS-COCO   (c) VOC

Fig. 4. Attack in A-M is more effective

Furthermore, as shown in Fig. 5, the external area in the graph represents the improvement in the performance of our method compared to DBA attacks. In contrast, the central area represents the performance improvement of distributed combined attacks over CA. In contrast to DBA, which uses uniform pixel-level geometric shapes as triggers, our method uses edge structures for distributed backdoor injection that impacts the global model more significantly. This result indicates that our method can further enhance the attack performance compared to DBA.

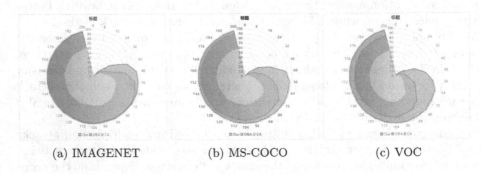

(a) IMAGENET   (b) MS-COCO   (c) VOC

Fig. 5. Unleashed the attack potential of DBA

In the A-S attacks Fig. 6, the toxicity level is set to the maximum ($\lambda = 0$). To ensure fairness, we set the number of A-S attack rounds to be 1/4 of the

A-M attacks. As shown in Fig. 7, in the 50 rounds of attacks, all attack ASRs experience an initial increase followed by a decrease. This is because, in A-S attacks, malicious clients are selected only once, leading to the weakening of the global model's backdoor by benign updates. DBA's ASR remains at around 50% during the entire attack cycle. On the other hand, on the IMAGENET dataset, CA's attack convergence is slightly higher than that of DBA and our method. This is because, in the A-S method, centralized attacks have a more substantial impact on the gradient of the global model.

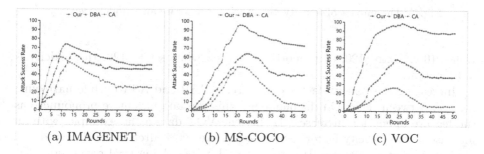

| (a) IMAGENET | (b) MS-COCO | (c) VOC |

Fig. 6. Attacks in A-S mode are more persistent

However, our method's persistence is significantly higher than DBA and CA on the COCO and VOC datasets with more features. For example, after 20 rounds of attacks on VOC, DBA's attack success rate remains above 80%, while DBA only has 55%, and CA only has 20%. The toxicity of the backdoor is almost ineffective. This indicates that our method has more remarkable persistence.

4.3 Trigger Factor Analysis

This section mainly evaluates the impact of the toxicity intensity factor and trigger position on attack performance in the A-S attack scenario. There are two reasons for this. First, the trigger factor includes trigger TS, trigger gap TG, and trigger location TL. The trigger generation rules subject TS and TG to certain constraints. Second, A-S attacks are closer to real-world scenarios. Therefore, in each experiment, we fix the value of one factor and analyze the other factor. ASR represents the attack success rate, and ACC represents the accuracy of the global model after injecting the last trigger. ASR-t represents the success rate of attacks after t rounds following a complete trigger implantation cycle. ACC-t is the central accuracy after t rounds.

As shown in Fig. 7, note that setting $t = 20$ is because the convergence of attacks in A-S occurs around the 20th round as shown in the experiments in Sect. 4.2. ACC may experience a slight decline, but after several rounds of updates, benign updates gradually dilute toxic updates, and ACC eventually returns to normal. To better analyze this process, we transform the range of

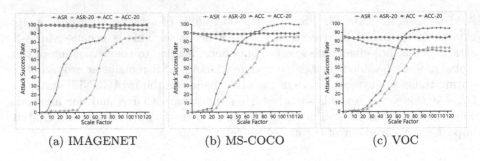

(a) IMAGENET   (b) MS-COCO   (c) VOC

Fig. 7. The impact of toxicity on attack success rate and model accuracy

values (0, 1) into (120, 0) proportionally, i.e., when set to 120, the toxicity is most potent.

Increasing the toxicity factor can increase ASR and ASR-t while narrowing the gap between them. On the one hand, this gap becomes more pronounced as the feature dimension increases. Taking the VOC data as an example, with an increase in the toxicity factor, ASR reaches over 90% after the 80th round and remains almost unchanged. However, it still proves the critical conclusion that it positively impacts ASR-t. On the other hand, with the increase in toxicity factor, the drop in central accuracy becomes more pronounced. This is because malicious updates disrupt more benign connections in neurons. Therefore, a balance is needed when choosing the toxicity factor.

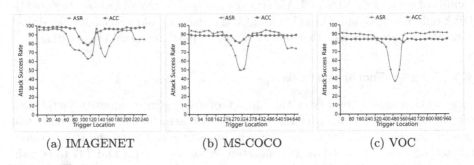

(a) IMAGENET   (b) MS-COCO   (c) VOC

Fig. 8. The impact of trigger location on attack success rate and model accuracy

In the assessment of trigger placement, we moved the trigger from the bottom left corner to the center and then to the top right corner to evaluate the impact of trigger placement on the attack. Since the samples in the three datasets have different ratios, the x-coordinate takes values corresponding to the resolution. As shown in Fig. 8, taking VOC as an example, when x = 0, the trigger is injected in the bottom left corner of the image; when $x = 480$, the trigger is injected in the center of the image; when $x = 960$, the trigger is injected in the top right corner of the image.

We observed that the variation in TL results in an almost U-shaped curve in ASR. This is because the central part of the image typically contains the main target object, and the trigger's feature intensity is weaker than that of the target, causing the model to ignore it. This observation becomes more pronounced as the sample features increase. For example, in VOC, when TL is around 480, which is the center of the image, ASR drops sharply to 40%. As TL gradually moves to the top right corner, ASR also decreases to some extent due to the limited injection space, resulting in some local triggers not being injected.

In addition, compared to the other two datasets, the IMAGENET data set exhibits a 'W'-shaped curve, which is an exciting discovery. It can be observed that when TL is in the center of the image, ASR drops sharply, but there is a brief improvement in the following ten rounds. This may be due to smaller targets, and when the trigger's edge structure coincides with the target's edge structure, it leads to enhanced trigger features, resulting in a temporary increase in ASR.

5 Conclusions

The security of federated learning models has become a hot topic of current research as the increasing popularity of federated learning. In this paper, in order to protect a federated learning system from attacks, we study the problem of generation of backdoor attacks and propose a new type of distributed backdoor attacks that are generated by dynamic triggers through application of composite techniques. We first design a global backdoor trigger for benign samples through an auto-encoder. It is then decomposed according to specific geometric decomposition rules and injected separately into multiple malicious clients for training. Subsequently, it generates attacks to the global model through a distributed approach that are harder to be detected than the existing backdoor attacks generated through a centralized approach. Through extensive experiments, we found that in the standard federated learning environment, compared to other attack methods, our attack method has a higher success rate and better persistence in both single-shot and multi-shot attack scenarios. It can successfully evade classical robust federated learning methods. Additionally, we thoroughly assessed two critical factors of triggers to explore their properties and limitations. Our results indicate that this dynamic composite backdoor is a more powerful attack for federated learning.

Acknowledgment. This work is supported by Science and Technology Development Fund of Macao (FDCT) #0015/2023/RIA1 and Macao Polytechnic University Research Grant RP/FCA-14/2022.

References

1. Byzantine, E., Veit, A., Hua, Y., Estrin, D., Shmatikov, V.: How to Backdoor Federated Learning (2020)
2. Chan, S.H., Dong, Y., Zhu, J., Zhang, X., Zhou, J.: BadDet: backdoor attacks on object detection. In: Karlinsky, L., Michaeli, T., Nishino, K. (eds.) ECCV 2022. LNCS, vol. 13801, pp. 396–412. Springer, Cham (2023). https://doi.org/10.1007/978-3-031-25056-9_26
3. Chen, J., Song, L., Wainwright, M.J., Jordan, M.I.: Learning to explain: an information-theoretic perspective on model interpretation (2018)
4. Chen, X., Liu, C., Li, B., Lu, K., Song, D.: Targeted backdoor attacks on deep learning systems using data poisoning. arXiv preprint arXiv:1712.05526 (2017)
5. Fang, M., Cao, X., Jia, J., Gong, N.Z.: Local model poisoning attacks to byzantine-robust federated learning (2020)
6. Fung, C., Yoon, C.J.M., Beschastnikh, I.: Mitigating sybils in federated learning poisoning, July 2020. arXiv:1808.04866 [cs, stat]
7. Gao, Y., Xu, C., Wang, D., Chen, S., Ranasinghe, D.C., Nepal, S.: STRIP: a defence against trojan attacks on deep neural networks. In: Proceedings of the 35th Annual Computer Security Applications Conference, pp. 113–125, San Juan Puerto Rico USA, December 2019. ACM (2019)
8. Jagielski, M., Oprea, A., Biggio, B., Liu, C., Nita-Rotaru, C., Li, B.: Manipulating machine learning: poisoning attacks and countermeasures for regression learning, September 2021. arXiv:1804.00308 [cs]
9. Li, S., Xue, M., Zhao, B.Z.H., Zhu, H., Zhang, X.: Invisible backdoor attacks on deep neural networks via steganography and regularization, August 2020. arXiv:1909.02742 [cs]
10. Li, X., Qu, Z., Zhao, S., Tang, B., Lu, Z., Liu, Y.: LoMar: a local defense against poisoning attack on federated learning, January 2022. arXiv:2201.02873 [cs]
11. McMahan, H.B., Ramage, D., Talwar, K., Zhang, L.: Learning differentially private recurrent language models, February 2018. arXiv:1710.06963 [cs]
12. Muñoz-González, L., Pfitzner, B., Russo, M., Carnerero-Cano, J., Lupu, E.C.: Poisoning attacks with generative adversarial nets. arXiv preprint arXiv:1906.07773 (2019)
13. Nguyen, T.A., Tran, T.A.: Input-aware dynamic backdoor attack (2020)
14. Peri, N., et al.: Deep k-NN defense against clean-label data poisoning attacks, August 2020. arXiv:1909.13374 [cs]
15. Pillutla, K., Kakade, S.M., Harchaoui, Z.: Robust aggregation for federated learning. IEEE Trans. Sig. Process. 70, 1142–1154 (2022). arXiv:1912.13445 [cs, stat]
16. Selvaraju, R.R., Cogswell, M., Das, A., Vedantam, R., Parikh, D., Batra, D.: Grad-cam: visual explanations from deep networks via gradient-based localization. In: Proceedings of the IEEE International Conference on Computer Vision, pp. 618–626 (2017)
17. Shafahi, A., et al.: Poison frogs! Targeted clean-label poisoning attacks on neural networks, November 2018. arXiv:1804.00792 [cs, stat]
18. Sun, G., Cong, Y., Dong, J., Wang, Q., Liu, J.: Data poisoning attacks on federated machine learning, April 2020. arXiv:2004.10020 [cs]
19. Sun, Z., Kairouz, P., Suresh, A.T., McMahan, H.B.: Can you really backdoor federated learning?, December 2019. arXiv:1911.07963 [cs, stat]
20. Tian, Z., Cui, L., Liang, J., Shui, Yu.: A comprehensive survey on poisoning attacks and countermeasures in machine learning. ACM Comput. Surv. 55(8), 1–35 (2023)

21. Wang, H., et al.: Attack of the tails: yes, you really can backdoor federated learning, July 2020. arXiv:2007.05084 [cs, stat]
22. Xie, C., Huang, K., Chen, P.-Y., Li, B.: DBA : distributed backdoor attacks against federated learning (2020)
23. Yang, Q., Liu, Y., Chen, T., Tong, Y.: Federated machine learning: concept and applications. ACM Trans. Intell. Syst. Technol. **10**(2), 1–19 (2019)
24. Zhang, H., Cisse, M., Dauphin, Y.N., Lopez-Paz, D.: Mixup: beyond empirical risk minimization. arXiv preprint arXiv:1710.09412 (2017)

Author Index

A
Adni, Fahd   33
Aziz, Rezak   162

B
Badr, Youakim   128
Banerjee, Saumya   96
Banerjee, Soumya   128, 162
Belaoued, Mohamed   80
Berruet, Pascal   64
Bouzefrane, Samia   96, 111, 162

C
Conord, Pierrick   111

D
Djenna, Amir   80

E
El Madhoun, Nour   111
Elmarkez, Ahmed   64
Erradi, Mohammed   33

G
Gebauer, Sven   17
gentschen Felde, Nils   49

J
Jakubeit, Philipp   1

K
Kastrup, Swantje   49
Kazem, Hussein   111
Kesraoui, Djamal   64
Khoumsi, Ahmed   33

L
Li, Yuli   178
Lifa, Nourdine   80
Liu, Xuehua   178

M
Mesli-Kesraoui, Soraya   64

O
Oquendo, Flavio   64

P
Peter, Andreas   1
Pöhls, Henrich C.   17
Posegga, Joachim   17

S
Saad-Bouzefrane, Samia   128
Scharnböck, Fabian   17
Shen, Hong   178
Spielvogel, Korbinian   17

T
Tamani, Nouredine   146

U
Unni, Pranav   96

V
van Steen, Maarten   1

W
Wang, Jian   178

Z
Zhou, Hua   178
Zhu, Xiaoyang   128

Printed in the United States
by Baker & Taylor Publisher Services